THE
"UGLY AMERICAN"
IN THE
ARAB MIND

Also by Mohamed El-Bendary

The Egyptian Press and Coverage of Local and International Events (2010)

Related Potomac Titles

The Al Jazeera Effect: How the New Global Media Are Reshaping World Politics
—Philip Seib

American Avatar: The United States in the Global Imagination
—Barry A. Sanders

Simple Gestures: A Cultural Journey into the Middle East
—Andrea B. Rugh

Public Opinion and International Intervention: Lessons from the Iraq War
—Richard Sobel, Peter Furia, and Bethany Barrett, eds.

THE "UGLY AMERICAN" IN THE ARAB MIND

WHY DO ARABS RESENT AMERICA?

Mohamed El-Bendary

Potomac Books
Washington, D.C.

Published in the United States by Potomac Books, Inc. All rights reserved. No
part of this book may be reproduced in any manner whatsoever without written
permission from the publisher, except in the case of brief quotations embodied in
critical articles and reviews.

Library of Congress Cataloging-in-Publication Data
El-Bendary, Mohamed, 1966–
    The "ugly American" in the Arab mind : why do Arabs resent America? /
Mohamed El-Bendary. — 1st ed.
        p. cm.
    Includes bibliographical references and index.
    ISBN 978-1-59797-673-2
    1. United States—Foreign relations—Arab countries. 2. Arab countries—
Foreign relations—United States. 3. United States—Foreign public opinion,
Arab. 4. Anti-Americanism—Arab countries. I. Title.
    DS63.2.U5E6 2011
    303.48'2174927073—dc23

                                                        2011019990

Printed in the United States of America on acid-free paper that meets the
American National Standards Institute Z39-48 Standard.

Potomac Books
22841 Quicksilver Drive
Dulles, Virginia 20166

First Edition

10 9 8 7 6 5 4 3 2 1

To my parents, and
to fellow Arabs and Americans
who work diligently toward better understanding
between their peoples

CONTENTS

1   HOW IT ALL BEGAN

How do Arabs view America? How do Arabs learn about America? There is a dearth of information on how the Arab media cover the West, particularly the United States. There are a number of books in English on how the U.S. media view Arabs but almost none on how the Arab media depict America, particularly during the George W. Bush administration. The aim of this book is to identify the picture of the United States in the Arab world over the past few years and how this picture is orchestrated in the increasingly diverse broadcast and print Arabic-language media—from Al-Jazeera to Al-Arabiya and Abu Dhabi satellite television channels, from *Al-Hayat* to *Al-Ahram* and *Al-Nahar* newspapers. How will Bush be remembered in the Arab world? How was the 2008 election of his successor, President Barack Hussein Obama, perceived?

Following the September 11, 2001, tragedies and the U.S. attack on Afghanistan and invasion of Iraq, many Arabs began to conceive of Bush's America as their enemy. This sentiment of anti-Americanism also began to rise in countries that maintained good ties with the United States, such as Jordan, Egypt, Saudi Arabia, Qatar, Morocco, Kuwait, and Oman. An Egyptian study on a sample of students from Cairo University in 2002 found that 72 percent of respondents held negative perceptions of the United States in comparison to 28 percent who showed positive attitudes. An American was portrayed as a hostile individual who does not respect other people's rights. Among the words used to depict the United States were "tyranny," "supremacy," "deceit," "pro-Israeli," "enemy," "terrorism," "hypocrisy," and "ethical decay."

Some 44 percent of total respondents said they aspired to watch American movies and television series while 56 percent said they did not.[1] On the other side, a study completed right before the 9/11 tragedies, also conducted by Cairo University's School of Mass Communication, found that the image of the American way of life among Egyptian youths was positive, with many of them desiring to travel to the United States to achieve the American Dream. They stressed that they aspired to reside in a land where the chances of living and freedom are better.[2]

A naturalized U.S. citizen of Egyptian descent, in 2004 I returned to live in Egypt, and I was astonished by how the Arab media negatively portrayed the "land of the free" and mocked the American Dream. Many of the Egyptians I spoke with often criticized the United States and its foreign policy in the Middle East. A seventy-five-year-old Egyptian told me that in no other time of his life had he seen so much resentment and observation of U.S. politics by Arabs. During the time I have spent in Egypt, it has felt as if America is losing the struggle for the hearts and minds of Arabs because of what Arabs call its aggressive nationalism and militarism, utter support of Israel, and failure to improve relations with Muslim nations. Regrettably, the United States seems to have lost the moral high ground in the Arab world. Hence, I believe there is an urgent need on the part of U.S. politicians, private institutions, and ordinary Americans to better understand the Arab mind and the cultural and political forces that shape its way of thinking—rather than display the empty slogans and stereotypical thinking I witnessed on television screens during the thirteen years I spent living and working in the United States.

I arrived in the United States in October 1988 and left my land of dreams in June 2002, nine months after the September 11 tragedies took place, mainly to teach international communications abroad and conduct field research on the Egyptian and Arab media; this book is one of the products of that research. The period I spent in the United States was the most prolific of my life, and I felt great joy when I gained my U.S. citizenship in 1993. I received my undergraduate and graduate degrees from two different U.S. universities, and I lived and worked in the nation's capital and four different states: Louisiana, Missouri, Illinois, and California. I hold good relationships with many American friends and colleagues, but I have remained strongly tied to Arab and Middle Eastern culture. Although I was taught at American journalism schools, I have been neutral in my views and have never denounced or promoted one culture over the other; I aim at promoting understanding among cultures rather than instigating the so-called clash of civilizations. In most of this book—which I wrote entirely while in Egypt—I merely play the role of a conveyer or carrier of Arab views to my fellow Americans and those in the U.S. media who have been busily trying to find an answer to the question, why do they hate us? These views are not mine; they are purely Arab ones: translation and analysis of a selection of hundreds of opinionated articles (op-eds, editorials, columns) and programs from the Arabic-language media. By "media" I essentially mean Arabic newspapers, magazines, television, radio, books, and the Internet. When the terms "press" and "journalism" are used, they refer to both print and broadcast media. On a few occasions, there are similarities in names of newspapers; to avoid confusion, I pinpoint who owns them.

This book primarily serves as an introduction to how Arabs view the United States in the aftermath of 9/11 and the American invasions of Afghanistan and Iraq, mainly five months before Bush won his second term in office in 2004 to roughly two weeks after President Obama delivered his speech to the Muslim world from Cairo University on June 4, 2009. In studying the Arab media commentary on the United States during this roughly four-year period, I sought answers to the following questions: What do Arabs see as characteristics of American culture in the post-9/11 era? Why do Arabs resent America? Are the media of some Arab states more disposed toward anti-American stances than others? Has there been a shift in the negative discourse on America in the Arab media following the election of Obama? I hope that this book will aid in the process of how American foreign policy in the Middle East is shaped and in improving America's image in the Arab world.

The book uses an analytical writing approach to document the negative impressions of America in the Arab world. It does so in eight chapters. In chapter 2 I offer an overview of the Arab media. Chapter 3 examines how America's rise as the world's superpower has been worrying to Arabs who believe that the United States is out to occupy their land and dominate their culture, and how the Bush government and neoconservatives added to this fear. The chapter also offers a snapshot of how Arabs portrayed the American president's visit to the region in January 2008. Chapter 4 shows condemnation of American policy in the Middle East and U.S. endeavors to control Arab oil and further empower Israel and weaken the Palestinians, in a so-called conspiracy to establish a Greater Middle East in which Israel acts as a hegemon. The chapter reveals that although Arabs oppose Iranian policy in the Middle East and its efforts to own nuclear power, they also oppose any U.S. military action against the Persian state. Chapter 5 raises questions on the principles upon which U.S. democracy has been founded and reveals Arabs' ridicule for

Washington for trying to "export" these principles to the Arabs. They argue that before Washington tries to promote democracy in the Arab world, it should first get its own house in order, citing cases of human rights violations in the United States and the Abu Ghraib and Guantánamo Bay prison scandals. Chapter 6 scrutinizes how the "land of dreams," which many Arabs craved to immigrate to in the past, has lost its charm in the Arab mind. This is due to Washington's post-9/11 policy on terrorism, which Arabs accuse of arousing discrimination and hostility toward them.

As this book underscores, the United States continues to face huge challenges concerning its public image in the Arab world. Whether this anti-Americanism in the Arab world will diminish with the arrival of President Obama is a question that deserves study, and chapter 7 is an attempt to do so. The chapter examines whether or not Arabs have been optimistic about Obama's rise to power and the factors upon which they base their judgments. The time period selected for the study is November 6, 2008, a couple days after Obama was elected, to February 1, 2009, roughly ten days after his inauguration. In chapter 8 I offer my concluding comments without any sense of antipathy but with the aim to raise the spirit of dialogue between Arabs and Americans and improve America's image in the Arab and Muslim world. I also offer a quick analysis on how the Arab media saw in Obama's speech to the Muslim world a glimpse of hope toward bridging the divide between the two cultures.

On top of deep divisions in social classes in the Arab world, Arabs are now digging in their heels for ways to counter U.S. dictates. But why do Arabs scold and view Americans as ethnocentric, materialistic warmongers? Is there truly a clash of cultures between "us" and "them"? Most importantly, how is such criticism (or hatred) expressed among Arabs? Regrettably, most Americans today are unaware of how they are portrayed in the Arab media. While in the past it was Washington's "biased policies" and not U.S. values that mainly shaped Arabs' negative opinion of America, today positive attitudes toward U.S. values, people, and products are declining among Arabs. Arabs see the 9/11 tragedies as offering neoconservatives in Washington a carte blanche to rule the world and turn it into a dangerous place; Arabs are denouncing U.S. foreign policy as "coca colonialism" and calling American culture the "Big Mac culture."

Fear of American imperialism is deeply engraved in the minds and hearts of many Arabs today. This is causing a rise in a religious piety founded on refutation of the West. In constructing America as the "Great Evil," a few of the Arabs I spoke with often referred to a U.S. history of violence and discrimination against blacks. (This view of America as a racist nation was reiterated less after Obama's election.) Arabs speak more of a tyrant America and less of their own Arab autocratic regimes. They portray America as an invading force, a rising empire that is targeting their people. They cry loudly of the injustice that Uncle Sam is inflicting on them, often admonishing America's notion of democracy. American involvement in Iraq and Afghanistan, support for Israeli assaults on Lebanon and against the Palestinians, and talk of attacking Iran have all fomented fears among Arabs, fuelling the stereotype that America is an anti-Arab, anti-Muslim nation. This was mirrored in the unwelcoming sentiment in the five Arab states President Bush visited in January 2008—particularly in Egypt, where he had a brief visit with President Hosni Mubarak, who had not visited the United States since 2004.[3]

I first felt this rising anti-American sentiment in the Arab world in January 2004, when I came to Egypt on a short visit from New Zealand, where I was teaching at the time. Egyptians were enraged by the U.S. capture of Saddam Hussein. Wherever I went it seemed that everyone was talking about Saddam, who no longer was viewed as a tyrant but as a hero, the only Arab leader to stand up to America. Saddam's humiliating capture by the United States raised his popularity among Arabs and unleashed potent anti-American currents. A few spoke of how the Americans drugged him, or else he would have assassinated himself. Others said that he was captured during the war but that the Americans kept it a secret to use in case things went wrong for them in Iraq. Many called on prominent Egyptian lawyers to enlist with the Jordanian-based Arab Lawyers Union and defend Saddam. Soon after his execution, which Arabs witnessed on their television screens, many voices in the Arab media began planting harmful images of Americans. It was at that time that I began considering coming back to the Arab world to write a book that documented the motives behind the mounting anti-Americanism in the region.

What further motivated me to write this book were the results of three opinion polls conducted in the Arab world. One poll was carried out by a well-established Egyptian magazine, the other two by the Washington-based Arab American Institute/Zogby International (AAI/ZI). The three polls showed alarming evidence of how the ongoing conflicts in Iraq and Palestine are deepening the rift between Arabs and Americans, with the image of the United States in the Arab mind being worse than ever. One AAI/ZI poll was conducted between February 26 and March 10, 2007, and surveyed 3,400 Arabs in the countries of Egypt, Saudi Arabia, Jordan, United Arab Emirates (UAE), and Lebanon.[4] Respondents in the five Arab countries showed deep concern and fear for stability in the region because of America's invasion of Iraq. They exhibited negative attitudes toward America's role in Iraq, with the following percentages: 68 percent in Saudi Arabia, 70 percent in UAE, 76 percent in Lebanon, 83 percent in Egypt, and 96 percent in Jordan. Of particular concern to those polled was the degree to which the war bolstered neighboring Iran and intensified the danger that Iraq may unravel in a civil war spilling over the broader region. "The Bush Administration finds itself in a bind of its own making, created by entering into this conflict without a clear understanding of its consequences," noted AAI president James Zogby. "But this same bind has also placed our Arab allies in an equally difficult situation—one with even more troubling options."[5] The other AAI/ZI poll was released in December 2006 and was based on face-to-face interviews with a total sample of 3,500 natives of the countries of Saudi Arabia, Egypt, Morocco, Jordan, and Lebanon.[6] In general, results showed that overall Arab attitudes toward America had worsened since 2002. The reason behind this increase in anti-Americanism was U.S. policies in Iraq and Palestine. "Uncertainty resulting from these two conflicts has significantly dampened Arab confidence in prospects for economic development and political stability," said the survey finding. Furthermore, attitudes toward American values, people, and culture had declined. American policy toward Lebanon also accounted for some negative sentiment.[7] As table 1 exhibits, the poll showed that overall U.S. favorable/unfavorable ratings in Saudi Arabia, Egypt, and Lebanon were largely unchanged, but the negatives had hardened. In Morocco and Jordan, the favorable U.S. rating had dropped considerably.[8]

Table 1: Opinion of the United States

	2002		2005		2006	
	Fav (%)	Unfav (%)	Fav (%)	Unfav (%)	Fav (%)	Unfav (%)
Egypt	15	76	14	85	14	83
Jordan	34	61	33	62	5	90
Lebanon	26	70	32	60	28	68
Morocco	38	61	34	64	7	87
Saudi Arabia	12	87	9	89	12	82

Note: The results shown here are based on the "favorable" and "unfavorable" category, but interviewees were also asked whether they were "not familiar enough to make a judgment."

The poll by *Rose El-Yossef* was published in the highly politicized Egyptian weekly magazine in April 2007, and it focused on Egyptian youths' perception of America and Israel.[9] It showed that gender and social class play a role in affecting Egyptian youths' attitudes toward U.S. policies and values, for there was a difference in opinion between boys and girls and between the affluent students of the American University in Cairo (AUC) and the rest of Egyptian youths. All of those polled, however, believed that America is run by a small group of Zionists who support Israel financially and militarily and violate the rights of Arab countries. They argued that while Israel wants Palestine, America desires to control the entire Middle East. Overall, there were favorable opinions about American education, technology, and freedom. America, said the respondents, is a civilized state that respects work, value of time, and the intellect. It is democratic in everything it does except when dealing with the Arabs, when it then becomes dictatorial. When asked whether or not they watch American movies, 75 percent of girls polled said yes because they reflect American reality and have high capability; they did not like the "obscene scenes" in some of them, despite the fact that such movies may reflect real-life stories. They also complained that every now and then there appear new movies that defame Arabs. Twenty percent of girls said they do not watch American movies for they introduce nothing new or because they prefer to watch other foreign movies. The remaining 5 percent said they sometimes watch them because they are mostly fantasy movies. On the other side, 70 percent of boys said they watch American movies because they tell what is happening and often focus on high-caliber and exciting issues. Twenty percent said they do not watch American movies because they dislike them, do not have time to do so, or because they prefer Arab movies. The remaining 10 percent said they watch some of them merely for enjoyment or for a desire to initiate an Arab response toward movies that associate them with terrorism and barbarism. Another reason given was to understand American public opinion, which, according to respondents, often goes in Israel's favor. All AUC students surveyed (100 percent) said they watch American movies.

Sixty percent of girls said they do not wish to travel to America because the country is a nightmare and Americans despise Arabs and Muslims; or they prefer to travel to Arab countries, where there is stability; or they would rather stay at home because they do not wish to travel. Twenty percent of girls said they wish to travel to America, mainly for better knowledge or to walk freely in the streets without facing molestation, and then return to Egypt. The remaining 20 percent had other reasons for wanting or not wanting to travel to the United States, such as America is their dream, they have relatives there, Americans do not agree with what Washington is doing, or America has now become a frightening place. Conversely, 55 percent of boys said they do not wish to travel to America because it has become an enormous deceit or because they do not accept living as second-class citizens. Others said that America mistreats Muslims, citing the torture of Muslim prisoners at Abu Ghraib and Guantánamo Bay as an example. The remaining 45 percent of male respondents said they desire to travel to America in search of better learning and to benefit from its freedom. Others said they wish to go there mainly for tourism or to seek job opportunities. Of the male AUC students, 60 percent said they desire to travel to America because the country respects work, the intellect, tourism, and civil liberties. The remaining 40 percent said no due to their love for Egypt or because since 9/11 America mistreats Arabs. Interestingly, 90 percent of female AUC students said they wish to travel there to study, learn about different cultures, or because America respects civil liberties. The 10 percent left said they do not wish to travel to America for they find it hard to travel and leave their beloved homeland behind.

When asked whether or not it is better for Egypt to approach and strengthen its ties with America, girls contended that it is better in order to avoid clashes with a mighty superpower and to gain from America's advanced technology. According to them, in the absence of strengthened ties, Washington could claim that Egypt is producing nuclear weapons, and their country could experience what Iraq, North Korea, and Iran have. Others said why not stand up to America one single time. There were also those who stressed that Egypt should increase ties with America mainly for maintaining peace in the region, but it should sever such relations when Israel invades Arab lands with Washington's consent. Boys, on the other side, said increasing relations with America when Egypt is strong has meaning, but if doing so is merely to avoid America's evil, then it is nonsense; there were times in the past, they said, when Arabs approached America and gained nothing in return. America, in their view, spreads oppression and corruption in the Arab world, and thus it is better to stay away from it. Others said it is better at present to approach and deal moderately with both Washington and Jerusalem, for America is the strongest country in the world and controls Egypt's main supply of food, corn, which Cairo imports annually with millions of dollars. They added that the issue is business and national interests, and it is not to Egypt's advantage to be America's enemy. All AUC students held that dealings with Washington should be judged based on each situation, but generally strengthening relations would make Egyptians understand America better. They added that Egypt benefits from U.S. aid in the areas of technology, the arts, and economics, but America certainly does not want Egypt to gain full benefit.

Undoubtedly, the Arab media recycle incomplete images of Americans. In a sense, what Hollywood has been doing to Arabs and Arab and Muslim Americans—paralleling them with terrorists such as Osama bin Laden and dictators such as Saddam Hussein—the Arab media are now doing to Americans: planting fear and revulsion of them in the Arab culture. Americans need to understand Arabs better if they are to break these cultural barriers and counter this rising anti-Americanism in the Arab consciousness. Americans should not take the criticism and distorted images exhibited of them in the Arab world with utter despair but as a propeller toward understanding their roots. Perhaps Arabs are undereducated about America and its people, or perhaps they are not. What is known for sure is that the time has come for Arabs and Americans to work consistently toward a better understanding of each other and toward a culture of trust, not just between them but also in the entire Middle East.

The strength of this book lies in its ability to bring an abundance of information and details—all examples were originally written or broadcast in the Arabic language—about a topic that could arouse anger and suspicion in the hearts and minds of the many Americans who idealize their notion of government, democracy, and freedom. It offers its readers answers to why this anti-Americanism is spreading in the Arab world and how the Arab media are propagating it in the Arab psyche. It also moves to broadly examine U.S. foreign policy in the Middle East and America's standing in the world, an issue of concern to many. The book should be of great value to ordinary readers, Middle East experts, and members of the U.S. government, particularly those serving on the U.S. House Committee on Foreign Affairs. I hope it will be a step for promoting mutual understanding not just between Arabs and Americans but among all people of the world.

In choosing a title for the book, I borrowed the phrase "ugly American" from the 1958 novel by Eugene Burdick and William Lederer.[10] The main theme of the novel, which portrays several real people whose names have been changed, is that America is losing the battle with Communism in Vietnam and the struggle for the hearts and minds of people in Southeast Asia because of U.S. arrogance and a failure to understand their local culture. The phrase "ugly American" has become part of the lexicon of Americans, often referring to the thoughtless and demeaning behavior of Americans abroad.[11] I often heard it while living in the States but never really knew from where it originated until my editor at Potomac Books referred me to the novel and suggested injecting its title into my own. I saw this as plausible, for the argument

I make in this book is that American policy in the Middle East under the Bush administration was haunted by the same mistakes as U.S. policy in Southeast Asia. In fact, many Arab commentators have compared America's mistakes in Iraq to those in Vietnam.

2 THE ARAB MEDIA: A BRIEF LOOK

A true journalist is one who is not afraid when writing and does not write when afraid. MUSTAPHA AMIN, journalist and cofounder of Egypt's Akhbar El-Yom Publishing Group

In this chapter, I briefly measure the contours of the Arab media and what one may call the mixed media culture that engulfs the Arab world today. Generally, the media are tools to inform, persuade, or mobilize a mass public. They are a forum for the exchange of ideas and the spread of truth. They are meant to play a pivotal role in what philosopher Jurgen Habermas called the "public sphere."[1] The press, in Harold Lasswell's view, plays a surveillance role.[2] Hence, argued Gaye Tuchman, "news is a window on the world."[3]

The Arab world consists of twenty-two Arab countries, with varied social, political, and media systems. It has a population of about three hundred million and land occupying 10 percent of the earth. The Arab region has numerous natural resources, including oil, natural gas, uranium, and iron. Arab states produce 28 percent of the world's total oil. In all, 63 percent of the earth's oil reserve is in the Arab world. Because of these economic and strategic factors, the region has been of great importance to the United States, with Washington consistently trying over the years to maintain good ties with Arab states, particularly the Gulf ones. Lately, however, political acrimony toward U.S. policy in the Middle East has been fueling a vibrant anti-American charge in the Arab world—and the Arab media have been busy reporting on it.

The media in the Arab world are becoming important institutions; they play a crucial role in shaping the opinion of Arabs. The number of newspapers and satellite channels has risen in the Arab world over the past few years, according to news editor and popular columnist Salama Ahmed Salama, but Arab governments continue to exercise some power over them. Restraint and shutting down of papers have become daily news in many parts of the Arab world. Salama praised the Federation of Arab Journalists for establishing a center to document cases of press freedom violations in the region.[4] A 2008 survey by the Washington-based Freedom House on the state of press freedom worldwide reported that the modest progress some Arab states, particularly Lebanon, Egypt, and Syria, had achieved over the past few years came to an end in 2007.[5] The "depressing pattern of the Arab media these days" seems to be "one step forward, two steps back," observed journalism professor Lawrence Pintak of the American University in Cairo.[6]

The emergence of the Arabic-language press goes back to the nineteenth century. European colonialists (such as Napoleon Bonaparte) and missionaries brought the printing press along with them.[7] While Arabs in Lebanon, Syria, Egypt, and Iraq have been involved in the media for almost a century, a number of Arab Gulf states did not have newspapers until the 1970s. The idea of a cross-border pan-Arab media emerged in the late 1970s and 1980s.[8] Following the eruption of the Lebanese civil war in 1975, some Arab publications began publishing from Europe, particularly from London. For example, major daily newspapers such as *Al-Hayat, Asharq Al-Awsat, Al-Quds Al-Arabi,* and *Al-Zaman* are published out of London. Lebanon's major newspaper *Al-Nahar* prints an international edition out of Paris. Egypt's giant *Al-Ahram* newspaper also has an international edition that prints out of London. A popular Arab weekly magazine published out of London is the Saudi-owned *Al-Majalla.* The Lebanese weekly magazine *Al-Hawadith* also published out of London for a few years before moving back to operate from Beirut. With London being the home base, these pan-Arab media developed a new notion of Arabism and constructed an arena for the marketplace of ideas.[9] They play a pivotal role in how Arabs perceive and interpret local and international events. Nonetheless, London has slowly been losing its standing as the hub of pan-Arab media.[10]

Today, with the rise of rich and powerful media tycoons in parts of the region, the Arab media seem to be divided between the haves (the Arab Gulf states) and the have-nots (Morocco, Jordan, Egypt, Sudan, and Lebanon). Over the past two decades, because of the oil revenue boom that came in the 1980s, the Saudis have acquired and launched many of the nongovernmental pan-Arab media channels, from *Al-Hayat* and *Asharq Al-Awsat* to the Cairo-based Arab Radio and Television (ART), from the Middle East Broadcasting Corporation (MBC) and Al-Arabiya television station to Orbit and a major chunk of Arab Satellite (Arabsat). These Saudi-owned publications and satellite television channels reach almost every Arab capital and many Middle Eastern and African nations. A leader in extending free-based satellite broadcasting to the Arab world, Orbit delivers more than twenty-four television channels plus radio to many parts of the world. It is owned by the Mawarid Group, a multibillion-dollar media conglomerate of Prince Khalid bin Abdullah. The group also has separate business operations in Lebanon, Morocco, Egypt, Tunisia, and Syria.

Culturally, content of the Arab media has helped in creating the images and promoting the paradigms that define Arabs' relations to and expectations of Americans. The Arab media vary from one political system to another, from one country to another, and from one theme to another. Unlike in the West, where the media are dominated by big capital, Arab media are strongly tied to culture and traditions with some political patronization. Most of the Arab media are government-owned or are controlled by government; they reflect governments' policies and influence and are influenced by them. Tahseen Al-Khiat, a media expert, views the Arab media as "regrettably" having no influence on the decision-making process in the Arab world.[11] Ismah Ibrahim, a consultant at the Palestinian Authority, believes that the primary function of state-owned Arab media is to promote the image of Arab governments and support their policies. He argued that there is a need for a unified Arab media that promotes the viewpoints of all Arabs.[12]

It is important to stress to the reader once again that most of the print and broadcast media in the Arab world serve the interests of their governments. As journalist Sherif Hatatah wrote in the Egyptian Nasserite Party paper *Al-Arabi*: "If we look closely at most of the newspapers, magazines and television channels operating in our Arab media, we will find that they are supported mainly by either a bureaucratic state regime or wealthy individuals. . . . Hence, it is natural that they are generally directed to serve the interests of those who fund and control them, even if they do that with a level of intelligence that can hide their goals."[13] Even the popular Qatari-owned Al-Jazeera would not permit criticism of the Qatari regime, noted Egyptian businessman Naguib Seweriss in an interview with Egypt's Al-Oula television station.[14] Furthermore, Pintak has pointed out that there are stories leaking that the Qatari royals have demanded Al-Jazeera take it easy on Saudi Arabia in a bid to protect Sunni unity in the face of Iranian danger to the region.[15]

Media Liberalization vs. Government Control

With the end of the Cold War, many Arab leaders lost the strong support they were getting from Moscow or Washington. This is particularly true for Arab states that were heavily dependent on the Soviet Union, such as Syria, Libya, and Yemen. This has had an effect on the structure and content of their media systems. Over the past two decades, the news media in the Arab world have become an industry, a major one. Today, because of globalization, media reform is the catchphrase in countries such as Jordan, Morocco, United Arab Emirates, and Bahrain, though many Arab journalists fear that is all just public-relations propaganda. In 2008, for example, it was said that Egypt was drafting a proposal to privatize its state media sector, but Cairo later denied that.[16]

Currently, there is a boom in the satellite television industry in the Arab world. It is easy to wake every morning and hear of a new channel being launched. In the past, most Arab television stations were entirely dependent on government funding for their operations. In the last few years, however, we have begun to witness television stations such as Al-Jazeera, Al-Arabiya, Abu Dhabi, and MBC depend on advertising as a means of funding. Media analysts have argued, though, that there are still "states that fund some Arab satellite channels in return for an Arab TV channel adopting and defending their policies and exerting its efforts to attack their opponents."[17] We are also seeing a rise in the number of private, nongovernment-owned newspapers, particularly in Egypt. Over the past decade, Egypt has witnessed the launching of a large number of newspapers independent from government influence, with many of them being characterized as yellow papers. It is said that the country's mainstream independent newspapers number roughly twenty-five. As I sit here in the city of Benha, about forty miles north of Cairo, I see an Arab media in a transitional period. I see the state media behemoth and a rapidly growing opposition press that uncovers government corruption and misdemeanor. The one thing they both seem to agree on is that America is an invader with an anti-Arab ideology.

It is worth mentioning that in February 2008, Arab ministers of information adopted a charter aimed at regulating the booming satellite broadcasting industry, which officials at times accuse of spreading lies and inciting conflicts. The satellite broadcasting charter allows authorities to withdraw permits from satellite channels considered to have offended Arab leaders or national or religious icons. Arab intellectuals criticized the charter and denounced it as a means of censoring media freedom. Qatar was the one country reported to have refused to endorse the charter.

Print Press

The *Jurnal Al-Iraq* (Journal of Iraq), published in 1816, is considered the first newspaper to be printed in Arabic (it was also published in Turkish). The Egyptian newspaper *Waqai Misriya* (Official Gazette) was founded by Mohammed Ali Pasha during his rule (1805–1848) of Egypt. The first Arabic daily newspaper was published in Lebanon in 1873. On the other side, the first Arab newspaper to be published in English was the *Egyptian Gazette*, which continues to print today. As for academic journals, Egypt's *Al-Siyassa Al-Dawliya* (International Politics) was founded in 1965. It is published quarterly by the giant Al-Ahram Press Group.

Today's Arab newspapers are of three genres: national (progovernment), party, and independent. The characteristics of partisan newspapers in the Arab world have changed over the past few years, particularly in Egypt, with papers growing so much stronger than their political parties that one can argue that without party newspapers there can be no parties. It is hard to get accurate circulation figures of newspapers and magazines in many Arab countries, but based on information I gained from contacting Arab media sources directly and from the 2008 edition of *Editor & Publisher International Yearbook*, newspapers with high circulation are *Asharq Al-Awsat, Al-Hayat, Al-Ahram*, and the Lebanese *Al-Nahar*. Weekly magazines with high circulation figures are *Almussawar, Al-Hawadith, Sabah El-Kheir*, and *Al-Majalla*. Popular monthly magazines include *Al-Arabi, Al-Hilal*, and *Wijhat Nathar*. Almost all Arab states operate government-sponsored news agencies, the most prominent of which are the Kuwait News Agency (KUNA), the Middle East News Agency of Egypt (MENA), and the Saudi News Agency.

Broadcast Media

Television and Pan-Arab Satellite TV Boom

In many ways, Arabs' perception of America nowadays is vigorously shaped by the stories that appear on television screens. The largely unfettered approach of transnational Arab broadcasters is widening the public sphere. Television news and talk shows affect and influence Arabs' political views and the way they perceive America. Because of high illiteracy, "broadcasting is the most widespread, powerful means of communication in the Arab world," according to Hussein Y. Amin, chair of the Department of Journalism and Mass Communications at the American University in Cairo.[18] For instance, over 55 percent of Egyptians have begun to depend on satellite television channels and the Internet as sources of information.

It is a normal practice in the Arab world for a government to own television and radio. Such ownership was inherited from European colonialists; the French and British placed television and radio under government control to be used as propaganda tools. After the end of colonial rule in the Arab world, independent Arab governments put the broadcast media under their control. In the 1950s, television was aired on a limited basis in Iraq and Lebanon. In most of the remaining Arab states, television did not begin until the 1960s. By 1975 all Arab states had their own television stations. Jordan began broadcasting in 1968, Bahrain in 1972, Oman in 1974, and Yemen in 1975. Over the last fifteen years, though, Arabs have witnessed an incredible rise in the number of transnational Arab satellite television stations, such as Al-Jazeera, Al-Arabiya, and Abu Dhabi TV. This is due in part to the first Gulf War in 1991, during which Arabs learned about Iraq's invasion of Kuwait through CNN. Currently, Arab satellite channels reach almost every Arab capital and many Middle Eastern and African states; major channels stretch as far as Europe and America. There are over three hundred satellite television channels broadcasting in Arabic from the Gulf to the Atlantic Ocean.[19] This boom has led many Arabs to tune in to pan-Arab satellite channels and turn off their local TV channels.[20] A large amount of these private TV satellite channels are owned by businessmen—members of the ruling governments or their loyalists. They are used mainly for political and social influence—a form of prestige— but others believe they can be used as tools for countering Western influence on Arab culture.[21] Certainly profit is also a goal, since satellite television channels are a moneymaking industry in the Arab world.

A few initiatives have been taken to counter Saudi dominance in the broadcasting industry: the launching of major satellite channels such as the maverick Al-Jazeera in 1996, Lebanon's LBC in 1996, the Syrian Arab News Network (ANN) in 1997, Egypt's Nile TV in 1998, and Abu Dhabi TV in 2000. Al-Jazeera is a progressive news and talk show satellite TV station founded by the emir of Qatar and is considered to have some influence on shaping Arab public opinion. It is the most watched news channel in the Arab world, with over forty million viewers. In early 2007, it launched a sister channel in English, known as Al-Jazeera International. Even though Al-Arabiya and Abu Dhabi TV also cover news and compete with Al-Jazeera, they are less contentious in their reporting. Al-Arabiya's all-news format tends to have a preference for financial news. Table 2 documents the development of major satellite channels in the Arab world:

Table 2: Development of major Arab satellite channels

Date	Name	Country Affiliation	Ownership
1990	ESC	Egypt	State
1991	MBC	Saudi Arabia	Private
1992	Dubai EDTV	United Arab Emirates	State
1993	JSC	Jordan	State
1994	ART Orbit RTM	Saudi Arabia Saudi Arabia Morocco	Private Private State
1995	STV	Syria	State
1996	LBC-Sat Future International Al-Jazeera	Lebanon Lebanon Qatar	Private Private Private
1997	ANN	Syria	Private
1998	Nile Channels	Egypt	State
2000	Abu Dhabi TV	United Arab Emirates	State
2003	Al-Arabiya	Saudi Arabia	Private

Source: Compiled by the author after consulting various newsletters, public relations releases, and Naomi Sakr, *Satellite Realms: Transnational Television, Globalisation and the Middle East* (London: IB Tauris, 2001).

Radio

Radio stations, like TV channels, are also in abundance in the Arab world and are mostly state-owned. Governments hold control over their editorial content, much more than they do with television stations. Radio first began broadcasting in Egypt and Morocco in the 1920s. Saudi Arabia opened its first radio station in 1948; Kuwait in 1952; United Arab Emirates, Oman, and Qatar in the 1970s. To escape government control, Arabs are beginning to launch their own online radio stations. One creative example is

Ammannet.net, which was founded by Daoud Khuttab, a Palestinian journalist. Awarded Jordan's first private radio license, Khuttab described it as a
multimedia community-oriented station.

Internet

The Internet is currently the fastest growing media form and is said to have
changed the flow of information throughout the world. It allows users to exchange information faster than at any other time in the history of humanity.
According to Nua Surveys, the Internet was first introduced in Egypt in 1993
via the founding of a small university network. Commercial Internet use
started in 1996, when connectivity was introduced to private Internet service
providers, resulting in a boom in the number of users at home, at business, and
at cyber cafes.[22] While Internet access was originally restricted to a very small
number of Arab elites, this notion is slowly changing. For a significant number of today's Arab editors, publishers, and reporters, embracing new tech-
nologies and the concept of a free press are becoming matters of economic
survival or professional pride—and sometimes both. There is also the oppor-
tunity for some Arab journalists to link faster with their Western counterparts.

The availability of the Internet among Arabs, particularly in the oil-rich
Gulf states, is growing. There are plenty of Arab journalism and media re-
sources of interest out there. One can read major Arabic daily newspapers on-
line—from *Al-Hayat* to *Asharq Al-Awsat*, from *Al-Ahram* to *Al-Nahar* and
Al-Quds Al-Arabi. Arab newspapers published in English, such as the *Jordan
Times*, *Oman Observer*, *Gulf News* of the United Arab Emirates, the Lebanese
Daily Star, and Egypt's *Al-Ahram Weekly*, are also available online. Major
Arabic magazines include *Almussawar*, *Al-Hawadith*, and *Sabah El-Kheir*.
Online media are also in abundance. The oldest Arabic online newspaper is the
Saudi-owned *Elaph*, which was first published in 2001, and there is the
Ammannet.net online radio station referred to previously. There is also a bur-
geoning blogging community in the Arab world, causing a lot of disturbance
to some Arab regimes.

How is the economic gap in the Arab world affecting media technology in
the region? Do reporters in the Arab world have full and free access to the
Internet? How much has Internet use benefited the free flow of information in
the region? How are Arab rulers dealing with this fast and new technology? These
are all questions that deserve to be studied but are beyond the scope of this book,
which primarily focuses on how the Arab media portray the United States.

Professionalism and Journalistic Ethics

The institutional foundation of journalism in the Arab world differs significantly from the Western ideal. For example, the way Arabs perceive and construct the Iraq War is, in many ways, influenced by Arabs' heritage and the varied political systems in their states—from authoritarian to democratic. Journalists, particularly those at the state-owned media, often censor themselves to avoid punishment and please their editors, who are frequently appointed by their governments.

Press freedom is said to be the foundation on which any democracy can be erected. Although there has been much improvement in Arab journalism, it still does not exactly set a high standard. The print and broadcast media of many countries in the Arab world have been trying to breathe on their own and find their places on the map of the New World Order. Among the challenges they face are the rise of new media technology, government-press relations, editorial independence, use of opinion polls to measure the public's attitude toward politics, the institution of a pluralist society, and the promotion of representation of women. The Arab youth is also not well represented in the Arab media.

Arabs must realize that for their media to be truly independent, they must be free, not only from government control but also from political and commercial pressures. Furthermore, Arab journalists and editors must not deceive their readers by spreading lies and misconceptions; they must always defend the truth and listen more to what their readers, viewers, and listeners want. At times, it is hard for a scholar of Arab journalism to distinguish between advertising, publicity, and news, particularly when elections are running. During national feasts or independence days, some Arab countries place a full page or more in major Arab newspapers, often with pictures of presidents or kings. Westerners are unaccustomed to such a practice. They would see it as weakening the press's detachment from government.

In the past, Arab governments entrusted the press with the responsibility of "guiding" citizens in the ways of the regime. Today, these concepts of media control are slowly being dismantled in the Arab region, with the concept of "guidance" being replaced by the terms "responsible" and "information." Countries such as Morocco, Kuwait, and Lebanon are making progress toward a free, Western-style press. How much of that is true? What role can the United States and American journalists play in assisting reporters in those states to establish a free and responsible press that is compatible with that in the West? In conclusion, after reading the Arab media commentary on the United States presented in this book, I believe that further research is badly needed on the following issues:

- Professionalism and dominant journalism standards in the Arab world.

- The social responsibility argument in the Arab world: Arab journalists often argue that when they cover events, they pay extreme attention to the social and cultural structure of the society in which they live. That, according to them, should not be viewed as censorship but respect for their culture and traditions.

- The ideals of objectivity in the Arab media and how they differ from Western ones. What establishes a good, fair, and objective story in the Arab press?

- The various types of constitutional rights Arab journalists have and the interaction between the press and ministries of information in the Arab world. What types of restrictions exist?

- How is the Arab press operating in monarchy systems different from that operating in state systems?

- Do we need those ministries of information in operation in many parts of the Arab world today?

3   THE AMERICAN EMPIRE

In the vision of the Right in the Bush Administration, an empire does not expand through love. GAMIL MATAR, Egyptian writer

To completely resent the culture of the other is a mistake; however, imitation, subordination, and being content with consumption is a grave mistake. HANNA MENA, Syrian novelist

The American culture of Big Mac, jeans, and fast food is invading the world, with the Hollywood culture of violence and sex having a negative impact on Arab culture. AL-HILAL, Egyptian magazine, November 1998

When I hear you I believe you, but your actions make me wonder. Arab proverb

Most Arab intellectuals tend not to deny that they live in the age of the American empire. The American imperial project began in the 1890s, after the end of the Civil War, and had spread over the world by the 1990s, according to Mohamed Hasseinein Heikel, former editor in chief of Egypt's *Al-Ahram* newspaper and advisor to President Gamal Abdel Nasser. With the end of the Cold War, the United States has moved from being a superpower to a hyperactive power, added the Arab world's most popular journalist. He described the United States as a "private sector empire" serving individual and corporate needs and stressed that it holds economic influence different from past empires, such as the Roman, Ottoman, or British, which predominantly served general needs. He accused the country of using the media as a tool in its campaign to rule the world.[1] Like Heikel, foreign policy expert Abdel Moneim Said believes the United States is dominating the world in a way different from that of past empires. "Perhaps past empires controlled more land, but America is not just controlling land; it is controlling the sky and beyond," wrote Said. "It is certainly disturbing and angering to many Arabs that there seems to be a kind of imbalance in the universe and the everlasting laws of balance among nations."[2]

America's clout as a superpower emerged following Washington's opposition to the British-French-Israeli attack on Egypt in 1956, argued former Egyptian ambassador to the United States Ashraf Gharbal, who believes that Western leadership has fallen from Britain and France to the United States.[3] America has aimed at widening its hegemony; its dreams have expanded to identify the whole world as part of its borders.[4] Today's United States is armed with all the tools needed for cultural, political, and economic manipulation and military destruction.[5] "It aspires to proclaim: 'I am the one and only nation in the world.'"[6] Yet Washington, in the view of Professor Said Al-Lawandi, has used all "means of distortion" to hide its "colonial plans."[7] It would be a mistake, he suggested, to believe that this "'American madness' began as a result of the September 11 attacks, for it is well established that the American imperial project began earlier. The September 11 terrorist attacks have merely accelerated its momentum by getting the American public ready to accept and agree to the necessity of dispatching American forces to all parts of the world to preserve the country's national security."[8]

A number of Arabs have predicted the demise of the American empire. Adel S. Bishtami spoke of the injustice the United States has employed to dominate the world, as embodied in its attempts to control Arab oil. He forecasted the failure of America's colonial ambitions in the Arab world and the downfall of its imperialism.[9] The fall of the United States, however, would have repercussions, cautioned Mahmoud Al-Saddani in his bestseller *America Wika*. "America is the greatest and biggest empire that history has ever known," he wrote.[10] "Simply, America is not a state; it is a continent," added the popular Egyptian journalist known for his muckraking. But unlike past empires, if it falls the "whole world will fall with it, because its economy dominates the globe."[11] He lamented the collapse of the Soviet Union, which he described as the "cracked wall" on which weak nations leaned to oppose American tyranny. Al-Saddani prognosticated that law will take its turn on the American empire, as it has done to past empires. "We pray that the next century will be better than the American one," he said.[12]

In the view of Lebanese/Syrian author Nazzar Basheer, the American empire differs from past empires in that it does not merely aspire to achieve victory against its enemies but to wipe them out. America's terrorist weapons vary according to geography, and Arabs and Muslims have always been targets of the tyranny of American imperialism, he wrote. "The enemy has realized from the beginning the power of the Arab world and Islam, and how they pose a direct threat to America's existence."[13] History, said Al-Saddani, never supports the weak or the poor. From the time Christopher Columbus discovered America, white Europeans began eradicating Native Americans, even though they were fully welcomed by the latter. "America slaughtered an entire population and crushed a flourishing civilization," alleged Al-Saddani.[14] Through the "biggest crime that history has ever known, the American empire has been established, and it remains the empire of violence and might." Citing the right for gun ownership in the United States, Al-Saddani lamented that this culture of violence has continued in the fabric of American society and is reiterated in Hollywood movies.[15] He asked us not to forget what the United States did in Hiroshima, Vietnam, Korea, Chile, and Guantánamo. He continued, "An empire which is founded on murder will continue to practice murder, and you will not know from where death comes—from gangs or police, from people or government. Everyone kills; everyone is a killer."[16] Fear, he cautioned, dominates the American empire. "If Israel has eradicated half of the Palestinian population, its crime is then only half of that of America, and when you discuss the issue with an American he will think you are an idiot or crazy. What is the problem with eradicating half of a population?"[17] Al-Saddani concluded, "This is the American psyche, the American mood. This is the American history without decoration or coloring—a connected chain of crimes which, in the view of Americans, culminated in good."[18]

Neoconservatives: Between the Right and the Far Right

With the ascendance of neoconservatives to power in Washington, Arab intellectuals began describing the United States as a right-wing country and capitalist empire that disregards social equality and aims at dominating other nations. Neocons, cautioned Al-Lawandi in 2005, aspire to weaken Arab identity and its symbol, the Arab League. They desire to achieve the dream of the Greater American Empire, as exhibited by their "invasion of Iraq, subordination of Europe and changing the dimensions of the 'old' Middle East region."[19] Neocons in the Bush government, such as Vice President Dick Cheney and

Secretary of Defense Donald Rumsfeld, believed that the United States should be a hegemon on the world center stage.[20] Heikel cited how a U.S. law granting a U.S. president the right to issue assassination orders against foreign political leaders was cancelled by President Gerald Ford but was later reenacted by George W. Bush in his "holy war" against terrorism.[21]

According to Raji Inayet, when it came to America's development, neocons moved from dependence on the power of knowledge to reliance on the power of the armed forces. He said that by having Bush in office, neocons increased their might: "The gang of neoconservatives has succeeded in controlling America, its President, and push for a U.S. war on Afghanistan and another on Iraq—both have not yet been finished. It has begun hunting for new wars with Syria, Iran or North Korea, with the possibility of turning on Venezuela or Cuba after that." Welcome to the age of the neocons, he said.[22] When trying to resolve conflicts, neocons in Washington atrociously refused any intervention from international or nongovernmental U.S. institutions. They often argued that America must not fall into the trap of the "policy of appeasement which the British used when dealing with Hitler; hence, anyone who disagrees with Washington today or opposes its hegemony on world affairs is likened to Hitler and his politics."[23] Consequently, stressed Waheed Abdel Mageed, neocons put back on the table the notion of war after it had been abandoned following the two world wars that left millions of people dead. To dominate the world, added Mageed, the Bush administration made war a "focal tool in international relations."[24]

Alas, the scandals of the Bush team were numerous, and Arabs were watching, asserted *Al-Khaleej*, a United Arab Emirates newspaper.[25] With the rise of neocons to power, American politics lost its credibility, wrote Morsi Attallah—who chairs the board of the giant Cairo-based Al-Ahram Press Group—in a piece in *Al-Ahram* newspaper.[26] Neocons are a bunch of fools who target Arabs, posited the Saudi paper *Al-Hayat* in 2007,[27] and their acts confirm that "American futility will not stop as long as this Administration has one day left in Office," added *Al-Thawara*, a Syrian paper.[28] They "carry the slogans of revisiting ethics" and "entirely depend on the activities of the 'religious institution,'" suggested Gamil Matar, director of the Arab Center for Development and Futuristic Research, in a piece in the Egyptian magazine *Al-Hilal*.[29] Via an "undeclared pact with AIPAC and Israel," neocons used major Christian churches to "promote views that are hostile to others," commented the Jordanian paper *Al-Rai*.[30] These "evangelists" wrongly believed that the United States should not only eliminate the threat of terrorism but also "disseminate

American thought worldwide, under the pretext that if U.S. culture is threatened abroad Americans will be exposed to danger," argued *Al-Ahram*.[31]

Certainly neocons have used religion as a tool to gather world power and achieve their goals in the Middle East, stated the Yemeni paper *Al-Thowrah*. Fighting terrorism and establishing democracy were at the forefront of the justifications they employed as "a motto for pushing the world to fight Islam and Muslims."[32] After the 9/11 attacks, wrote Nasreen Murad in the United Arab Emirates paper *Al-Bayan*, Washington used a "vicious military assault to invade the world, starting with weaker regions" such as Afghanistan and Iraq, under the "slogan of fighting 'Muslim terrorism.'"[33] According to some Arabs, the right-wing Bush administration employed the war against terrorism as an instrument for launching World War III on the Arabs. "There is no future for the neoconservatives in America," hypothesized a Libyan political analyst in an interview with the Libyan television channel Al-Jamahiriya.[34] These radicals have indulged the United States in a bloody and endless conflict in Iraq, and the question is what their future will be like after Bush is gone, stated the Saudi paper *Asharq Al-Awsat*.[35]

The politics of neoconservatives unquestionably weakened America, and the Bush administration resorted to the "politics of arm-twisting," concluded Salama Ahmed Salama, one of the Arab world's most distinguished political commentators, in a piece in *Al-Ahram*.[36] In a commentary in *Al-Hayat* on the changes that America might undergo in the future and the possibility of Barack Obama, an African American Democrat, winning the 2008 presidential election, Matar cautioned that it would be a mistake for Arabs to anticipate the "end of the neoconservatives" because their so-called war on terrorism will stay put. He wrote, "The end of the neocons has not yet come, and it may take long before it happens."[37] This position was supported by Attif Al-Ghamri, a prominent political analyst and a former U.S. correspondent for *Al-Ahram*. He conjectured that the neocons' "aggressive foreign policy," which had ruled the White House, National Security Council, and U.S. Middle East institutions since 2002, would not end with their departure in 2008; America's elite decision-makers—both Republicans and Democrats—and the public, he said, will continue to believe that "democracy in the Arab world is the safeguard for national security in the United States." Al-Ghamri added that such a belief is a modification of a theory first embraced by neocons: "Muslim terrorism is the enemy."[38]

The Bush administration surpassed all that is permissible, with its members lying to and threatening Arabs. President Bush claimed repeatedly that "his War against Iraq does not differ from America's war against Nazism and fascism," said Matar, who believes the "catastrophic" situation America is facing would not have happened if there were not individuals in power catering to certain lobbies and representing radical views. In his *Al-Hilal* piece, Matar placed neoconservatives into two groups: "imperialists" and "religious visionaries." Imperialists dream of establishing the "pillars of a long-lived empire ruling the world without any competitor. At the forefront of those belonging to this 'category' are: President George W. Bush, Donald Rumsfeld, Condoleezza Rice, and, to some extent, Richard Cheney." Religious visionaries, on the other side, believe that America has a mission. "Some see it as a mission of a crusade; others perceive it as a moral duty originating from the traditions of Western civilizations. President Bush is also in this category, with Attorney General [John] Aschroft and others who conjure up a vision to the President that he is the shadow of god on earth." Matar accused members of the latter group of being responsible for increasing tension among civilizations in the world, particularly between the Muslim world and the United States.[39]

In a commentary titled "United States in a State of Dismantling," Annis Al-Nakash argued in the Lebanese paper *As-Safir* that under a neocon government, America was "losing both its military and economic influence. . . . The most foolish Administration that history has ever witnessed has resulted in the dismantling of the U.S. and its morals."[40] Neocons believe they should seize the chance of America's status as the world's superpower to achieve the "project of an American empire," said Heikel in an interview with Al-Jazeera.[41] Safi Nazkazim described Rumsfeld as the "secretary of war," arguing in his *Al-Hilal* article that he resembled Robert McNamara, "the Vietnamese war criminal."[42] This description was reinforced by another piece in *Al-Hayat*, which characterized the secretary of defense as the "engineer of the offensive on Iraq."[43] Karam Gabr of Egypt's *Rose El-Yossef* magazine predicted that Rice would grow more "vicious and violent" during her last days in office.[44]

The might of neocons grew under the Bush administration, observed the Egyptian magazine *Almussawar*, with their influence reaching the media and dictating the content of newspapers and television stations.[45] In order to boost America's military and economic superiority globally, *Al-Ahram* argued, neocons exercised power to break the traditional tie between national sovereignty and the security of a state.[46] This "contentiousness of the American military is the result of the neoconservatives' view that the bipolarity of the old world system has fallen," stressed prominent commentator Abdel Wahab Al-Missari in the United Arab Emirates paper *Al-Ittihad* in early 2008. Sadly, though, these hardliners "do not understand that such unipolarity cannot continue."[47]

They must realize that they have brought America to a state of defeat, noted *Al-Hayat*,[48] and that their "New American Century" project has failed, posited *Akher Saa*.[49] "I am sure Bush and the neoconservatives will be kicked out of Iraq," said one caller on the Cairo-based Iraqi TV channel Al-Baghdadia.[50]

Many of the faults of American politics in the Middle East are the works of neocons, of Bush and his zealot henchmen, stressed Salama in the Egyptian magazine *Weghat Nazar*. He added that they have left their nation in a deep miasma, referring to Rumsfeld as playing a main role in "sinking America in the Iraq quagmire."[51] In spite of its failure, neocons continue to defend their policy in Iraq, observed *Al-Thawara*.[52] In "Americans Gain Results of Their Mistakes," Makrim Mohamed Ahmed, head of the Egyptian Journalists Syndicate, indicated there may have been no escape for the Bush administration from the neocons' flawed politics. Citing Palestinian-Israeli violence, troubles in Pakistan and Iraq, and tension over Iran's nuclear program, in his *Almussawar* article Ahmed saw the Bush administration as being in the middle of a "frantic storm."[53] The London-based Palestinian paper *Al-Quds Al-Arabi* characterized the Bush administration as a "Zionist, right-wing, Christian Administration."[54]

Wherever neocons go, they spoil everything, wrote Abdullah Kamal of *Rose El-Yossef* in 2006. The editor in chief of the Egyptian magazine added, "American politics has resulted in 'sympathy' for Musab Al-Zarqawi, Mullah Omar, Osama bin Laden, and turned Hassan Nasrallah into a leader." Kamal asked readers to consider who is responsible for these blunders and the continuation of violence. He answered, "It is a disastrous American Administration and a futile Secretary of State" who opt to dominate the world.[55] The chief editor of *October*, Ismail Montassar, sarcastically portrayed the "inhabitants" of the White House as poor and unwise because of their failure in Iraq and Afghanistan.[56]

In an attempt to win hearts and minds in the fight against terrorism and offer a positive vision of America in the Arab world, the Bush administration appointed Karen Hughes in March 2005 as under secretary of state for public diplomacy. Upon her appointment, an article in *Asharq Al-Awsat* called on her to remember that improving America's image can be achieved by "policies" and not "propaganda."[57] Following her resignation in December 2008, the Syrian paper *Al-Baath* accused Hughes of failure, adding, "The problem, as it seems, was in that she did not realize the dimensions of the mission she was entrusted with and the reason behind the hatred of American politics in many parts of the world."[58]

The crumpling of a bipolar world and the rise of neocons to power are the reasons for American tyranny today, argued *Al-Ittihad* in 2008, but neocons were unaware that such unipolarity might not last for long, since a "Russian-German-French bloc could emerge, with the possibility of China joining in."[59] Actually, argued *Al-Ahram*, "the most important lesson which the [Bush] Administration should gain . . . is that power is not the best means to solve the world's problems." If neocons believed that excessive force was the only way to confirm U.S. supremacy, all indicators proved they were wrong.[60] "I believe there will come a time when the world calls on the four-member gang"—Bush, Rumsfeld, Cheney, and Paul Wolfowitz—to stand trial, observed an Iraqi political analyst who claimed that all the United States was trying to do was save face. He made these comment to the Egyptian satellite television channel Nile News.[61]

In this somewhat antagonistic atmosphere, it is natural for jokes about America to spread in the Arab media. Such humoristic depictions of America are best manifested in caricatures. For example, on August 5, 2008, *Asharq Al-Awsat* ran a caricature of a giant human body with the face of an American resembling Uncle Sam showing from behind it. On the belt around the waist of the giant human body are written the words: "The Bush Administration."

President Bush: A "Dangerous Fanatic"

Anti-Bush feeling began heightening among Arabs when they felt that an attack on Iraq was imminent. From the moment America attacked Iraq in March 2003, Arabs started mocking Bush and portraying him as the worst leader in America's history. In many ways, noted one author, Bush acted as if he were a "holy ruler on this earth."[62] Such criticism and mocking of Bush were conveyed not just in political books and the press but also in fiction. In a political fantasy titled *Kidnapping of a President*, Egyptian journalist Samia Sadeq told the story of the kidnapping of President Bush by four American boys, while in the meantime an Islamic resistance group falsely claims it detains him. The boys, whose loved ones suffered in the Iraq War, hold President Bush in a small cage—similar to that in the Abu Ghraib prison—with wild dogs chasing him. They place on the Internet scenes of him being tortured. In one scene Bush is electrified; in another an Iraqi girl drags him on the floor with a rope. The Islamic group shows similar pictures, and people around the globe wonder who the true Bush is. The White House denies the kidnapping of the president, stressing that Bush went into hiding; it claims that the four boys and the

Islamic group have shown images that merely look like the president. The author also brought into her work scenes of racism on the part of Bush against African Americans.[63]

Bush's "war on terror" speech and his "propaganda wars" in Iraq and Afghanistan enraged Arabs, and many considered the U.S. president to be a greater threat to world peace than Saddam Hussein. While in Egypt, before and after Saddam's death, I heard many on the street speak of how Iraqis were better off under Saddam's rule than under the forces of the United States and its allies. They often depicted the American president as a dictator and a narcissist. On the cover page of one of its issues, *Rose El-Yossef* featured a manipulated photo of Saddam's execution, in which his head has been replaced with that of Bush.[64] The Jordanian paper *Al-Arab Al-Yawm* likened Bush to a Nazi and portrayed him as the spiritual father of neoconservatives.[65] In a piece in *Al-Khaleej*, Emil Eamen condemned Bush's policies for being founded on Darwin's principle of survival of the fittest.[66] Regretfully, in the age of power, "whatever Bush desires he gets," concluded *Al-Gomhuria*, an Egyptian paper, in 2007.[67]

Ghassan Hussein of *Asharq Al-Awsat* believes that although Arabs do not regret the end of Saddam's regime, they—from a political point of view—accuse Bush of overthrowing an Arab government.[68] "The one who should be tried today is President Bush," said Hassan Omar, an expert on international law, in an interview with Al-Jazeera.[69] Recourse to violence became a characteristic of Bush, noted Mohamed Barakat, chief editor of the Egyptian paper *Al-Akhbar*.[70] After America's failure in Iraq, the Egyptian magazine *Al-Mawkef Al-Arabi* wondered, "Does not Bush think about committing suicide?"[71] The Jordanian paper *Ad-Dustour* contemptuously likened what Bush did in Iraq and Afghanistan to what hurricane Katrina did to "America's poor south." It added, "Violence leads to violence, oppression to oppression and torture to torture, exactly like the feelings which American politics provokes."[72]

Certainly Bush is neither a politician nor a statesman, asserted Mohamed Ali Ibrahim, editor in chief of *Al-Gomhuria*. He tried to appear as the "custodian of democracy and the one responsible for its prosperity worldwide. Such role is constructed for him by his assistants."[73] These acts by the Bush administration fed the furies of anti-Americanism in the Arab world. Bouthaina Shaaban wrote in *Asharq Al-Awsat*:

> The center of the problem in the strategy of the younger Bush and his team in Iraq and the Middle East is that they think the Middle East is

far away from the United States. They believe that what they are doing here behind the rivers does not affect events inside the United States, or that the human values of the Arabs differ from those of the Americans. Thus, within the prejudiced values of that team, there is nothing wrong in slaughtering Iraqis . . . and using the Western mass media, with their biased concepts, to help in obstructing all these crimes from Americans and saving America and its future from the causes of war.[74]

Ahmed Hamrouch of Egypt's *Sabah El-Kheir* magazine expressed doubt that Bush consulted with any of his officials around him before making his decisions.[75] Arabs have described U.S. policy under President Bush as a "stick and carrot" one—obey and you will be rewarded or else you will be punished. In some ways, this is similar to Bush's message in the aftermath of the 9/11 tragedies: "Either you are with us, or you are with the terrorists." Arabs, cautioned the Tunisian paper *Al-Chourouk* in 2007, must realize that any move Bush takes in the Middle East is not aimed at resolving the region's conflicts but at improving his administration's hurt image from its plight in Iraq and Afghanistan.[76] In *Al-Hilal* Nazkazim accused Arabs of caving in to the Bush administration. "Our submissiveness," he lamented, "has reached a level that makes an idiotic and ignorant person like George W. Bush dare tell us about our religion."[77]

Criticism of Bush and America was mingled at times with religious connotation. Consider this, for example, from the Kuwaiti magazine *Al-Nahda*: "Bush and America are, without a competitor, the pharaohs of the age. They have, and still do, spread corruption on the earth. . . . We ask that God make the end of these pharaohs similar to the end of the de facto Pharaoh, if not even worse, so the world enjoys true security and comfort under the rule and system that God desires for his people."[78] Bush believes he was "sent from God to earth to plant the laws of ethics" but forgets that "he is the top terrorist in the world," posited *Al-Wafd*, an Egyptian paper, in 2007. After all, he invaded Afghanistan and Iraq and caused immense suffering to weak nations. The Egyptian paper added, "Arabs must wake up and not follow that fascist who plans to assassinate the region's few remaining nations before he departs from the White House."[79]

Rashad Kamel, chief editor of *Sabah El-Kheir*, wondered how often Bush spoke of terrorism and extremism and called on nations to fight them, "forgetting about the terrorism and extremism that America has practiced against innocent peoples worldwide under his leadership." He asked readers to examine the state of the world since Bush assumed power—the "destruction and devastation" spreading in the "name of democracy, reform and the New Middle East." A Coptic Christian, Kamel asked readers not to believe Bush when he spoke of democracy, fighting terrorism, helping the poor, or the teachings of Christ: "How many times did Bush say that he is acting based on an inspiration from the sky, and that he is executing the teachings of Christ, and that God ordered him to fight Saddam Hussein, and he did?" He stressed, "The 'Christ' promoted by the neoconservatives—that gang which has kidnapped America and controlled Bush himself—is one that wants to sink the world into a sea of blood and killings. . . . Bush can do a lot to change the Arab world's view of him. He can put pressure on the American state of Israel to establish a Palestinian homeland."[80]

The U.S. leader's policies have damaged America's image abroad, burdened the country with economic problems, and most importantly proved Washington's failure in making the world unipolar, contended one article posted on Alarabiya.net.[81] In a 2007 interview with Egypt's Al-Oula television channel, Maha Abdel Fattah, a journalist who lived in the United States and covered foreign affairs for Egyptian newspapers, emphasized that Bush's administration was the nastiest in the history of the United States.[82] Arabs supported President Jimmy Carter when he said that Bush's foreign policy was the worst in America's history, observed *Al-Arab Al-Yawm*.[83] But was Bush worried about Carter's remarks? The president must be "tired of thinking about how history will judge him," contended *October*.[84]

Bush's policy in the Middle East proved to be an utter failure, claimed *Al-Ittihad*, with his administration offering unprecedented support for the "Zionist state." This was clearly manifested in the speech he delivered to the Knesset in May 2008.[85] The U.S. leader, in the opinion of Mohamed Ali Ibrahim of *Al-Gomhuria*, failed in his long war on terrorism, and his invasion of Iraq "inflamed sectarian riots." He added, "Instead of Bush being a messenger of freedom, democracy and human rights, he has become the first to violate them."[86] To justify the military attack on Iraq, Bush and his team had to "falsify historic facts" and create "numerous lies," argued *Ad-Dustour*.[87] In short, the American president "wants but cannot achieve, desires but does not accomplish," said Heikel on Al-Jazeera. In occupying Iraq, Washington had a set of goals planned; however, Bush found himself entering into a nightmare, added Heikel.[88]

The Bush administration should have comprehended that any empire founded purely on military power will not thrive, stressed *Al-Thawara*. The Syrian paper contemplated: "But will the captains of the neoconservatives in the U.S. be convinced of that before it is too late?"[89] If Saddam Hussein destroyed Iraq once, concluded a commentary in *Al-Ahram*, "George Bush and his friends destroyed it a thousand times."[90] The picture of America was not the same after Bush assumed power. "Change has begun in the United States and withdrawing from Iraq, whether it takes place today or after a year, will not stop" it, said *Asharq Al-Awsat*.[91]

His 2008 Visit to the Middle East

Bush's tour to the Middle East began with a red-carpet visit to Israel on January 9, 2008, and ended with a stopover in Egypt seven days later. The U.S. president also visited Kuwait, United Arab Emirates, Bahrain, and Saudi Arabia. The main goal of the tour, according to the White House, was to activate the peace process between Palestinians and Israelis, which began in Annapolis on November 27, 2007, and to gather support against Iran. The president's visit to the five Arab countries, Israel, and the West Bank provides a chance to reflect on the image of Bush and American Middle East policy in the Arab world. How did Arabs view the tour, Bush's longest to the region since he assumed power in 2001? Did it achieve its goals and was it considered successful?

Arab media coverage primarily focused on the Palestinian-Israeli conflict and Washington's confrontation with Tehran. Most Arabs were suspicious of the trip and showed reservations about Bush's ability to strike a Palestinian-Israeli peace agreement before his term ended. They described it as a publicity stunt aimed at (1) improving the U.S. leader's image before his departure, (2) showing more support for Israel, and (3) gathering momentum for a possible strike against Iran. Commentaries ran with screaming headlines: "George Bush in Our Homelands Walking on a Carpet of Our Blood," "The Leader of Destruction," "Hate You Sir but Value Your People," "You're Not Welcomed." Others portrayed the U.S. president as an American cowboy who knew nothing about world affairs and only used the language of force. For example, *Rose El-Yossef* ran on the cover page of its January 12, 2008, issue the headline, "Raven of Peace: Bush Welcomed but Not Ever Easy." A raven in Arab culture is a symbol of destruction; the connotation is that Bush is a man of destruction.

Numerous were the goals that Bush's trip aspired to achieve, argued *As-Safir*. The United States wanted to prove that a Palestinian-Israeli peace deal, particularly after the Annapolis conference, was possible, of course within the framework of an Israeli-American plan. It sought to indicate that its embroilment in the Iraq quagmire did not hinder Washington in forming an international alliance to fight terrorism.[92] Yet in reality, Bush's trip was meaningless because the atmosphere in the region was not ready for peace, said political analyst Mohamed Abdel Hakm Ziyab in an interview with Al-Jazeera. It was tense and neither the Israelis nor the Palestinians were prepared to initiate a constructive dialogue. He added that U.S. politics is dominated by political institutions, and the "Zionist lobby" strongly influences how Washington's Middle East policy is shaped.[93]

Like Ziyab, Nasser Al-Yahamdi felt that the Middle East was in a complicated situation, and he accused Bush and his "henchmen" of being responsible for the deteriorating conditions in Iraq, Afghanistan, Iran, Palestine, and Lebanon. Al-Yahamdi made his point in a commentary in the Omani paper *Al-Shabiba*.[94] The Egyptian magazine *Akher Saa* ran a story headlined, "Bush in the Region without an Agenda."[95] The Syrians viewed the tour as more of a public relations campaign, with *Tishreen* newspaper running a column under the headline, "Not Welcomed."[96] Similar to *Tishreen* and *Akher Saa*, Abdullah Kamal of *Rose El-Yossef* expected early on that Bush's trip would not bring any positive results and called it a public relations stunt by which the American president could inject a few quotes into his memoir: "I do not think that the few days he will spend in our countries and among our people will make us forget what this destructive American President—who made of our countries an experimental field for his foolish policies and plans—has done."[97]

Renowned Saudi journalist Gamal Khashkgi wondered if Bush could truly change history in the eleven months in office remaining for him at the time. "Welcome honorary President to our world which your ancestors have made complicated and in which you have followed their footsteps," he observed in *Al-Watan*, a Saudi paper.[98] Writing in the Bahraini paper *Akhbar Al-Khaleej*, Fahmi Hewadi, a distinguished political commentator, said he felt pity for those Arabs who waited anxiously for Bush's visit, hoping that the American president could bring any good for them.[99] "Bush's trip will only bring Bush's results," according to *Al-Bayan*,[100] for he comes to the region with a fake mission of peace, asserted *Al-Thawara*.[101] The central goals behind the visit were to "isolate Iran, push Arabs to normalize relations with Israel, gain the largest profit from oil, and increase support for U.S. military presence in the region," stressed Lebanese writer and politician Saadallah Mizraani in his country's paper *Al-Akhbar*.[102]

Zahir Magid declared in the Omani paper *Al-Watan* that Bush would leave the region after receiving "red carpets of Arab blood."[103] He has a "dark record written with Palestinian and Iraqi blood," wrote Mustapha Samy in *Al-Ahram*. According to him, the main objectives behind Bush's tour were planting

hatred between Palestinian leader Mahmoud Abbas and Hamas leaders, causing a rift in relations between Arab states and Iran, and offering Israelis the
"green light to slaughter more Palestinians and invade Gaza." Samy continued,
"The American President's visit was not about establishing peace in the Middle
East; it was about Israel's security and draining Arab wealth and powers within
the framework of the neocons' strategy."[104] Writing in *Ad-Dustour*, political science professor Hassan Nafah had a similar take on the story, predicting no
positive outcomes for Palestinians and Arabs from the visit and no shift in
Bush's "persistence to continue serving the Zionist project until his last moment at the White House."[105] Nothing would come of Bush's visit but more
of the same unfulfilled promises, reiterated *Al-Bayan*.[106]

Certainly, conjectured the online Annabaa Information Network, the U.S.
president hoped to win Arab support in order to suppress Iran's growing influence in the region.[107] *Almussawar* carried an editorial by its chief editor,
Abdel Kader Shohaib, in which he argued that Bush was selling to Arabs
"cheap talk" while offering Israelis "all support for their horrible occupation"
of Palestinian land. He added that in return for all this "gibberish talk," Bush
was attempting to win Arab support in a new military endeavor against Iran.[108]
In "Bush: Harvest of Evil," Mohamed Abdel Nour of *Sabah El-Kheir* condemned the American president's legitimatization of the Israeli occupation of
Palestine and accused him of spilling Palestinian blood and inflaming conflicts in the region during his two terms in office. "The stupid American stub-
bornness is imposing its catastrophic results on the Middle East," cried
Nour.[109] *As-Safir* cautioned that Arab states must realize that success of Bush's
tour would mean great failure for the Arabs.[110]

There were some Arabs, though few in number, who viewed Bush's tour favorably, arguing that the American president truly wanted to improve his
image before leaving office by striking a peace deal between Palestinians and
Israelis. They argued that although Bush's trip did not propose anything new
and confrontation between Washington and Tehran continued to intensify,
Arabs must not deny that the tour was aimed at reaching a balance in the region—aside from America's support for Israel, improving America's image in
the region, reducing the price of oil, and frightening the Arabs of Iran. Babil
Ghishan, a Jordanian writer, claimed that Bush's trip was important, even
though his speeches and comments were pro-Israeli. He added in his interview
with the Iraqi television channel Al-Iraqiya that Bush's mission offered Arabs
a chance to convey their views to the U.S. administration.[111] Writing in *Al-
Ittihad*, Ahmed Amiri asked Arabs to remember Bush's positive actions, from

liberating Iraq from Saddam Hussein's tyranny to countering the Taliban's oppressive rule in Afghanistan and Iran's growing influence in the region. "He is
the first American President to declare that he supports the establishment of
a Palestinian state," said Amiri. Arabs must admit, he added, that "Bush is
neither an angel nor a devil. He is the President of the only remaining superpower in the world. A world in which there will be no peace and stability without a price or blunders, and without good either." Amiri's article was titled
"George Bush's Good Deeds."[112]

It should be noted that almost all Arabs who did not oppose Bush's visit
to the Middle East doubted that he had the skills and charisma needed to
strike a just solution to the Palestinian cause or contain the bloodshed in both
Iraq and Afghanistan before he left office in January 2009. "Better late than
never" is a proverb Aishaa Al-Mari used in an article in *Al-Ittihad* to describe
Bush's tour. She wondered whether his last trip to the region could bring any
positive results.[113] In an interview with Al-Jazeera, Gihad Khazen, a popular
political analyst and former editor in chief of *Al-Hayat*, stated his belief that
Bush came to the region with a strong desire to strike a peace deal between the
Palestinians and Israelis. He said he wanted to "stand by the president—although Bush never stood by anyone—for I believe he honestly wants a solution to the Palestinian cause founded on establishing a Palestinian state side by
side with the Israeli state." Khazen added, "I do not doubt his intention; I
doubt his ability."[114] In the same vein, Palestinian political analyst Ghada Al-
Koroni suspected Bush did not have the political skills needed to get
Palestinians and Israelis to reach a peace settlement. Al-Koroni's point of view
was broadcast on Al-Sharqiya, a Dubai-based Iraqi television channel.[115]

The conclusion is that Bush's presence in the Arab world was quite undesirable, both from the viewpoint of intellectuals as well as ordinary citizens on
the street who saw very little hope of a considerable change taking place in
American policy in the Middle East. In "Arabs without Bush," Mohamed
Sabreen of *Al-Ahram* argued that many Arabs began to feel a sense of comfort
as Bush's departure neared, but he cautioned that the American agenda will not
disappear. What is more likely to change, he said, is America's manner, with
Washington using "soft power"—diplomacy—instead of military power. The
Middle East after Bush's presidency will be the same as the Middle East during
and before, with Arabs surviving in "false American promises" while Israel gains
all the support it needs.[116] The American president's trip failed "remarkably," alleged *Al-Quds Al-Arabi*.[117] "The winners from Bush's tour are Israel and the
U.S., and the losers are the Palestinians and all the Arabs," stated *As-Safir*.[118]

Coca Colonialism

American imperialism today is very strong due to U.S. advancement in technology and mass media, wrote Nahed Hatr.[119] Uncle Sam is a "giant nuclear monster" that wants a lot from Arabs, including protection of U.S. interests, normalization of relations with Israel, and dismantling of Arab organizations such as the Arab League. In short, America desires to restructure the Arab region to its own interest and in Israel's favor.[120] Under American hegemony, wrote Galal Amin, a professor of economics at the American University in Cairo, the "United States and Israel are ready to do the impossible in order to destroy development, obstruct democratic growth, place hurdles in the face of cultural and educational reform, and stand against bringing about any effective image for Arab cooperation or Arab nationalism."[121]

If we consider the Cold War to be the third world war, the war on terrorism is the fourth. It is "tied to economic globalization, a North vs. South war aimed at protecting and popularizing American public life, which is purely founded on consumerism and squandering," wrote Al-Lawandi.[122] Consumerism, he added, dominates American culture, for "everything can be sold and bought, including ethics and principles. And why not? Do not we breathe in the sphere of a monstrous globalization that deals with humans, values and ideas as a commodity that succumbs to market values and turns into banknotes and currency at the end?" History is no longer "human actions succeeding and accumulating over years"; it has become "similar to a movie whose actions take place in the alleys of Hollywood," concluded Al-Lawandi.[123]

Globalization is by all means an American invention. The globalization that the United States wants to impose on the world is modeled after the Romans.[124] According to Mohamed Said Ahmed Al-Maceer, it means nothing but the "enforcement of American hegemony with all its clout, tyranny and corruption," but "we Muslims can stand against American globalization with our culture, capital and good of our land."[125] Heikel called on Arabs to grasp that America's dealing with the world is based on a commercial culture of buying and selling, with everything of benefit seen as legal. "The American Empire knows how to take but not how to give. And when it gives it calculates interests in double," he continued. That explains why the United States did not take part in World War I of 1917 and World War II of 1939 until 1920 and 1941 respectively.[126]

Operating in a purely capitalist culture, Americans enjoy owning and consuming world resources, particularly cheap oil, alleged an article in *Al-Ahram* by acclaimed political commentator Al-Sayed Yassin. In that sense, the "United States of America is the world and the world is the United States of America," he noted. The global system has no choice but to work toward reconstructing the unipolar world into a multipolar one.[127] In this age of American globalization, posited *Sabah El-Kheir*, there is a sense of political absurdity in the hegemony of one nation. "Now Iraq is being attacked and then Iran, Darfur, [North] Korea."[128] In an interview with the Egyptian radio station Sout Al-Arab, Mohamed Gabr, a professor at Damascus University in Syria, spoke of a fake American globalization that aspires to dominate Arab culture.[129] The main perpetrator and profiteer of inciting fear of violence and terrorism is a "globalization founded on a culture of buying and selling," commented Professor Amin in *Al-Hilal*.[130]

Celebrated novelist Bahaa Taher tackled in more than one of his works the issue of Western dominance on Arab culture and the tension in relations between the East and West, without proposing solutions. His work is more focused on the human aspects of his heroes and heroines—rather than their race or ethnicity—in the hope that a tolerant dialogue between Easterners and Westerners can emerge in the end. In his masterpiece *Sunset Oasis* he told the story of an Egyptian married to a Western woman who is obsessed with ancient temples. This affects her marriage and makes her careless of her husband.[131] In an interview with *Sabah El-Kheir*, Taher, who worked at the United Nations in Geneva as a translator for over a decade, expressed doubt that there will be a happy marriage in future relations between the West and the East, between America and the Arabs. He added:

> This tension between the East and West will remain. From our side, we feel that the West is more superior, and that it is a colonizer, particularly because of its continual support of Israel. The West looks at the East as if it wants to devour it through legal and illegal immigration. The troubling question that remains is this: Should we take the West as it is and do as Japan did and turn into Westerners in our own countries? Should we resent the West completely as Yemen did during the days of "Imam" and Afghanistan under the "Taliban" or should we take one part of it and reject another?[132]

The importance of the relationship between politics and the military in the American imperial project cannot be overlooked, stressed Heikel in *Weghat Nazar*.[133] The United States has a long history of illegal intervention, commented *Al-Ittihad*; after all, its establishment led to the elimination of Native

Americans. It believes in a theory that grants it the right to penetrate borders and change the destinies of nations.[134] Ali Al-Siyar wrote in *Akhbar Al-Khaleej*:

> The United States, before growing arrogant, was the ideal model whose path world nations aspired to follow. Its behavior began to change once the gunfire of World War II had gone silent. The giant state, which prominent journalist Mustapha Amin described as "The Laughing America," has become an austere state with claws and tusks; its foreign policy is drawn by its intelligence. It has become similar to a home inhabited only by snakes and vicious monsters. Its intelligence men were hunting people on the streets under the pretext that they had been spying for the Soviet Union. Driven by a desire to dominate the world, they threw them in jails.
>
> In the years that followed World War II, we saw it launching wars on Vietnam and Korea under the allegation of countering the spread of Communism and in a bid to win the Cold War that was taking place between the two superpowers. We then saw it aspiring for what is more than Vietnam and Korea. It began transporting its wars to a Middle East region rich in oil resources. Israel is all of a sudden born under the protection of President Harry Truman to become the watchdog for U.S. interests in the region. From that time on, countries of the region became destined to endless wars, with battles ceasing in one place only to erupt in another. The U.S. has sadly chosen to be the first terrorist state in the world, and this is making it lose all its bets.[135]

In Heikel's view, which he expressed on Al-Jazeera, America came out of the Cold War fragmented and aimed at controlling an exhausted Middle East region.[136] The American imperial project that emerged following the collapse of the Soviet Union is based on securing oil and protecting Israel, said Amin Mshaqba, a political science professor at Jordan's University of Higher Studies. "The main American goal is to have hegemony on the region by dividing it," added Mshaqba in an interview with Jordan, a Jordanian satellite television channel. The United States now has control over the Gulf states and, as a result, over oil.[137] American hostility in the Middle East has made the world less secure, stressed Hamad Al-Majed of *Asharq Al-Awsat*. He argued that Arabs are anxious to see a new Cold War emerge between the United States on one side and Russia and China on the other. He wondered if American occupation of Iraq and Afghanistan and its double-standard policy in the Middle East would have taken place had the Soviet Union not collapsed.[138]

Since it has become the world's only superpower, the United States believes it "holds the keys for truth and is capable of uniting the world via marketing and under the pressure of its stick," claimed *Al-Quds Al-Arabi*.[139] It wants the twenty-first century to be the American century, according to Nile News, one in which the world follows whatever it says.[140] In a debate on U.S. foreign aid to Egypt titled "What Does U.S. Aid to Egypt Mean," the secretary general of Egypt's New Wafd Party, Munir Fakhri Abdel Nour, argued on Al-Oula that after the Cold War America tried to impose its culture on the world, as it had done in Japan and Germany following World War II.[141] He said that Egyptians refuse any pressure from the United States exerted under the "aid card." Americans, he added, have hindered Egypt's reform measures and its march toward democracy. "My advice to them is to leave us alone."[142] Egypt should not be another state of the United States, cautioned Mustapha Bakri, chief editor of the Egyptian *Al-Osboa* newspaper and a member of the Egyptian Parliament.[143]

America views the world's countries today as "either nations that pay bills or ones that cave in," said Anisa Fakhrou in *Akhbar Al-Khaleej*. "It believes that Arab oil should be the world's oil, a world on which it sits on top."[144] And it has succeeded, for "we beyond doubt live in the age of the pax-Americana," stated *Al-Hayat*.[145] The American empire now dominates the world arena, backed by its "superior military power, boundless economic capacity and advanced technological initiatives," observed *Al-Ittihad*'s Yassin, who believes that such dominance began long ago but strengthened following 9/11.[146] In a similar take on the issue, Yassin wrote in the Kuwaiti paper *Al-Qabas*: "The danger of American hegemony and its threat to world peace did not clearly manifest themselves until after the 9/11 terrorist attacks and following President Bush's declaration of a war on terrorism—a war that, according to his definition, includes the whole universe and lasts forever."[147]

Fiercely criticized were Bush's unilateralist policy and his doctrine that maintained, "You are either with us or against us." The Bush doctrine, argued *Al-Bayan*, has its roots in the era of McCarthyism in America, the arms race with the former Soviet Union, and policies of containment and alliance-building.[148] The arrival of neoconservatives in Washington revealed the "colonial face" that the United States had been trying to hide, emphasized *Al-Gomhuria*.[149] Under the pretext of fighting terrorism, the "U.S. hawks and neocons have put a plan to dominate 'the five continents' and accomplish the 'American Century project,'" according to *Al-Wafd*.[150] What Bush promised, alleged *As-Safir*, was a war against any society that refused to join American culture and support its goals. "We were actually waiting for Bush to talk about the culture of peace and about democracy and human rights, and to call us to the table of a true liberal American culture, which we do not deny the presence and influence of on the world," argued the Lebanese paper.[151] Instead what the United States has done is penetrate Arab culture and mass media establishments, wrote Salaheddine Hafez, vice editor in chief of *Al-Ahram* and general secretary of the Federation of Arab Journalists.[152]

The United States has become a police state, claimed *Al-Bayan*, enflaming wars and conflicts all over the globe.[153] Very simply, contended Ibrahim of *Al-Gomhuria*, America now wants to control the world. "In spite of the U.S.'s denial that it is intending to dictate the creative chaos that Condoleezza Rice mentioned last year, all America's acts indicate that it is on its way to spreading such chaos in third world countries and Arab states, in Egypt and other states in particular."[154] Arabs' problem with successive U.S. administrations, commented *Al-Ahram*, is that "we, Western Europeans, Russians and Chinese believe—after thousands of years of experience—that power does not make peace; it is peace that makes peace. But the United States believes only in power and nothing else; hence, we see it superior in technology and not superior in civilization, and there is a deep difference between the two."[155]

On this rising American hegemony, Hussein Ahmed Amin wrote in the Egyptian paper *Al-Masry Al-Youm*: "America does not stop at highlighting the 'positive' aspects of its own culture, but it also cares about pointing out the 'negative' sides in the societies that it dominates, such as the Islamic one. This is meant to ostracize any feeling of guilt or consciousness-hurting, which dominators may feel due to their tyranny in directing other societies and different systems and religions."[156] While the Arab and Muslim public feels "injustice, subjugation and unipolar tyranny, the public in America and the West feels the pleasure of a civic victory," noted Taha Al-Amri in *Al-Thawara*. This is because "American forces have got into Iraq, the Gulf region, Africa and Asia for the first time since [the United States] was founded nearly two and a half centuries ago." He added that a number of neocons believe that the scattering of U.S. troops around the world and their invasion of other countries are not colonial acts but civic and humanistic ones. Al-Amri's article was titled, "Only by Justice and Freedom World Stabilizes."[157]

Criticism of the American empire continues relentlessly. When America wants to implement something, it does so, said Ibrahim Shukab, a military analyst, on Nile News.[158] As a superpower, the United States uses its entire media to dominate the world, said Abdullah Kamal on Al-Oula. It is the "worst power that the twenty-first century has known."[159] In a piece in *Al-Hilal*,

Matar accused the U.S. media of knowing a lot about U.S. troops' wrongdoings in Iraq but refusing to report them. According to him, these offenses include "behavior of officers," "inefficiency of American forces," "squandering of money, corruption, bribery and torture in prisons and detention centers." But the U.S. media, he said, "responded to the call for 'nationalism' and the claim that publishing anything harmful to President Bush or the U.S. military establishment would expose the lives of military officers abroad to danger."[160]

Because the United States is the world's only superpower, posited *Al-Masry Al-Youm*, it is no longer shy about granting "documents of good deeds" to any country or region.[161] *Akhbar Al-Khaleej* called the United States the "first lady of the universe."[162] America wants the current unipolar world to remain as it is and for America to be the "world hegemon," commented columnist Rageb Al-Banna in *October*. It does not desire any competition from other entities, such as the European Union, China, Russia, or India. "What interests us is how this American strategy will affect the Arab world." He accused the United States of cunningly maneuvering to establish "a new regional security system in the Middle East to ensure that its interests in the region are protected. It is purely nonsense for the U.S. to say that its objective is to make the region enjoy democracy and human rights. These are nothing but mere slogans in a political campaign that seeks to hide its true intentions."[163]

It might be of importance to note that at times Arabs have reprimanded their governments for caving in to the United States. In a piece in *Sabah El-Kheir* titled "Where Are the Arabs," Salwa Al-Khateeb accused Arabs of avoiding and pulling out from "political conflicts and depending more on what the world decides, or rather on what America decides." She believes that a new map is being drawn for the "Middle East, depending essentially on dividing Arab communities on racial, tribal and religious basis."[164] This is sad because some non-Arab countries, such as Iran and Venezuela, are no longer afraid and are standing up to American hegemony, contended *Al-Ahram*.[165] "Arab nations have become a bite in the vicious Western jaw," lamented the head of the Yemeni delegation at the fortieth session of the Council of Arab Information Ministers in Cairo in 2007, which was aired on Al-Oula.[166] Currently there is no Arab leader who can make a decision against the United States, argued Khdr Al-Birae of the Palestinian Syndicate of Journalists in an Al-Jamahiriya interview.[167] "We have to deal with America as an adversary" or else it will always dominate Arabs and their culture, concluded a political science professor at the American University of Beirut in a debate broadcast on Future, a Lebanese television channel.[168]

United Nations of America

In their condemnation of American supremacy, the Arab media called on the United Nations to assert its authority and role globally within the provisions of the UN Charter. In the face of American might, wrote Al-Lawandi, the United Nations stands today as a "not valuable machine, costly and bureaucratic. Its only use is to support the efforts of the vital state: America." He added that there is a widening belief among Arabs that the United States wants to replace the international governmental agency with NATO.[169] The United States has never been interested in having the UN play an effective role in resolving regional conflicts.[170] This growing American influence on the UN was revealed during the country's invasion and occupation of Iraq, with Washington threatening members of the Security Council with cancelation of previously signed trade agreements.[171]

Writing in *Al-Hayat*, Mustapha Al-Fiqi, an author and chairman of Egypt's People's Assembly Foreign Affairs Committee, asserted that the United Nations "has abandoned its vital role and message for civilization, turning into a tool at the hands of a hidden power that plays with the destinies of world nations, behaves disproportionately and mixes religion with politics."[172] The United States has demolished faith in the UN, rendering it futile and irrelevant, stated *Akhbar Al-Khaleej*.[173] The UN, reiterated Kamal Rasheed of *Ad-Dustour*, has become a tool of the United States. Of America's eighty-one vetoes at the Security Council, forty-one have been against Arabs and Muslims.[174] A piece in *Al-Bayan* likewise reprimanded world democracies for failing to modernize the UN Security Council: "Where is world democracy, you who call for it, when a minority of five countries in the Security Council controls the 186 nations that represent the majority of world nations?"[175]

Isolationism of a Big Mac Culture

The United States has a history of political isolation and economic independence, according to many Arab intellectuals who visited the United States and studied American culture and politics. Its culture of materialism and isolationism emerged long ago. In September 1953 Zaki Naguib Mahmoud went to the United States to serve as a visiting philosophy professor for a year at both the University of South Carolina and Washington State University. He documented his visit in a diary, which a couple of years later was turned into a book called *Days in America*. He described his first impression of Americans as "helpful, kind, generous and friendly."[176] Americans, wrote Mahmoud, have a "spirit of adventure"; after all, running from religious persecution in Europe was how they established their new life.[177] Nevertheless, he lamented their sense of isolationism, religiosity, and materialism, and he cited how South Carolina's *Columbia Record* and *State* newspapers cared first about their state's affairs, with "world affairs coming last."[178] Similarly, Mustapha Amin, a journalist and newspaper founder, spent a year in the United States in the late 1930s and wrote a book about his stay titled *The Laughing America*. Amin said that as an "Orientalist" he could not understand the spirit of materialism that dominates American life: "Everyone in America talks about money."[179] Contrary to the Arab world, where spiritual values exist, money comes first in America, even before humans, cried Fouad Zakaria, a political sociologist. "America," he added, "is the most materialistic society in our modern world."[180]

There is something unusual about the American society, with everyone rushing to enjoy the moment.[181] Everyone is in a race against time, with an "American believing that everything in today's world, as well as in yesterday's world, can be bought with money."[182] Within this framework, power comes before principles in American daily life. When dealing with Americans, one has to be persistent and keep pushing, for an American will not respond automatically to what you need just because he or she believes that you have a right.[183] Attif Al-Ghamri remarked:

If America is a homeland and a nation like others, it is also, and with the same degree, a "belief" in the emotion of Americans. This connotes that their country is a model society for the world to emulate. This is in addition to the element of distance of a country encompassing a continent and not just a single state. They also feel that their country is big and the world outside is small; that it is rich and other countries are poor; and that they are on top and the rest are at the bottom or below.[184]

He further noted that Americans' belief in their country has led U.S. politicians to perform just as actors do, resulting in U.S. presidents getting elected despite their unawareness of political affairs. "From on top of the ship of advertising and marketing promotion they jumped to the leadership seat."[185]

According to Saudi academic Bassem Khafagi, the U.S media have excelled at employing the American personality to promote American foreign policy projects aimed at dominating other nations and used as a ploy by Washington to "intervene in the international affairs of other nations."[186] He believes that the American people always feel that they are "saved from all laws of the universe and are capable of doing what others see as the impossible."[187] On the structure of U.S. politics and personality, Al-Ghamri stated: "Politics in America is a dramatic art with contradictions, dissimilarities and struggle for power. Perhaps that is due to the nature of a complicated political system that has characteristics different from any other political system in the world. Perhaps the existence of Hollywood as the capital of moviemaking in the world and an inspirational center for the American dream has its effective role on the American personality in life and on politics to a larger degree."[188] Al-Ghamri added that the United States has a "different language of political talk and well-established think tanks" capable of influencing the political life.[189]

An American, regretted Khafagi, does not care much about what takes place outside his country "unless that has a direct effect on his daily life. That is why an American did not care about Middle East problems until after September 11."[190] The notion of American imperialism is founded on isolationism, noted Nile News, on the United States "being a separate entity from the rest of the world."[191] An Arab knows a lot about America, but an American knows little about Arabs, argued a Sudanese writer in an article in *Asharq Al-Awsat*.[192] Most Americans care only about their daily lives "within the parameters of health care: health insurance, social security insurance, retirement pension, higher prices, and taxes," noted Egypt's consul general in New York, Sherief Al-Kholi, in an interview with *Almussawar*. "After September 11, they have woken up to realize how little they know about the world outside. Naturally, they have started to believe all the information provided to them by the media, which are the sole supplier of information and often side with Israel. These media cover issues without any sense of objectivity and often focus on the negative."[193]

Ahmed Youssef of the Egyptian paper *Al-Arabi* believes all Americans live on the edge, struggling for their survival. They live in a "persistent state of disturbance because there is a thin line separating success from failure, winning from losing. . . . This is the American way of life, which they want to impose on us so that we lose our identity and belief in ourselves and in turn become wandering spirits."[194] Americans, unlike Europeans, are very simple in the way they deal with each other, wrote Omro El-Shabaki in *Al-Masry Al-Youm*. In the view of El-Shabaki, a political analyst at *Al-Ahram*, American culture takes full advantage of the skills of an individual and breaks the barriers of race, color, and religion. He added, "Different from its European counterpart, the 'American model' makes you feel that if you are poor then that is your problem, or it is lack of skills which forbids you from becoming rich. Most of the acts of social securities, which a European state shoulders for its poor, are absent in America, thus the percentages of crimes and violence in the U.S. are much higher than in all European states."[195] Americans know nothing about the world, cried Libyan president Moammar Qaddafi in an interactive lecture he gave from Tripoli to students of the Oxford Union in Oxford, Britain, broadcast on the BBC World TV channel on May 20, 2007. Americans only know what is of interest to them, stated *Rose El-Yossef*.[196] Amid an abundance of media channels, they are becoming less knowledgeable about their surroundings, declared an article on the Lebanese website Annabaa.org.[197]

While America has opened up and embraced globalization, Americans have become more isolated, said Al-Birae on Al-Jamahiriya.[198] "Americans are among the world's most ignorant when it comes to knowing other cultures. An American feels it is sufficient to belong to the 'American Republic'; his knowledge of geography is very limited to his knowing the difference between Californians and New Yorkers, or Los Angelenos and Washingtonians," said El-Shabaki following a conference he attended at Georgetown University in Washington, D.C., on Muslim movements in the Arab world. This lack of knowledge on the part of Americans "has made it easier for the current Administration—the worst in U.S. history—to shape the pictures of good and evil in front of the ordinary citizen, with Arabs, Islam and Muslim movements being equated with absolute evil and Israel with utter good," added El-Shabaki in a 2007 article in *Al-Masry Al-Youm*.[199] In a piece in *Al-Hilal*, Matar (who said he had participated in conferences and meetings in which U.S. politicians, diplomats, journalists, and academics took part) blamed American officials—Republicans and Democrats alike—for blindly supporting the foreign policy of their government "without stopping for a minute to ask how such 'blind' support could cause catastrophes for America and its people."[200]

There is a lot of humor to be sensed when Arabs portray American culture. For instance, one *Al-Ittihad* newspaper caricature showed the figure of a huge American seeing the world through the lenses of a dollar sign—"world through American eyes"—and smoking a cigarette on which is written, "The American rescue plan." The phrase "poor nations" is placed over the head of an impoverished, weak man standing small in front of the huge American figure.[201]

4 AMERICAN POLICY IN THE MIDDLE EAST

Politics is the art of fooling people. ANIS MANSOUR, Egyptian writer

There is no hope of having the minimum capacity to counter Israeli haughtiness without having the minimum will to resist the United States. JOSEPH SAMAHA, Lebanese thinker

The global media—and I do not exclude Arab ones—do not see the Palestinians but in one of two frames: a Palestinian holding a knife in his hand or with a knife at his back. MAREAD AL-BARGHOTHI, Palestinian poet

Traditionally, many Arabs believe, American foreign policy in the Middle East was aimed at maintaining the territorial integrity of Israel, keeping the Middle East out of the orbit of Communism, controlling oil, and enhancing peace and stability in the region. According to Fouad Zakaria, the United States expanded its influence in the Arab world after World War II, becoming the deciding factor in "political causes that determine the destiny of Arab nations."[1] With the collapse of the Soviet Union, some of America's foreign policy goals became outdated, and an era of estrangement in relations between the United States and the Arabs began. Today, the popular thought among Arabs is that American policy in the Middle East is founded on two major factors: controlling Arab oil (as seen in Iraq) and further empowering Israel and weakening the Palestinian cause. Arabs believe that for a just and

47

durable peace to be established between them and the Israelis, the United States must play the role of an honest broker in the Middle East. In fact, mourned Nahed Hatr, "the whole world has an interest in peace and stability except Washington," which is mainly interested in spreading chaos.[2] To counter U.S. influence in the Middle East, cautioned Attif Al-Ghamri, there has to be a joint Arab stance.[3]

For many years now, wrote Mohamed Al-Said Edrees in the Egyptian paper *Al-Ahram*, Washington has had an interest in the Arab world because of its "special relation with Israel, interest in Arab oil and desire to benefit from the region's strategic place."[4] Overall, Arab commentators perceive the Bush administration's Middle East policy as a total failure. They believe these failed policies are the main cause behind the negative impressions of the United States in the Arab world. "The Americans have done great damage to this area. They've got Egypt out of the equation and made Saudi Arabia run after them," said Mohamed Hasseinein Heikel in an interview with Robert Fisk of the British daily *The Independent*.[5] The Arab world's most acclaimed journalist contended in an interview with Al-Jazeera that Bush's policy in the Middle East aimed at controlling Middle East oil, insuring Israel's security, and abolishing the Palestinian cause.[6]

Attif Abdel Gawad, a journalist, believes that Arabs, particularly in Saudi Arabia, doubt America's honesty in achieving peace in the Middle East. He made his point to the Egyptian television channel Nile News.[7] In a commentary titled "Israel and America: As If They Are Twins," *Al-Ahram* said, "America's relationship with the Arabs is a sad one, for Arabs know well that what America cares about in the Middle East are oil and Israel." This, it added, is "withdrawing every bit of passion, love or respect for the U.S. in the hearts of Arabs."[8] Safwhat Sobhi Fanoos, a political analyst, said in a discussion on the Sudanese satellite television channel Sudan that America justifies its stationing of military troops overseas, particularly in Arab and African countries, on two factors: fighting terrorism and insuring the free flow of oil.[9] America, said Nile News, invaded Iraq to pursue its Greater Middle East project, counter growing Iranian influence, and protect Israel. "Is not America in such a terrible situation to be able to initiate a peace dialogue with Syria and Iran?" asked an Iraqi political analyst in an interview with the Egyptian television channel.[10]

The destruction of Iraq, Lebanon, and Gaza and failure in Afghanistan are America's vision of a "New Middle East," alleged numerous Arab commentators. Arabs nowadays are faced with "an American occupation of Iraq and a

Zionist occupation of Lebanon and Palestine," cried one participant at a conference on national security in the Arab world held in Tripoli and aired on the Libyan satellite television channel Al-Jamahiriya. The United States is spreading a culture of fear in the Arab world, said another participant.[11] If U.S. troops withdraw from Iraq, stressed Turki Al-Hamd in a piece in the Saudi paper *Asharq Al-Awsat*, the world's superpower will face a political and economic challenge. Iran's influence in Iraq and the region will grow, with many Middle Eastern states inching toward accepting and dealing with Tehran, "not out of love for Iran but out of hatred of Israel." Al-Hamd cautioned that the United States would then become more of an open target for global terrorism. America should search for a solution not just for its crisis in Iraq but for its predicament with the whole world, he continued.[12]

Farag Shalhoub of the Palestinian paper *As-Sabeel* accused Washington of laboring to divide and redraw the Middle East map to its advantage and to Israel's benefit. The United States does not just want to "hunt only two birds with one stone, but more than that."[13] Its experiment in Iraq is a minimized example of its Greater Middle East project, said the Egyptian magazine *Almussawar*.[14] Shamefully, the Arab world has become a battleground because of Americans' appalling politics, wrote Abdullah Kamal, chief editor of the Egyptian magazine *Rose El-Yossef*. "They ruined Iraq, corrupted Lebanon, did not secure Palestine, destroyed Somalia and never rebuilt Afghanistan and Sudan." Kamal continued, "As if we were victims in the *Silence of the Lambs* movie, U.S. politicians feed us cooked slices of segments of our brains." In 2006 the chief editor derided Condoleezza Rice's politics in the Middle East and described her as an unsuccessful secretary of state who stood watching while Israel attacked Lebanon: "She . . . has not achieved peace," and the "politics of her Administration supports hatred and propagates antipathy." He blamed her for not demanding that Israel stop its attack on Lebanon and for instead "speaking softly and quietly of a 'New Middle East.'" Rice, he added, "is an artist, a musician who plays the piano; but her ideas are like knives and her plans are like daggers. No matter what shrewdness and softness she employs when stabbing, she is at the end stabbing." Generally, noted Kamal, American foreign policy is one of violence and killings. "Realistically, the American sentiment no longer has compassion that can move when seeing this number of casualties, for U.S. politics has gotten used to subsequent killings. I do not think that a few hundred casualties in Lebanon, resulting from a 'supreme' military operation like the one Israel is carrying out, can be compared with the hundreds of deaths that fall daily in Iraq, where the first surgery for the birth of a New Middle East was undertaken," concluded Kamal. His article was titled, "The Futile: A Mockery of the 'Horrible East.'"[15]

Greater Middle East Project

The way Arabs interpreted America's project for a New Middle East may be shocking to many Westerners. In the view of Said Al-Lawandi, a political scientist, reforming the Middle East became a matter of national security for the United States. Americans, he said, "write history in the way they wish," and he asked Arabs to consider how the United States tried to change the history of the Middle East by separating its past from its present.[16] The Greater Middle East project was a Bushian colonial project that extended from Pakistan to Morocco with the aim of helping Israel to dominate the region, Al-Lawandi said. The intent was to "melt Arabs into a larger ocean and weaken Arab and Muslim 'identity' in the region, turning its people into a minority constituting no more than 40 percent of the total population of the Greater Middle East."[17] In short, the idea of a Greater Middle East aimed at "unifying American strategy, simplifying the region's problems, dispersing attention off the Palestinian-Israeli conflict," and incorporating Israel as an essential part of it. To achieve this, the United States raised the "slogan of a war on terrorism, spread of nuclear weapons and dictatorship" in the region.[18]

America's campaign for the establishment of democracy in the Middle East was a cunning maneuver to gain advantage in the region and achieve its Greater Middle East project.[19] The Bush administration did not establish a plan for withdrawing from Iraq before occupying it because it never intended to leave.[20] It wanted to eliminate any threat to America's national security coming from the region and change the status quo in the Arab world, not out of love for the Arabs but as a step toward securing its interests in the region.[21] In that sense, the American initiative for a Greater Middle East was a "new chapter of the strategy of Mr. Bush and his collaborators of neocons and international thieves." The initiative, in Hatr's view, granted the United States the right to interfere in the internal affairs of Arab nations; it imposed a geopolitical frame by which America could define the identity of Arabs and determine the Palestinian cause within a new regional order that granted Israel full partnership and hegemony. Thus, Americans were demanding that Arabs give up (1) sovereignty, (2) identity, (3) the Palestinian cause, and more.[22]

In a piece in *Asharq Al-Awsat*, Attallah Mohajerani decried America's notion of a New Middle East, for it meant "Israel and the Other." In doing so, he made reference to Edward Said's book *Orientalism* and how the late Palestinian American intellectual used the terms "the West" and "the Other."[23] Intelligently, in his masterpiece America supports the Israeli war on Lebanon for it believes it can construct a new path for a New Middle East, claimed *Al-Ahram*.[24] According to the newspaper, the United States does not want "our Arab world" in a leading position in the region.[25] "The 'Greater Middle East' project, which embodies the de facto dimensions of the American imperial project, mainly depended on an Israeli role until the War on Iraq and its occupation, which is considered the real entrance for imposing the 'Greater Middle East' plot on the ruins of the Arab system," argued Edrees in *Al-Ahram*. He added that the U.S. project failed because the Middle East has become an authority on spoiling American projects.[26]

Speaking at the Doha Conference for Dialogue of the Islamic Schools of Thought held in Qatar in January 2007, the president of Egypt's Al-Azhar University, Ahmed Mohamed Al-Tayeb, conjectured that the American-advocated New Middle East project meant a division of Arab and Muslim countries. "The new colonial powers are still working to undermine our unity," he said.[27] The goal of the project was to redraw the regional map and place Israel at its center, commented *Al-Ahram*.[28] It meant exterminating all opposition in Iraq, Palestine, and Lebanon, said the Bahraini paper *Akhbar Al-Khaleej*.[29] The Jordanian paper *Ad-Dustour* wondered, "When will there be those among us who trust and expect good coming from America?"[30] Writing a day ahead of the Annapolis conference for Middle East peace held in late November 2007, the head of the Egyptian Journalists Syndicate, Makrim Mohamed Ahmed, maintained in a piece in *Al-Ahram* that when dealing with the Arabs the United States should realize that the politics of the carrot is better than the politics of the stick.[31]

There is no doubt that America planned to attack either Iran or Syria as an escape from the Iraqi quandary, but the deficit in the U.S. budget proved a hurdle, said Mohamed Abdel Hakm Ziyab, a writer and political analyst, in an interview on Al-Jazeera.[32] Ibrahim Qaod wrote in the Egyptian magazine *Akher Saa*:

> This time specifically, America and Israel want an Arab-Muslim grouping to target Iran. . . . They want to wipe out all forms of resistance on Arab lands, be they in Iraq, Lebanon, Palestine, Sudan or Somalia. Hence, during Bush's rule, U.S. proposals multiplied, from the Greater Middle East to the creative chaos re-disintegration and re-composition of the Arab region. All forms of opposition and resistance to the

American project were considered acts of terrorism (all Arab resistance organizations being included in this classification).[33]

Israel's presence in the region will help achieve America's dream of the Greater Middle East project, which aims at dividing the region based on ethnic and sectarian background, stated Abdel Wahab Al-Missari, the Arab world's most distinguished expert on Zionism, in a 2006 commentary posted on Aljazeera.net.[34] But in 2007, Qaod of *Akher Saa* cautioned that the project faced difficulty, if not failure. He added, "Washington has worked with all its strength to push Palestinians toward division and supported a movement inside Fatah to abort the Mecca agreement. It has backed the loyalist team in Lebanon against the opposition movement and stood against any solution to end the country's escalating crisis. It endeavors to place Darfur under direct international monitoring and supports rebel sects in the region. It also got rid of the rule of Islamic courts by supporting Ethiopian intervention."[35]

The destruction that the United States has caused in Iraq supports Israel's role in the region and opens the door for it to work freely and without threats toward achieving its greater project, wrote Rageb Al-Banna in the Egyptian magazine *October*.[36] "The New Middle East will not be the newborn that Ms. Condi [Rice] has wished for, and I do not rule out it becoming a nightmare disrupting her sleep," contended the popular columnist Fahmi Hewadi in 2006 in *Asharq Al-Awsat*.[37] Her "creative chaos theory has religious dimensions rooted in beliefs of the neocons and derived from the principles of the Jewish religion," commented Mohamed Al-Shibani in the Kuwaiti paper *Al-Qabas*. That theory aspired to achieve America's political goals globally by provoking conflicts in troubled regions ruled by despotic and oppressive regimes. Al-Shibani said that Rice used the theory successfully when she served as a Soviet Union consultant in the Ronald Reagan administration.[38]

Conspiracy against Arabs

Conflicts and wars in the Arab world—from Iraq in the far north to Lebanon and Palestine at the center to Sudan in the south and Somalia on the edge of the southeast—have led a portion of ordinary Arabs and politicized elites to believe in the existence of a conspiracy against the Arabs. Supporters of the conspiracy theory believe there are outside forces—fingers often point at the United States and Israel—aiming at dividing the Arab world, controlling the Gulf region's oil, and insuring Israel's security. Those who oppose the theory contend that the Arab world is merely experiencing conflicts as in other world regions, such as Eastern Europe and central Asia. In *America to Where!*, Raji Inayet listed by date over a dozen of what he called U.S. atrocities and conspiracies against the people of the Middle East. He contended that, beginning with the Reagan administration, the United States enacted a major conspiracy to dominate the world following the collapse of the Soviet Union: "From the time Ronald Reagan came to power that conspiracy was initiated by a group later known as neoconservatives." The neocons lived with the hope that after the demise of the Soviet Union the United States could establish a global empire. Inayet added that the "idea of an American empire is in essence an exploitative movement by big arms dealers and oil dealers aimed at doubling their profit."[39] He concluded with the question, "Is it rational then, after all that, [for America] to ask: Why do nations of the Middle East hate the U.S.?"[40]

According to Saudi writer and diplomat Abdullah Mohamed Al-Nasser, America has planned tactics with Israel to break the Middle East region by political tricks and by provoking conflicts among Arabs. It has succeeded in dividing Arab unity on the Palestinian cause, an issue on which Arabs once held strong consensus.[41] The Greater Middle East project has been nothing but an American conspiracy against the Arabs, wrote Al-Lawandi. Citing French sources, Al-Lawandi stressed that evidence of violence and terrorist activities tied to al Qaeda and Muslim groups was fabricated. He said, "We are victims of lies, false claims and fabrications [stating] that America did not fire randomly" but rather was a "wounded state avenging its honor." With extensive media campaigns, Washington turned such lies into indisputable facts.[42] Galal Amin, a professor of economics at the American University in Cairo, accused America of conspiring against Egypt and of being the reason behind the bad situation that Egyptians live under today.[43] In *Creative or Destructive Chaos*, Mustapha Bakri (an Egyptian journalist and member of the Egyptian Parliament) cited how David Welch, when serving as the U.S. ambassador to Egypt, stated in a press conference in Cairo that he would grant one million dollars to nongovernmental Egyptian organizations in support of democracy and reform in the North African state. This "Western, Zionist, American money" was used as a tool for exercising pressure on Egypt to accept America's new plan for the Greater Middle East project, added Bakri.[44]

Like Bakri, Mohamed Ali Ibrahim, chief editor of Egypt's *Al-Gomhuria* newspaper, believes that America is employing a conspiracy to break states worldwide in the manner that was used in Ukraine and Georgia.[45] *Asharq Al-Awsat* noted that a few books were published claiming that it was the United States and not al Qaeda that carried out the 9/11 attacks, and that it was not truly Saddam

Hussein who was hanged but a representation of him.[46] On Al-Jazeera's popular TV program *Counter Opinion*, Nasser Qandeel, chairman of the Middle East Media Center, accused America of funding extremists in the Middle East and stressed that the real war for Arabs is with the United States.[47] "No one says the truth in Washington nowadays," contended the United Arab Emirates paper *Al-Khaleej*.[48] "America is a liar, and anyone who believes in anything it says is a fool," said seventy-year-old Mohamed Madbolli, who owns a popular Cairene bookstore, in an interview with the Egyptian television channel Al-Oula.[49]

Ad-Dustour alleged that there is a "conspiracy to divide Iraq into three regions: one in the north for the Kurds, another in the south for Shiites, and a third in the middle for the Sunnis." It admonished U.S. policy in the Middle East and stressed that the Iraqi people have lived united in peace for centuries and Arabs will not accept any attempt to divide them.[50] This attempt to split Iraq into small, feeble states is "part of a bigger plan drawn by international Zionists to divide the larger Arab world," argued Omani writer and researcher Mohamed bin Said Al-Fatisi in an article in the Omani paper *Al-Watan*.[51] On the much-admired *Panorama* program of the Abu Dhabi satellite television channel of the United Arab Emirates, a few callers spoke of a U.S. conspiracy to divide and rule the Arabs. One guest on the program, journalist Abdullah Al-Sinnawi, did not rule out the existence of numerous conspiracies against the Arab world. Another guest, Burhan Ghaluin, a political sociology expert, took a different view, arguing that there are no conspiracies but mainly strategies, and the strategy of the United States has always been founded on "securing oil and protecting Israel."[52]

Egyptian diplomat Mohamed Munir Zahran warned of the existence of conspiracies to divide Arabs and control their resources. "Modern imperialism and neocolonialism embrace the slogan of the former British empire: 'Unite by dividing,'" he wrote in the Egyptian magazine *The Diplomat*. Arabs have witnessed "conspiracies by superpowers to divide the Arab world, the most recent of which was the U.S.-British invasion of Iraq in March 2003, which came in violation of international law and under false pretexts that brought catastrophic results to the Iraqi people," added Zahran.[53] In a piece in the Egyptian paper *Al-Osboa*, Bakri condemned the U.S. Congress's decision to divide Iraq into regions based on religion and race and under a federalist state. He called it a U.S. conspiracy to divide the region within the plan of a New Middle East. He cautioned Arabs to be aware of such a conspiracy, stressing that after Iraq the United States will target other Arab states. Bakri asked Arabs "not to reduce the magnitude of the conspiracy."[54]

In a piece in the Egyptian magazine *Al-Hilal*, Gamil Matar asked readers to consider why the Bush administration failed in its Middle East "adventures," particularly in Iraq. He expressed his belief that the United States is driven by a desire to erect "a new moral and political world structure. . . . There is a frenzy in Washington with the idea of structuring a new regional system in the Middle East, swallowing up, if possible, the Arab League or weakening it to the extent of being inefficient or nonexistent."[55] Within this context, cautioned Tayib Tizini in the United Arab Emirates paper *Al-Ittihad*, the American-Israeli alliance works painstakingly to inflame sectarian violence in Arab states, particularly in Syria and Lebanon, and Arabs must be fully aware of that.[56] Ali Lagha, a Lebanese academic and scholar of Islamic thought, believes that Western efforts have been exerted to divide the Syrian-Lebanese alliance. "This death dance must stop," observed Lagha in an interview with the Lebanese television channel Lebanon. There is no such thing as al Qaeda, he cried. "Al Qaeda is an illusion" created by the United States.[57]

American politics, said *Al-Gomhuria*, has been founded on the principle that "ethnic or religious conflicts among citizens of any country, or countries, offer [the United States] the legal cover to intervene and control these countries by dividing them into small states, which it later reorganizes according to its vision and interests."[58] Arabs, observed *Al-Khaleej*, with all their religious backgrounds, have been victims of these American conspiracies; they are unarmed and slaughtered daily in Palestine and Iraq.[59] The Lebanese paper *As-Safir* went so far as to claim that it was an American-Israeli conspiracy that led to the assassination of Palestinian leader Yasser Arafat.[60] "Was not the Zionist movement a conspiracy?" cried Khdr Al-Birae, a Palestinian journalist, in an Al-Jamahiriya interview. Arabs cannot deny that there is an American-Israeli conspiracy to control the Middle East region, he added.[61] The United States maneuvers to "deepen Palestinian division and intensify conflict between the Fatah and Hamas movements," noted *Al-Akhbar*, a Lebanese paper.[62] Similar to *Al-Akhbar*, retired Egyptian brigadier general Taha Khalil agrees that there has been a U.S.-Israeli conspiracy against the Palestinians from the day Israel was founded. He expressed this in an interview by the Saudi television channel Ein.[63]

Within this vapor of anti-Americanism, some commentators also denounced the Camp David peace accords, which were signed between Egypt and Israel in 1978, as a conspiracy against their people. Farid Abdel Khaleq, a Muslim scholar in his nineties, is one such commentator. A member of Egypt's banned Muslim Brotherhood group, Khaleq charged Arab rulers of corruption and added, "Camp David was wrong because Israel benefited the most from it." In his interview with the Kuwaiti satellite channel Al-Adala, he called on Arabs to become powerful and build a strong community that holds no hatred toward anybody. It is only by being strong that Arabs avoid being exploited and dominated.[64]

Other Arab analysts took different views that did not fully support the conspiracy theory. Arabs cannot be held captive by the theory of conspiracy, but they cannot also be prisoners of the theory of good intentions, said Abdel Raziq Al-Dahish, editor in chief of the Libyan *Al-Jamahiria* newspaper, in an interview with Al-Jamahiriya.[65] On Al-Jazeera, Heikel expressed a similar position, arguing that although he did not uphold the conspiracy theory, scholars cannot deny the existence of conspiracies when they examine history.[66]

Desire for Oil

Arabs see oil as a main factor behind U.S. hostility toward them and the invasion of Iraq, a country that controls 11 percent of the world's oil reserve. America's plan to control Arab oil began following World War II, argued renowned political commentator Al-Sayed Yassin in *Al-Qabas*, and has continued since then.[67] "From the first day Bush came to power, he aimed at controlling the Middle East and the region's oil," stated Heikel on Al-Jazeera.[68] Controlling oil and protecting Israel are the two main goals of U.S. policy in the Middle East, pointed out *Akher Saa*.[69] "If support for Israel comes first in U.S. policy in the Middle East, protecting oil fields comes right after that," remarked an article in the Saudi paper *Al-Hayat* by Mustapha Al-Fiqi, chair of the Foreign Affairs Committee at the Egyptian People's Assembly.[70]

In the view of the Omani paper *Al-Shabiba*, the United States went to Iraq not to help Iraqis or promote democracy but to control the country's oil and further ensure the security of Israel, a nation that often expressed to Washington a fear that Iraq was rising as a power in the Middle East.[71] The "current U.S. administration, including the younger Bush, are members of a major oil company headed by the older Bush," asserted the satellite television channel Sudan in 2007.[72] America is now in control of the wealth and oil of Iraq, claimed *Al-Gomhuria*.[73] Saudi satellite television channel Al-Arabiya considered the U.S. military presence in Iraq and the Arab Gulf states the result of a weak Arab system.[74]

Darfur

There were also reports that the United States wanted to intervene in Darfur because oil resources had been discovered there. The "American project" aimed at controlling the entire region, said Fathi Yakan, a Lebanese Muslim cleric who held a seat in the country's parliament. Consider Sudan: when oil was discovered there the Americans created the Darfur crisis, he added in an interview with the pro-Hezbollah satellite channel Al-Manar.[75] Washington's eye was focused on Sudan because of its strategic role and oil fields discovered there, noted the United Arab Emirates paper *Al-Bayan*. The extreme right wing in America also wanted to control the region's flow of Nile water resources.[76] These extremists in the United States were behind the escalation of violence in Darfur, according to Nile News.[77] Another article in *Al-Bayan* accused the Bush administration of interfering in Darfur mainly for economic and political reasons and not on humanitarian grounds. It accused Bush's agenda in the African state of being a colonial one.[78]

On Al-Jazeera's *Opposite Direction* program, Talaat Rimmah, a journalist and expert on African affairs, called the United States a devil and accused it of inflaming conflicts in Sudan and pressuring Khartoum to normalize its relations with Israel.[79] Egypt's *Al-Masry Al-Youm* newspaper accused the United States of provoking division among tribes in Sudan and other African states. It asked, "Why this media focus on the Greater Middle East project while overlooking America's great African century project, which is of no less threat? Is not Africa facing the danger of division?"[80] America sees Sudan as the gate through which it can enter Africa and separate its predominantly Arabic-speaking Muslim northern states from its black Christian southern states, noted Mahmoud Abdel Hakim Taha, a political analyst, in *Al-Gomhuria*.[81] However, contended *Al-Khaleej*, this U.S. attempt to separate southern Sudan from northern Sudan is nothing new.[82]

With oil, minerals, and uranium increasingly being discovered in African nations, said Taha, the United States has begun to show an interest in establishing military bases in Africa. It has started to realize the "economic importance of this continent, for America's military presence in Africa means opening up new markets for its products."[83] Citing the role the United States played in the issuance of UN decision 1706, which condemned the government in Khartoum for human rights violations in Darfur, Mohamed Ali Ibrahim admonished U.S. policy toward Sudan, saying, "This is how Washington wants to use the weapon of human rights against Arab or African countries."[84]

Support for Israel and Arab-Israeli Conflict

One factor that has harmed America's image in the Arab world is the country's unanimous support of Israel; Arabs believe that Israel is cashing in on the widespread anti-Arab attitude present in the United States since the 9/11 attacks. Arabs have often accused the United States, particularly after 9/11, of conspiring with Israel against them and their causes. "Members of the U.S. Congress saw no offense in supporting the neo-Israeli Nazism, which succeeded in convincing the American public to place the 9/11 terrorists and Palestinian mujahedeen in the same basket," wrote Abdel Aziz Hammouda, who served as a cultural attaché at the Egyptian embassy in Washington in the late 1980s and early 1990s.[85]

American foreign policy in the Middle East is goaded on by Israel, contended Waheed Abdel Mageed. Over the past decades, Israel and the Jewish lobby have been influential in the decision-making process in Washington, he added. "And now Israel reaps the fruits planted for it by the Jewish lobby, adding to this the investment gained from the September 11 attacks as if they did not happen but to benefit Israel."[86] The Zionist influence has deepened in the White House and within U.S. organizations, according to Hatr.[87] In this pro-Israeli atmosphere in America, noted Al-Ghamri, neocons held "Zionist beliefs" and formed an "alliance with the Likud." America's pro-Israeli policy, or the lack of a U.S. role in the Middle East peace process, will cause threats to U.S. interests in the long run.[88]

Israel protects U.S. interests in the region, observed Zakaria.[89] The Jews in America fully support Israel in everything it does, claimed former Egyptian ambassador to the United States Ashraf Gharbal. The American Israel Public Affairs Committee (AIPAC) "exercises pressure on decision-makers and on any American who dares criticize Israel, even if his criticism is driven by the will to protect the interests of the United States."[90] What makes Israel popular among Americans is the view that it is a "successful project that has achieved its goal," said Heikel, no matter the illegal or nonethical means employed in the process. Heikel likened the United States' "extermination" of Native Americans to Israel's "atrocities" against Palestinians.[91]

In the view of the Qatari paper *Al-Rayah*, Washington no longer plays the role of a neutral Middle East peace broker, with its main goal being the protection of Israel.[92] Following 9/11, an alliance between neocons and American Zionism was formed, stated *As-Safir*. Bush endorsed Israel as a Jewish state; it was no longer a "state for the Jews" but a "Jewish state" free from any other ethnic roots, hence the eradication of Palestinians went without any condemnation from Washington, added the Lebanese paper.[93] Since Bush proposed his solution of two states living side by side, the Middle East peace process did not move a step forward, observed *Akher Saa*.[94] The board chair of Egypt's Al-Ahram Press Group, Morsi Attallah, argued in *Al-Ahram* that with America's support Israel has violated all international mandates that call for the establishment of an independent Palestinian state.[95] From Madrid 1991 to Oslo 1993 and Annapolis 2007, Israel has escaped all peace initiatives, complained the Syrian paper *Al-Baath*.[96]

Because Israel shapes and plans U.S. policy in the Middle East, Arab-American relations have been dominated by Israeli interests, wrote Said Rafaat, who serves as editor of the Arab League's magazine *Arab Affairs*.[97] The influence of Zionism in America has resulted in American politicians keeping silent in the face of the Israeli slaughter of Palestinians, contended Anisa Fakhrou in *Al-Rayah*. Unless the United States stops its blind support of Israel, no just solution for the Palestinian cause will be reached, she added.[98] In spite of that, remarked *Akhbar Al-Khaleej*, some Arabs still trust in the role the United States can play as a peacemaker in the Middle East.[99] In a piece in *As-Safir*, Palestinian writer Fayez Rasheed wondered why Arabs believe that the United States can be a fair mediator between Arabs and Israelis. He reminded them that Israel is America's first strategic ally and Washington has always backed it, regardless of the "dozens of Nazi-style crimes" committed against Palestinians.[100]

In short, American politics in the Middle East is met with strong hostility and hatred due to the "U.S. Administration's recurrent stances and utter support of Israel while ignoring the rights of Palestinians. Adding to that is America's continued backing of despotic regimes in the region," argued the Egyptian paper *Al-Arabi* in 2007.[101] Such blind support of Israel could result in Washington "losing its Arab allies or those left of them," observed *October*.[102] America has inflamed the Middle East and continues to support Israel in its assassinations of many prominent Arab resistance activists, contended Mohamed Habash, a member of the Syrian Parliament, in an interview on Al-Oula.[103] In the face of this continued Israeli atrocity, "Where is the international community?" asked the Algerian paper *Al-Massa*. It added that Israel "always gains international protection in spite of its occupation of other people's land."[104]

The amount of arms the United States provides to Israel is more than what all other Arab states get from Washington, said Charles Ayoub, editor in chief of the Lebanese newspaper *Al-Diyar*, in an interview with the Qatari satellite television channel Al-Jazeera Mubasher.[105] When conflicts erupt in the Middle East, Washington always sides with Tel Aviv, wrote Al-Fiqi in *Al-Hayat*. Within this framework, America's support for Israel comes first, at times even before its own interests.[106] American leaders and officials are "hostages at the hands of Israel and Zionism," claimed *Akhbar Al-Khaleej*.[107] Jews in America control major economic and media organizations, alleged Lebanese political analyst George Naseef in an Al-Arabiya interview.[108] This, in Gamal Khashkgi's view, is resulting in more "suffering of the Palestinian people" and anger on the Arab and Muslim side. He added in his piece in the Saudi paper *Al-Watan* that Arabs have always longed for a comprehensive peace settlement with Israel, and that is why they have every right to be angry at the United States.[109]

America, said Heikel on Al-Jazeera, needs a protector of its interests in the region, and Israel is the choice.[110] With America's support, contended the Egyptian paper *El-Dostour*, Israel now has control over the Middle East.[111] In that sense, noted Al-Adala, America's imperialist project is the same as that of Israel.[112] The Kuwaiti television channel spoke of a "greater Israeli project" aimed at controlling the Arab world.[113] With America's support, this "Israeli colonial project" has been going on since 1946, said Hamada Al-Faranah, a member of Jordan's Lower House, on Al-Sharqiya, a Dubai-based Iraqi TV channel.[114] Americans want us to give up our honest resistance movement, and we say no to them, said Talal Irslan, a former Lebanese government minister, in a speech to students of Lebanese universities broadcast on Al-Manar.[115]

The Bush administration supported Israel in everything, said Al-Fiqi on Al-Jazeera.[116] Its road map for peace in the Middle East led to nowhere, argued Ahmed Maher, a former Egyptian foreign minister, in a commentary in *Asharq Al-Awsat*.[117] Through America's support, Israel always gets what it desires, wrote the distinguished Egyptian columnist Salama Ahmed Salama in *Al-Ahram*.[118] "Israel does not want peace," and this is clear from its acts, contended journalist Wael Al-Gheshi on the United Arab Emirates satellite television channel Al-Sharja.[119] "Why does America always support Israel?" cried Iraqi political analyst Waleed Al-Zoubidi in an interview with Future, a Lebanese satellite television channel.[120] The U.S. project in the Middle East will eventually serve Israel's interests, said Amin Mshaqba of the Jordanian-based University of Higher Studies in a 2007 interview with the Jordanian satellite television channel Jordan.[121] America wants to withdraw its troops from Iraq but it fears for Israel's security, said Al-Jazeera.[122]

The United States does not seem to want peace in the Middle East; it does not want to recognize facts and the rights of others, according to the United

Arab Emirates paper *Al-Ittihad*.[123] Alas, "we live in the Israeli Age," mourned the Jordanian paper *Al-Arab Al-Yawm*.[124] Under Bush, Washington lost the character of a honest and caring participant in the peace process due to its open support for Tel Aviv, noted Naseef on Al-Arabiya. The United States and Israel will be rejected in the Arab world until Palestinians and Arabs gain their rights, he added.[125] "What can protect Israel in the present and the future is the establishment of a just and durable peace in the Middle East and not the adoption of the politics of power and endeavors for domination," concluded the secretary general of the Arab League, Amr Moussa, in an article in *Arab Affairs*.[126]

Palestine

In *Renewal of National Thought*, Al-Fiqi argued that the "Palestinian cause is the Arab world's top issue. It has dominated Arabs' thought, politics, and way of dealing with the outside world for the past five decades."[127] In short, the Palestinian problem is the Arab world's main concern.[128] *Al-Gomhuria* contended, "The whole world was and still is against the siege of defenseless people in Palestine, daily destruction of homes over the heads of children and elderly men and women, and the politics of repression and collective punishment that Israel practices on the Palestinian people. But Tel Aviv does all what it desires . . . challenging all international laws and human customs under the protection of American veto."[129]

Arab observers vehemently and constantly criticize the unbalanced U.S. policy in Palestine, which they allege goes in Israel's favor and aims at dividing the Palestinians. American policy in the Middle East is unrealistic and un-challenging to Israel's refusal to establish a Palestinian state, said Ahmed Youseff Al-Qarai on Egypt's Radio Cairo.[130] "What is prescribed for the Palestinians is to accept a state without arms to defend its people," wrote Al-Banna in *October*. Sadly, this is the politics of America and Israel.[131] Every time Arabs propose a peace initiative, Israel "throws it in the trash bag," said Maher Al-Taher, a Palestinian, on Al-Manar. "Arabs must realize that Israel does not want peace" in the Middle East. It is now happy that the Palestinians are fighting each other and will work on intensifying internal conflict among them. With America's assistance, added Al-Taher, the Zionist state will work on ostracizing Gaza from the West Bank.[132]

Speaking on the fortieth anniversary of Arabs' defeat in the 1967 Six-Day War, military expert Talaat Muslim implied in an Al-Sharqiya interview that the Camp David peace accords abolished the Palestinian cause. Arabs, he said, did not lose Palestine in 1948 or 1967 but with agreements made with Israel in the 1970s.[133] Israel was created as a project to divide Arabs and Arab identity, said Al-Sharja. After the clashes between Hamas and Fatah, we now disdainfully hear of the U.S. administration, of Rice, speaking of the "rights of Palestinians," the United Arab Emirates satellite television channel said in 2007.[134] If there had not been an American occupation in the region, there would not have been such clashes between Hamas and Fatah, said the head of the Palestinian delegation at the meeting of the Council of Arab Information Ministers in Cairo in June 2007, which was broadcast on Al-Oula.[135] "The conspiracy theory exists, but it is foolish for Hamas to be deceived by it," concluded Emad Ghad, an expert on Israeli affairs, in an interview on the Omani satellite television channel Oman.[136]

The United States and Israel should realize that the deadlock in Palestinian-Israeli peace talks cannot be solved by force, cautioned Al-Gheshi in a piece in the Omani paper *Al-Watan*. Bush came to the region to coerce Arabs to "sell the Palestinian cause," but he made a grave mistake, he added.[137] "If the Palestinian ship sinks, we will all drown," stressed Al-Sharja.[138] Bush's Middle East map was based on a two-state solution, and that was when Hamas engaged in a peace dialogue, argued Al-Hiwar, a London-based satellite television channel.[139] The United States is the only country in the world that can resolve the Middle East conflict, by pushing Israel to settle its differences with Syria and the Palestinians, noted Ibrahim Shukab, a military affairs expert, on Nile News.[140] Karam Gabr, board chair of Egypt's Rose El-Yossef Press Group, wrote the following in *Rose El-Yossef* magazine a few days after the Annapolis Middle East peace conference:

> The Arab public should be angry with and revolt against the unjust and one-for-two policies of America. It should also be saddened by the death of Palestinian children and women. It has its rights and justification for such anger. But it should never hinder the efforts that we must hold to until we eventually achieve peace and establish a Palestinian state, with Jerusalem as its capital. Israel and Washington know well that there is not an Arab or a Muslim who would forsake Arab Jerusalem. And there will never be peace in the region if Jerusalem does not come back under Arab control.[141]

Because Arabs are preoccupied with how to get out of their own crises, they are incapable of playing an effective role when it comes to gaining the minimum necessities for Palestinians, stressed Abdel Nasser Al-Naggar in the Palestinian paper *Al-Ayyam*. "The effective political triangle in the region today is formed of the United States, European Union and Israel, and the cold peace cannot be reached without their agreement on any decree."[142] Experience has taught Arabs that Bush was the "most supportive president of Israel in the history of the United States," wrote Mazen Hammad in *Ad-Dustour*. His government backed more than one Israeli campaign to liquidate the Palestinian cause, as witnessed in the aggression committed in Gaza.[143]

Syria

Arab commentators criticized the U.S. pressure imposed on Syria and Lebanon, and Washington's continued search for pretexts to defend its intervention in their internal affairs. The Tunisian paper *Al-Sabah* accused America of interfering in the internal affairs of Syria and Lebanon and trying to impose its "hegemony on the region." It added that Syria has every right to restore the Golan Heights, occupied by Israel in 1967.[144] Egypt's *Al-Osboa* newspaper spoke of a fake "Israeli-American scenario" in which Syria is accused of having nuclear weapons and then is attacked by the United States.[145] American politicians know nothing but chicanery and deceit and employ fake cards to exercise pressure on other nations, such as Syria, said Al-Manar.[146]

In the opinion of *Akhbar Al-Khaleej*, the United States has been pushing Damascus to support its policies in the Middle East.[147] Those who mock Syria's position on the Israeli-American project in the Middle East do not realize the strain Damascus is under because of its support for the Palestinian and Lebanese people, observed Syrian ambassador to the United States Emad Mustapha in an interview with LBC, a Lebanese satellite television channel. He added that all U.S. policies in the Middle East are founded primarily on promoting Israeli interests.[148] It is unwise for the United States to keep pushing to isolate Syria, whose security is essential for the safety and stability of the entire Middle East, posited the Yemeni paper *Al-Ayam*.[149]

Lebanon

In his novel *Love in Exile*, Bahaa Taher told the story of the Lebanese people's suffering under Israeli bombardment, of the massacre of Palestinians at the Sabra and Shatila refugee camps in Lebanon in 1982, and the need for America to stop its support for Israel.[150] Arabs, including writer Sameera Rajab, believe that from Beirut, America and Israel will head to Damascus and Tehran. Lebanon went through war and later destruction (or creative chaos) as part of a plan, a conspiracy, by the United States to fulfill its dream of a "'Greater and New Middle East,'" Rajab claimed in a piece in *Akhbar Al-Khaleej*. She called on Arabs to resist the American colonial project, which she said began with Iraq and will go beyond the Lebanese border.[151]

In "What's in Bush's Gun Barrel?" the Yemeni paper *Al-Thowrah* cited how the Jordanian king cautioned President Bush of the possibility of the breakout of a civil war in Lebanon similar to that in Iraq. The paper predicted that Bush would, however, pay little attention to King Abdullah's advice.[152] America has always looked at Lebanon as a nation essential for maintaining stability in the Middle East and at Hezbollah as a terrorist group, said Oman.[153] But it does not want Lebanon to have a strong army capable of countering Israeli threats, noted *Akhbar Al-Khaleej*,[154] with Washington, according to Al-Manar, consistently working on weakening resistance forces in the country.[155] Similarly, journalist Ghalib Kandeel stressed on the Syrian television channel Syria that the key U.S. plan in Lebanon is to weaken the resistance movement. He cautioned, "The place of every Lebanese soldier is with resistance in the south."[156]

Washington has tried to provoke a Shiite-Sunni war in Lebanon, but so far it has failed, contended Ayoub on Al-Jazeera Mubasher;[157] in the view of Al-Adala, Hezbollah has succeeded in achieving its objective.[158] America's definition of terrorism should not include Hezbollah, said Hassan Al-Gonni, a professor of international law at the Lebanese University, in an interview with Future. Terrorism means killing innocent civilians, and Hezbollah never did that.[159] Al-Gonni, who opposes any attempt to disarm Hezbollah, added that all Arabs are aware that America wants only to secure Israel's interests. Israel was hurt in Lebanon, and it will attack Lebanon and Hezbollah in revenge in the future, said Abdullah Al-Ashal, an assistant to the former Egyptian minister of foreign affairs Ahmed Maher. He added in his interview with Al-Adala that continuing conflicts in Lebanon are to Israel's benefit.[160]

The United States' invasion of Iraq has moved Lebanon from stability to instability, asserted Hassan Nafah, a political science professor at Cairo University in Egypt, in an interview by Oman.[161] When Israel attacked Lebanon in July 2006, there was no international force dispatched to the country like the one headed by the United States to fight members of Fatah al-Islam in the Nahr Al-Bared camp, said Mohamed Al-Mosfir, a political science professor at the University of Qatar, in a Syrian news program.[162] Al-Fiqi admonished Israel's "massacre" in Kana and criticized what he called U.S. Zionist movements and their influence on the American public. "The exposure of Jews to what they talk about and identify as the 'gas ovens' at the hands of the Nazis does not grant them the right to undertake similar practices and crimes in other nations," wrote Al-Fiqi in *Al-Hayat*.[163] The world must admit that

Israel, with American encouragement, committed Nazi-style crimes in Lebanon, concluded *Akhbar Al-Khaleej*.[164]

Invasion and Occupation of Iraq

The U.S. invasion of Iraq in 2003 has become the catalyst for much anti-Americanism in the Arab world; after all, Arabs say, the Iraq War is the worst human catastrophe in the twenty-first century. To many Arabs, the "Land between the Two Rivers" has been the target of the most massive American propaganda campaign since the end of the Cold War. They continue to question the true motives behind America's invasion of Iraq. Al-Nasser accused the United States of behaving in the Middle East like a "god" that kills and tortures whomever it desires. He described the U.S. occupation of Iraq as a political and moral scandal for the whole world in general and the Arab and Muslim world in particular, cautioning that Arabs could meet the same fate as Native Americans, whom, he alleged, white Americans exterminated. Al-Nasser accused Washington of planting hatred and inflaming racial and ethnic division in Iraq, adding that the United States did not just occupy Iraqi land but seized Arab dignity as well.[165]

The Iraq War has left popular anger high in the Arab world, with Arab critics contending that for peace and stability to be established in Iraq, America must first withdraw its troops from the country. Division between Shiite and Sunni Muslims in Iraq is mostly incited by the United States, wrote Rafaat in *Arab Affairs*.[166] The occupiers of Iraq encourage and support extremists, alleged writer Hamid Al-Mokhtar in an interview with the Cairo-based Iraqi television channel Al-Baghdadia. He cited how the Shiite *intifada*, or rebellion, against Saddam Hussein was denounced by the United States for fear that pro-Iranian Shiites would gain power in Baghdad.[167] In the same vein, Ahmad Nufal, a political science professor at Jordan's Yarmouk University, expressed his belief in an interview with Jordan that America does not want a strong Iraq.[168]

In this ongoing Arab-America contest, the phrase "propaganda" has been used at times to describe American policies. Hassan Omar, an expert on international affairs, questioned the motives behind America's invasion of Iraq, drawing a comparison between the policy of lies of Joseph Goebbels, the German minister of propaganda from 1933 to 1945, and that of Washington.[169] "Since 9/11, all U.S. policies have been based on lies," noted Omar in his interview with Al-Jazeera. Bush "did not expect all that resistance in Iraq," he added. Iraqis today "dream of the [good] days of Saddam Hussein."[170] It is worth citing here that in glorifying Saddam after his execution, some Arab newspapers placed his photo on their cover pages, one in which he holds the Quran in his hand before heading to the gallows. Headlines called him a "hero" and a "martyr."

Other Arabs, including Hazem Al-Yousifi of Iraq's Patriotic Union of Kurdistan, disagree with that characterization, stressing that Saddam was a vicious dictator who humiliated his own people. In an interview with the Egyptian satellite television channel Al-Mehwer, Al-Yousifi said that Saddam committed many atrocities against his own people. Al-Yousifi expressed opposition to any withdrawal of foreign security forces from Iraq, including American troops, claiming that if America is defeated, the influence of the al Qaeda network in Iraq will grow stronger.[171] Fawzy Al-Atroushi, a political activist Kurd, also opposes U.S. withdrawal from Iraq, contending that Iraq has moved a step forward toward freedom and democratization: "The threat to Iraq comes not from America but from al Qaeda and Baath terrorists." In his interview with Al-Jazeera, Al-Atroushi praised Iraqi president Jalal Talabani—a Kurd and founder of the Patriotic Union of Kurdistan—for being the first freely elected president of Iraq. If the United States leaves Iraq, he said, the country will become fragmented. "We have to learn to deal with the mightiest colossus in the world. America is not an 'open evil,'" he added.[172] Americans, said Iraqi writer Seif Al-Khayat in an Al-Baghdadia interview, did not bring conflicts to Iraq; conflicts were lurking there before their arrival. He added that he does not support the conspiracy theory.[173] Adnan Al-Mufti, head of the Parliament of Kurdistan in Iraq, offered his thanks on Abu Dhabi to American and British forces for helping his people.[174]

However, the majority of Arab observers have concluded that the United States is in crisis in Iraq but refuses to admit it. In launching a war on Iraq, America used the "wrong weapon at the wrong time and in the wrong place," said one Middle East expert on Egypt's Sout Al-Arab radio station.[175] In a 2007 discussion on Al-Sharqiya, the director of the Iraqi Institute for Development and Democracy, Ghassan Al-Attiya, wondered what American soldiers were doing in Iraq: "The problem behind establishing national reconciliation in Iraq is U.S. presence." The government in Baghdad is an American government, he added, prognosticating, "Americans have a year or so before they leave, either by defeat or change of [U.S.] government."[176] Ali Kalidar, a journalist, made the same point on Al-Jazeera, stressing that U.S. troops should pull out of Iraq. A civil war will not, as some claim, break out in Iraq if America withdraws, for the reason behind violence in the country is the presence of U.S. troops, Kalidar added.[177]

A number of newspapers ran e-mails sent to them by Iraqis portraying the horrible situation they live under, which some described as the "Iraqi Holocaust." Winning in Iraq is not a matter of time, as Bush tried to convince Americans; the withdrawal of U.S. troops from Iraq will be Washington's next decision, asserted *Al-Khaleej* in 2007, for the situation in the country has been more catastrophic than under Hussein's dictatorial rule.[178] A poll conducted by Al-Jazeera's *Opposite Direction* program on May 29, 2007, and broadcast on the same day showed that nearly 92 percent of respondents believed that the United States must leave Iraq. On the same program, Fadel Al-Rabiai, a Shiite Iraqi writer, accused the "Shiite-Kurd alliance" of being a "puppet" for the United States. America's occupation of Iraq has brought nothing but disaster, he said. Americans must leave or else they will pay for their occupation, he continued. "Yes, Americans will be kicked out of Iraq," and the country after occupation will no longer be one of "dead bodies," he added. American troops in Iraq now are experiencing the "Vietnamese moment."[179]

The reason behind the ongoing instability in Iraq is U.S. occupation, proclaimed Mshaqba in his Jordan interview. "America holds control over Iraq and does not want Arabs involved," he said. It wants Iraq to be fragmented.[180] Alas, lamented *Akhbar Al-Khaleej*, Washington's crimes in Iraq have turned the country into the most dangerous place on earth.[181] It is poignant that the world is standing watching while one of its members is disappearing, said *Al-Massa*. "Iraq is falling into a catastrophe that could drag into it the Middle East region. The continued deteriorating situation in the country could lead to a wide Middle East war, bringing thereafter a third world war," added the Algerian paper.[182] Al-Banna wrote:

> By invading Iraq, the United States has succeeded in achieving three
> goals. The first is imposing hegemony on the region through its mili-
> tary presence in the heart of the Arab world, making the U.S. army a
> thorn in the side of Arabs. The second goal is implementing the process
> of having Arab oil under its control. The third goal is making the re-
> gion ready for a solution to the Arab-Israeli conflict in a manner that
> achieves Israel's vision and desires.[183]

Many have called on the United States to pull its forces out from Iraq and replace them with an Arab international peace keeping force under the auspices of the UN, similar to that adopted in Sudan. They cited the violations committed by U.S. security companies such as Blackwater. *Al-Gomhuria* stressed, "Canceling Blackwater's license is not enough. What is needed to protect Iraq now and in the future is the cancellation of the license of U.S. occupation."[184] President Bush is in a real crisis in Iraq, for he can neither withdraw nor continue staying there," said Maher in *Almussawar* in 2007. He added that the solution for Iraq is an agreement among Iraqi factions, which would encourage Americans to withdraw.[185]

As long as American occupation of Iraq continues, there will not be security in the Arab country, expressed Nufal. The existence of U.S. troops in Iraq does not just hurt the Iraqis but poses a threat to all Arabs, he added in his interview with Jordan.[186] No one can doubt this fact, said Ayoub on Al-Jazeera Mubasher. No one can doubt that the U.S. invasion of Iraq has hurt all Arabs.[187] The issue in Iraq is security and stability, and so far the Iraqis have neither, conveyed Mahdi Al-Hafez, an independent member of Iraq's House of Representatives, in an interview with the Lebanese-based Iraqi television channel Al-Sumaria.[188] "Now, after the U.S. has shown its failure in Iraq, as it did in Vietnam, Lebanon, Somalia and Afghanistan, resolving the current problems of the Iraqis and ending their suffering will not be accomplished until the U.S. departs from their homeland and power is handed to them," commented Issa Al-Zedejali in *Al-Shabiba*.[189]

All U.S. actions and plans in Iraq will fail due to strong Iraqi resistance, asserted Iraqi writer Raad Al-Azawi in *Al-Osboa*.[190] Democrats and Republicans now realize that victory has become impossible in Iraq, but they are reluctant to accept a defeat similar to that of Vietnam or Somalia, according to *Al-Khaleej*.[191] "America's vision for the future in Iraq was shortsighted," said Al-Hafez on Al-Sumaria. "The American project has failed."[192] According to the Saudi paper *Al-Riad*, the question that occupies the minds of Arabs today is: Where is U.S. politics toward Iraq heading and what are its dimensions?[193] Americans must admit that the Bush administration's involvement in Iraq led to strong instability in U.S. foreign policy decision-making, remarked *Akher Saa*.[194] What Bush experienced in Iraq was far beyond what he anticipated, said Heikel on Al-Jazeera. However, America will not get out of Iraq easily, he added. What will happen is a restructuring of its forces in the Middle East.[195]

Bush believed he would not meet resistance when invading Iraq, wrote Hewadi in *Al-Ahram*. He "set a fire in Iraq and was unable to put it out."[196] The Iraq War has cost the lives of over a million people, noted *As-Safir*.[197] It opened a big market for the U.S. arms industry and has left over seven hundred thousand Iraqi civilians dead and more than two million homeless, said

October.[198] Saad Mahyou of *Al-Khaleej* wondered in early 2007 whom should Arabs believe—Bush and the neocons, who claimed that victory in Iraq was still attainable, or presidential candidates Barack Obama, Hillary Clinton, and John Edwards, who called for withdrawal of U.S. troops from Iraq before the end of 2008? His answer: Arabs should not believe any of them. "Nobody says the truth these days in Washington." He added that Iraq was no longer a place of war between Americans and Iraqis; it had become a battlefield between Americans and Americans, between Americans in the White House and those who aspired to kick them out and take over power.[199]

Since World War II, wrote Samira Raghab in *Akhbar Al-Khaleej*, the "U.S. got embroiled in a number of wars from which it pulled out in one way or another, after facing strong resistance that caused it huge losses." But the U.S. war in Iraq was different from past conflicts, she added, for Iraq did not pose any threat to America's national security or interests in the Middle East. She grieved that today Iraq stands in total destruction. "Certainly withdrawal from Iraq will not be like previous U.S. pull outs, for in the name of Iraq and its people, Iraqis will not let them depart without paying a heavy price for what they have done," she said.[200] It was utterly foolish for Americans to think that they would be welcomed in Iraq, wrote Al-Zedejali in *Al-Shabiba*, and the only way out for America from the Iraq quandary is to withdraw its troops from the country. He continued:

> All who follow American foreign policy in Iraq must realize the number of blunders that the manufacturers of such policy have committed over the past two decades, be that during the Iran-Iraq War, after Iraq's fault of invading Kuwait, or the siege and starvation of the Iraqi people that followed, particularly the innocent children who died. Things got worse when the American Administration under the leadership of George W. Bush insisted on invading and occupying Iraq, committing by this a major historical blunder similar to that for which Iraq was punished.[201]

The conclusion from all this, remarked *Al-Gomhuria*, is that "no one believes America anymore or trusts in any statement it issues. Even the American people themselves do not trust in what their government says after it deceived them and the entire world" about the true reasons behind its war on Iraq.[202] When Bush asked Arab nations such as Jordan, Egypt, and Saudi Arabia (together with other Gulf states) to help the Iraqi government because it would support the security of their own countries, *Al-Thowrah* called it a "desperate request" from the American president. Describing Iraq as a battlefield filled with death everywhere, the Yemeni paper added that Arab states have enough problems of their own and that those who caused Iraq's agony should be held responsible. It citied the following verse by the popular Syrian poet Nazzar Kibbany: "'Whoever opened the doors should close them; whoever set the fire should put it out.'"[203]

America Is Weak

There were those who questioned America's power and capabilities, with particular focus on what they described as its military failure in Iraq and Afghanistan. The American empire is weakening and doomed to collapse, wrote Hatr. In the face of a rising, powerful China, the United States is losing its predominance in the global market, he added. Its military machines are failing in the guerilla wars in Iraq and Afghanistan.[204] Under the North Atlantic Alliance, Afghanistan is sailing on a "journey from one nightmare to another," observed Heikel.[205] After six years of war in Afghanistan, "America is still plunged in a fierce conflict against the Taliban forces, with its effects expanding to Pakistan," Salama stated in 2007 in *Al-Ahram*.[206]

The United States is growing feeble both politically and economically, and this is clearly manifested in how the value of its currency has been decreasing, *Al-Gomhuria* claimed.[207] In "Fancies of an Empire," Al-Banna argued in *October*, "American thinking these days mirrors the worry about the future of the American empire, with a number of thinkers reaching the level of cautioning about the collapse of the American system. This pessimistic way of thinking seems to be influenced by the historic failure of the politics of President Bush in his wars in Iraq and Afghanistan."[208] American troops have failed in their melee with resistance forces in Iraq, said Al-Gheshi on Al-Sharja.[209] With Iraq facing the threat of a civil war, the United States is reluctant to accept defeat and withdraw its troops, argued *Al-Khaleej*.[210]

In "A Roman Style Demise of America," Montassir Al-Zayiat pointed out in *Al-Masry Al-Youm* that with its wars in Iraq and Afghanistan the United States has fallen in the "trap of history"; it has aspired to become an empire— rather than a world superpower—that can stand forever. "Now things look different, and what a difference it has been between the condition of American soldiers before entering Iraq, waiting for roses to pour over their heads, and their status quo, which is full of melancholy."[211] When Americans invaded Iraq, said Iraqi politician Nouri Abdel Razaq Hussein on Al-Mehwer, they did not want any international involvement, for they believed they were strong enough and could do it alone. Now, he added, they are weak and should allow for international participation if the crisis in Iraq is to be solved.[212]

Americans today live in a "state of hysteria" regarding Iraq, contended Al-Zoubidi in his interview with Future.[213] They now call on Arabs to come and help, but only in the manner that Washington desires, Al-Attiya said on Al-Sharqiya.[214] The Iraqi people's strong resistance has shattered America's teeth, according to *Al-Arab Al-Yawm*.[215] The Bush government was encouraged to get into the war without being "cautioned about the Middle East's complexities, mystery and moving sand," noted *Al-Hilal*.[216] Despite all its skill with strategic tactics, the United States constantly falls into strategic blunders when dealing with the people of the Middle East, wrote Nabeel Omar in *Al-Ahram*.[217] "Lack of understanding of other cultures and civilizations is among the main reasons behind the collapse of the American empire," observed *October*.[218]

America's "strategy of imposing hegemony on the world has become a thing of the past," said Ali Nassrallah in the Syrian paper *Al-Thawara*.[219] The United States cannot "up the ante," or else it would have succeeded in ousting its historic enemy Fidel Castro, protecting the rule of Hamid Karzai of Afghanistan, or forcing Kim Jong Il of North Korea to cave in, noted Kamal of *Rose El-Yossef*.[220] The politics of the neocons has weakened America and raised hatred of the country worldwide, *Al-Arab Al-Yawm* contemplated, characterizing today's America as an "injured tiger."[221] Certainly, argued *Asharq Al-Awsat*, America's torturing of prisoners is an indication of its weakness.[222]

There is no doubt that America's involvement in Iraq has failed on all levels, politically, militarily, and ethically, said Mustapha Kamal Al-Said, an expert on Middle Eastern affairs, in *Almussawar*. Pulling out from Iraq is seen by the world's superpower as a big defeat, he added.[223] This defeat, in the view of *October*, has hurt the image and reputation of the United States and has resulted in the allied forces running from its "sinking ship" in Iraq and Afghanistan.[224] In the midst of the failure of America's dream of a unipolar world, Al-Missari envisioned in a piece in *Al-Ittihad* the rise of a Russian-French-German alliance (with the possibility of China joining in) to counter America and create a bipolar world.[225] America's "defeat in Iraq may be the beginning of the collapse of the empire of evil and an indication of a new stage in history," wrote Ahmed Shaheen in *October*.[226]

Caricature 1 is by one of the Arab world's greatest caricaturists, Mustapha Hussein, and it was published as a cover page of the monthly Egyptian magazine *Caricature*. It shows an injured U.S. soldier in Iraq with a broken leg and the word "Iraq" written in blood on the wall behind him. He screams over a telecom, "Oh! People, you've to understand: How can I withdraw? To do that, someone has to drag me out."

Caricature 1

Source: *Caricature* magazine, April 2007.

Challenge to Nuclear Iran

For the United States and Arab Gulf countries, Iran has been troubling, yet most Arabs reject any American attack on the nation. Iran is a neighbor of the

Arab Gulf states and the fourth largest oil producer in the world and OPEC's second largest exporter. In addition to owning 10 percent of the world's oil, the Persian state is rich in natural gas. It is a Muslim nation and has a population of over sixty million, with 90 percent of its citizens belonging to the Shiite sect of Islam. During Shah Mohammad Reza Pahlavi's rule (1941–79), the country was a strong ally of the United States, often used as a guard for the Arab Gulf states against any Iraqi threat. In the 1970s Iran seized three islands, then under the control of the United Arab Emirates, claiming that they were originally Iranian. Similar claims have been made by Tehran that the state of Bahrain, of which 75 percent of the population are Shiites, is an Iranian land. Tehran has also been accused of supporting Shiite Muslims in the states of Lebanon and Syria.

Since the 1979 Iranian revolution and ousting of the shah and rise of Ayatollah Khomeini to power, a cold war has emerged between the United States and Iran. During the Iran-Iraq War (1980–88), the Ronald Reagan administration adopted a dual-containment policy, selling arms to both Tehran and Baghdad. Since Iran's declaration in 2003 that it will continue to enrich uranium for its nuclear program, tension has escalated between Washington and Tehran. Tehran has never forgotten that Arabs backed Baghdad during the eight-year Iran-Iraq War, and many Arab Gulf states view Tehran with suspicion. "All that the Gulf states want from America is to use its power in the region to counter Iran," contended Ghassan Al-Emam in the Saudi paper *Asharq Al-Awsat*.[227]

Arabs have been embroiled in the Iranian-American conflict for some time. Iran has promised to set Arab oil ablaze and shoot fifty rockets a minute if it is attacked. Despite Iran's growing influence in the Middle East and Arab leaders' suspicion of Tehran, most Arabs have shown cordial gestures toward the Persian state. In late 2007, talks of normalizing relations between Egypt and Iran were underway. Saudi foreign minister Prince Saud Al-Faisal, like most of his Arab counterparts, stated that Iran is not an enemy. In October 2007 King Abdullah of Saudi Arabia met with President Mahmoud Ahmadinejad. The Iranian president was also invited to the opening session of the Gulf Cooperation Council's meeting a couple of months later. But tension with Iran remerged and intensified in 2008 following Tehran's opening of offices on the disputed Tunb islands, which the United Arab Emirates claims to be its own. In April of that year, Condoleezza Rice attended a Gulf Cooperation Council meeting with the aim of gaining Arab support against Iran. Five months later, the council denounced Tehran for opening those offices.

There are, nonetheless, differences in Arab opinion on whether or not the United States would, or should, attack Iran. Ordinary Arabs, particularly Syrians, Palestinians, Lebanese, Yemenis, and Egyptians, sympathize with the Iranians because of a similarity in cultural roots. They see Iran as a defender of Islam against Bush's "evangelical" invasion of the Arab and Muslim world, and they call on Washington to initiate a dialogue with Tehran in a way that benefits the Arabs. In "Iran and Gulf Security," the Tunisian paper *Al-Sabah* expressed an opinion that "containing the growing Iranian influence in the region does not necessarily require the use of force . . . nor does reining in the Iranian nuclear program in its turn mandate declaring a war on Tehran."[228] *Al-Arab Al-Yawm* stressed that although no Arab backs Tehran's policies, "Arabs should realize that destroying Iran means their own destruction."[229] *Al-Wafd* wondered why Washington continues to chase Tehran if evidence has shown that Iran does not own nuclear weapons nor is it currently pursuing a nuclear program that could pose a danger to the region's stability. The Egyptian paper added, "America should feel ashamed of itself, particularly considering that it was the first country to use such a destructive weapon to wipe out humans, stones and trees." The paper asked readers to remember Hiroshima and Nagasaki.[230]

Arabs, including the Gulf states, refuse the use of force against Iran due to the catastrophic circumstances that could erupt thereafter. Considering the ups and downs between Tehran and Washington, commented *Al-Ittihad*, the Arab Gulf states stand as "victims in a big chess game, which Washington plays on the stage of the Greater Middle East with the last rib of the 'axis of evil.'"[231] Those who call for military attacks on Iran, in the opinion of *Akhbar Al-Khaleej*, are not only "crazy" but "criminals" as well.[232] Any U.S. military attack on Iran would affect the security and stability of the region, asserted Ibrahim Qaod of *Akher Saa*. It would be a political, economic, and environmental disaster not just for the Arabs but for the entire globe, he added.[233] Iran has every right to become a nuclear power, proclaimed Al-Adala.[234] If Tehran's nuclear program is a peaceful one, why reject it, asked Libyan president Moammar Qaddafi in an interactive lecture he gave from Tripoli to students of the Oxford Union broadcast on BBC World on May 20, 2007.

According to Yemeni writer Ali Mohassein Hamid, there are two chief objectives behind the U.S. war against Iraq. The first is to maintain Israel's military superiority in the region; the second is to get rid of the Iranian regime and deprive the Persian state of the right to own nuclear arms. He stressed in his 2007 piece in *Al-Hayat* that what neocons truly want is to do away with the ayatollahs.[235] America might use the Iran card as a tool to frighten Arabs, claimed Al-Attiya on Al-Sharqiya.[236] The chances of the United States attacking Iran have never been as high as they are today, observed Makrim Mohamed Ahmed in *Almussawar*.[237] The United States plans to attack Iran, maintained *Al-Khaleej*, and its denial of that is part of a strategic deceit by the military.[238] Arab countries, asserted Mohamed Abdel Hady in *Al-Masry Al-Youm*, should not support or participate in "any U.S. plan against Iran that aspires for Israel—after dropping Egypt, Iraq and possibly Syria and Iran from the equation—to become the hegemonic state in the region."[239]

Asharq Al-Awsat cautioned Washington that its pro-Israeli politics helps Iran penetrate the Levant—Syria, Lebanon, and Palestine—and turn the three states against America and Arab regimes.[240] On Al-Jazeera's television show *More Than One Opinion*, Gihad Khazen stressed that Arabs are aware of the threat that Iran poses to the region, particularly to the Gulf states. The popular Arab columnist and former editor of *Al-Hayat* added that when Bush frightened Arabs of Iran during his visit to the region in January 2008, he was merely carrying an "Israeli message."[241] Al-Banna, on the other side, chronicled America's relations with Iran from the time Bush first ran for president and how he worked toward reducing tension with Tehran. "America has no friend; it has interests that compel it to antagonize its friends and befriend its enemies," he wrote in *October*. He added that America's relations with Iran could be a model for studying the relationship between ethics and politics within the vision of the Bush administration. Citing Iran's military power and the opinion of a former Egyptian marshal, Al-Banna expressed doubt that the United States will attack Iran.[242]

Arabs need a unified policy to counter America's growing influence in the region and the threat of a U.S.-Iranian war, said Abdel Aziz bin Sakr, director of the Gulf Center for Research, in an Al-Arabiya interview.[243] Iran wants to challenge the United States and will make no concession, and America is employing this against it, declared Anwer Eshqi, head of a Saudi-based Middle East policy organization, in a discussion with Future.[244] Neocons will try to pressure Bush to go to war against Iran, *Almussawar* warned in 2007.[245] The United States and Israel have a plan to strike Iran, said Mustapha Abdel Khaleq, a former Egyptian diplomat, on Nile News. But as long as America is in a crisis in Iraq, it is unlikely that it will hit Iran, he added.[246] Instead of attacking Iran and throwing the region into destruction, contended the Lebanese magazine *Al-Afkar*, the United States should put pressure on Israel to get rid of its nuclear arms.[247]

Undoubtedly, Iran is one of the nations that have benefited the most from America's invasion of Iraq, said political science expert Mohamed Al-Said Abdel Moneim in *Almussawar*.[248] Gabr of *Rose El-Yossef* believes that Iran was upset by the Annapolis Middle East conference because the United States was trying to bring Syria closer to other Arab states. He added that Iran may be able to put pressure on Hezbollah or Hamas to hinder peace efforts in the Middle East. "It cannot play, however, this role with Syria, for relations between Damascus and Tehran are tactical and not strategic. If Israel withdraws from the Golan, Syria will agree on normalizing relations with Israel."[249]

There were those who believed that Bush would go to war with Iran because that was the only way for him to keep U.S. troops in Iraq. Ismail Montassar of *October* was one of them, writing that the United States works toward "a real confrontation with Iran, even if it abandons its nuclear program or submits it for international monitoring."[250] The United States, said Nile News, should solve its problems with Iran, for the latter is pursuing a "peaceful nuclear program." When Iran violates that, the international community can and should then interfere.[251] In another Nile News debate, political science professor Midhat Hammad praised Iran's switch from the U.S. dollar to the euro as the official currency for its foreign trade.[252]

Bush told Arabs about the danger of the Iranian nuclear program but not about the threats of Israel's nuclear arsenal, cried the Saudi paper *Al-Riyadh*.[253] Israel is facing the danger of a rising Iranian influence in the Middle East, contended Rafaat in *Arab Affairs*.[254] Hence, Israel encourages the United States to strike Iran, said Nufal in a Jordan television debate.[255] Iran has worked laboriously to "foil the American project in the region," noted Mshaqba in the same debate on Jordan. Iran desires to drag America more into the Iraq quandary for its benefit. It is possible, added Mshaqba, for the United States and Iran to strike a deal over Iraq, allowing Tehran to have a nuclear program for peaceful use in return for its help in stabilizing Iraq.[256] In the same vein, Al-Hafez stated that Iraq could be used as a card by Iran for settling many of its issues with Washington. "Iran is an essential part in Iraq today," said Al-Hafez in an interview with the Iraqi Al-Sumaria television channel on June 18, 2007. It is worth mentioning here that during the broadcast Al-Sumaria asked viewers for a vote on whether or not they supported an Iranian-American dialogue on Iraq. In all, 42 percent of the respondents said yes and 58 percent said no.

In the view of Abdel Karim Al-Alougi of *Al-Arabi*, "Iran now plays a measurable role in the region—from Iraq to Lebanon and Palestine—with the support of resistance groups. It desires to undertake the same role as America in the region, and thus it is directly in the face of the U.S." He added that Bush would not leave Iraq for Tehran to control.[257] Nevertheless, Moneim of *Almussawar* believes that there is an "intersection for the American dream in Iraq and the Iranian dream in Iraq." Both parties understand that there is no choice but to deal with one another. Iran realizes that there is no alternative but to do business with the world's superpower, therefore it prefers peaceful cooperation and not a military confrontation.[258]

5 QUESTIONING AMERICAN DEMOCRACY

This is democracy, one day for us and another day against us. AL-MOATTI
EBEAD, Moroccan politician

*Devoid of decency, yet speaking a lot of it, exactly like America's talk about its
democracy, in which there is unprecedented surveillance on Americans in the
name of fighting terrorism. In it, there is the Guantánamo detention center,
a butchery of human rights unseen in any of the world's ugliest dictatorships.
And in Iraq—the model of U.S. democracy—there is America's biggest scandal:
Abu Ghraib prison.* AHMED RAGAB, Egyptian journalist

The United States has been pushing Arabs on the issue of democracy for a
long time, but many of them have interpreted democracy as a cover-up for
American dominance. Over the past century, Arab elites and intellectuals have
insisted on doing things their own way, complaining of inequities in American
democracy. They stress that the Jacksonian democracy existed with slavery and
the denial of women's rights. Their skepticism of the notion of American
democracy goes back to when discrimination against African Americans was
vibrant in the social fabric of American society. Following a visit to the United
States in the late 1930s, the great journalist Mustapha Amin was astonished
at how a nation that worshiped and idealized freedom was discriminating
against blacks. He spoke of how he witnessed hotels, bars, restaurants, and

cinemas displaying signs proclaiming that blacks were not welcome.[1] Similarly, Zaki Naguib Mahmoud, a philosophy professor who spent a year teaching in the United States in the early 1950s, was shocked by the segregation of blacks and how Native Americans had no right to vote and were "raped" of their country.[2] A decade later, political analyst Rashid Al-Barowny wrote an article in the Egyptian magazine *Al-Hilal* questioning American democracy and "a polity that makes of 20 million people second-class citizens for a reason no other than the color of their skin."[3] This belief of "a racist America" remains deeply engraved in the minds of Arabs and is often reiterated in the Arab media, particularly when the United States calls on an Arab state to open up and embrace democracy.

Another example that is worth citing goes back a couple of decades earlier. As the battle for the independence of Egypt and Sudan from British rule intensified, the weekly Egyptian newspaper *Akhbar El-Yom* began a campaign late in July 1947 in support of both nations' struggle for freedom. The paper printed drawings the size of a postcard, written in the language of each of the then eleven members of the United Nations Security Council; *Akhbar El-Yom* called on readers to crop these cards and mail them to delegates at the UN. The postcard addressed to the United States carried the words: "You Kicked England Out of America to Have an Independence Day. Why Shouldn't We? Liberate Egypt and Sudan."[4] All Arabs at the time felt that America would stand by their side, but Harry Truman's government later called on King Farouq, who ruled Egypt and Sudan from 1936 to 1952, to resume negotiations with the British. Egyptians were angered by Washington's decision, and *Akhbar El-Yom* published a caricature of the Statue of Liberty in New York with an Egyptian standing in front and disdainfully saying to President Truman: "When someone dies in Egypt we build a statue for him, and it seems that you have the same tradition."[5]

Muckraking journalist Mahmoud Al-Saddani spoke of numerous contradictions in the American way of life and democracy. The United States is the "only country that calls its government an 'administration' because it is not a state but a company, and its citizens are not the public but shareholders in that company," he said.[6] There is no such thing as absolute free speech, be it commercial or not, remarked Bassem Khafagi, director of the Cairo-based International Center for American and Western Studies. "American freedom is a huge historical dilemma," in the sense that an "American is free and not free at the same time."[7] Americans are free to do what they want and enjoy life, but they are tied in their general life because of media's control of the decision-making process.[8] Amin, who visited the United States more than twenty-five times over half a century, accused the country of promoting authoritarian regimes: "An American loves speed, and that is the secret behind American politicians forming an alliance with dictatorial states, since it is easy to deal with an individual ruler and difficult to deal with democratic countries."[9]

Since the end of the Cold War, the United States' image as a democracy has been shaken in the Arab world, according to Attif Al-Ghamri, a distinguished author and columnist at Egypt's *Al-Ahram* newspaper.[10] "America has lost a lot when Arabs feel that it exports to them arms, cars, airplanes, television, movies, video, and not the best that it has: democracy and human rights."[11] The George W. Bush administration promised to establish democracy in Iraq but ended up creating chaos and destruction in the Arab country. If the "horrible scenes" of Iraqi prisoners being tortured and the "shameful pictures" displayed on the Internet of Iraqi women held captive and raped prove anything, it is that "American culture is essentially founded on violence" and discrimination, asserted Nahed Hatr.[12] "I do not really think that Bush has the right to impose reform on any nation before he reforms the state of his own Administration, army and democracy," contended Raji Inayet. Bush's claim that America invaded Iraq to implement democracy was a lie for two reasons, he wrote. First, the practices of his administration in America were themselves undemocratic. Second, the history of successive republican administrations' dealings with totalitarian regimes has been founded mainly on making profit and not promoting democracy.[13]

In the view of writer and philosopher Fouad Zakaria, the American model is a unique phenomenon that cannot be repeated. It is astounding, yet filled with self-weakness. "The American model is increasingly imposing itself on us," he cautioned. He added that although many Arabs publicly refuse the American way of life, it is met with "growing admiration" in secret.[14] He accused the Arab media—naming the Egyptian media in particular—of being controlled by individuals whose aim is to "beautify" America's image. The United States, he went on, is described as a perfect model that would "uplift us from poverty to wealth and from weakness to power."[15] The American model puts no restrictions or limits on the activities of individuals in the financial field. Such a model, continued Zakaria, "is not suitable for a third-world nation, particularly in the Arab world," where resources are limited.[16] He added that the United States knows well that its model is suitable only for itself and will result in failure if applied to other nations, "but it simply does not care for what happens to others."[17] It employs the democracy card in the Arab world as a means to an end, believing that it is the only way to get Arabs to soften their thinking and accept America. Arab regimes, however, see democracy as a ploy by Washington to control their people rather than give them the upper hand.[18]

America does not want true reform or democracy in the Arab world and will use all means possible to achieve its goal and protect its interests, wrote Salaheddine Hafez, vice chief editor of *Al-Ahram* and general secretary of the Federation of Arab Journalists. It is the biggest betrayer of liberal principles and values, and when the United States talks about promoting democracy and liberal values, it is as if it were talking about marketing a product to export.[19] "To hide its 'colonial ambitions' in the region," Washington, with the help of the U.S. media, often raises the "slogan of democracy," wrote Said Al-Lawandi, an expert on international relations. After the United States occupied Iraq in April 2003, for example, the "American media began to speak about a promised, holy democracy in Iraq, and that was all 'lies,'" concluded Al-Lawandi. Instead of planting democracy in Iraq, the United States has filled the hearts of Arabs with hatred through its killings of innocent Iraqis.[20]

Principles of U.S. Freedom and Democracy

How do Arabs perceive the principles and morals of American democracy? How is that debate orchestrated today in the hearts and minds of Arabs? "The American political system is different from that in any other country," wrote Ashraf Gharbal, former Egyptian ambassador to the United States. "Americans are fascinated by what they call the balance of power in foreign policy," he added. To have an influence on a U.S. foreign policy decision, one has to address all parties, including Congress, the media, and public opinion.[21] Yet, the U.S. political system is far from being democratic, argued Nazzar Basheer. All the United States has are cosmetic forms of democracy; it is the democracy of elitists. It is a democracy of money, for if you are rich you can buy your way to government office.[22] The United States is purely a capitalist system, which arms and oil dealers control entirely—from the presidency to the judicial and legislative branches and the mass media.[23] Mohamed Kamal, a university professor, proclaimed in a piece in *Al-Ahram* that the U.S. Congress is different from other parliamentarian institutions in the world in that it is increasingly becoming a participant in the executive decision-making process, hence raising questions about the separation of powers as embedded in the American Constitution.[24]

As much as they scorn Bush, Arabs have also been making sport of George Washington's proclamation that America should be a model for the world.

"The mass extermination that capitalist America practices in the name of 'freeing nations from dictatorship'" brings to memory the "criminal" role its European founders embraced two hundred years ago, stated the Jordanian paper *Al-Arab Al-Yawm*.[25] "The process by which the United States gained its independence from British colonialism brought equality to all peoples, but it kept slavery alive for a century until the Civil War took place and abolished it," wrote distinguished columnist Ahmed Bahghat in *Al-Ahram*.[26] Even Thomas Jefferson was racist and often made discriminatory remarks against blacks, the Kuwaiti paper *Al-Qabas* pointed out.[27]

Arabs want democracy, "but an American-style democracy is an open lie," wrote prominent journalist and media commentator Gihad Khazen in the Saudi paper *Al-Hayat*.[28] The establishment of an American-style democracy would mean the disintegration of Arab entities, according to the Lebanese paper *As-Safir*.[29] In essence, an American democracy is merely one of "shape"; it is "founded on a huge arsenal of procedures and lacks ethics," alleged the Egyptian paper *Al-Arabi*.[30] After all, America has a long history of illegal intervention in other nations, from Vietnam to Iraq, argued *Al-Ittihad*, a United Arab Emirates paper.[31] The American invasion of Iraq was a "smack to all the principles contained in the American Constitution" and a violation of general freedoms that all American administrations have said they back, particularly the right for self-determination, observed commentator Gameel Kamal Georgee in the Egyptian paper *Al-Gomhuria*. The invasion revealed the "fragility and fakeness" of those American principles.[32]

When denouncing American democracy, Arabs have often referred to stories of Iraqis being tortured and women raped by American soldiers. When Arabs examine the situation in Iraq and the cruelty of American actions there, they can comprehend Washington's colonial ambitions and can see that the United States is far from being democratic, noted the Bahraini paper *Akhbar Al-Khaleej*. "It is a dictatorship working to plunder people's wealth and impoverish three quarters of the world's population for the sake of a few rich nations and transatlantic corporations" and nothing else.[33] Washington claims that we live in the "age of freedom, human rights, open skies and the one village," wrote Ahmed Shaheen in the Egyptian magazine *October*, "but it has been and still is the last to uphold these principles. It is the first to destroy and violate them. If there is freedom in Iraq, Afghanistan or Palestine, it is the freedom of killing, destruction and vagrancy."[34] Ahmed Hamrouch of the Egyptian magazine *Sabah El-Kheir* condemned American democracy for criticizing U.S. movie director Michael Moore for taking individuals to Cuba for medical treatment; the United States has been boycotting Cuba for decades and considers the country to be an enemy.[35]

In the view of award-winning novelist Bahaa Taher, neither Arab culture nor Western culture is democratic. In an interview with *Sabah El-Kheir* he said, "Democracy is absolute freedom, and I cannot describe a system or a state as democratic simply because it runs true elections, while in the meantime it exterminates other people . . . as witnessed in Iraq and Palestine. For this is nothing but clear dictatorship. To say that Western culture is democratic and that our culture is oppressive is wrong, for there exists oppression in both of them."[36] Like Taher, Arab journalists have asserted in their coverage that U.S. forces are committing massacres in Iraq. On May 20, 2007, the independent Egyptian television channel Al-Mehwer hosted a German investigative journalist with *Die Spiegel* magazine who showed photographs of an alleged massacre by U.S. soldiers in an Iraqi area known as Al-Hadditha. Viewers were glued to the box because these frightening photos of slaughtered Iraqis had not yet been published.

A few Arab commentaries have praised American democracy as a distinctive model. Commenting on the 2008 U.S. presidential elections, the Omani paper *Al-Watan* wrote, "In spite of all its foreign policy faults, the United States of America remains a unique model of democratic practice—the one nation capable of accommodating all its people with their different nationalities without regard to gender, color or ethnicity."[37] In a piece in *Al-Ittihad*, Khalil Ali Hdeer asked Muslims to remember the services that American democracy and Western nations in general have offered to them—from advanced medical achievements to technological inventions—and how they opened the doors of their universities for Muslims to study at them.[38] But such praise of American democracy, which is seldom witnessed in the Arab media, was often met with strong resentment and a religiosity proclaiming that an American-style democracy is anti-Islamic. Consider this comment, for example, from a Palestinian: "In God's name, what is happening to us?" lamented Ibrahim Assal Al-Ebadi of the Palestinian paper *As-Sabeel*. "Have we replaced religion with democracy? Has American democracy become a god for us to worship?"[39]

Manufacturing Democracy and Reform Abroad

President Bush called on Arabs to open up and embrace democracy in a speech he gave in November 2003. In the years that followed, many Arabs perceived Bush's promotion of democracy in the Arab world—some used the words "manufacturing of democracy"—as the cause of the rise of negative attitudes toward the United States in the Arab world. In their view, democracy cannot be given; it must be earned. Even if it could be given, they said they would not take it from Bush. With its occupation of Iraq, wrote Abdullah Mohamed Al-Nasser, the United States has hindered all endeavors for freedom and democracy in the Arab world.[40] America wants a democracy in the Arab world similar to that in Iraq, with half a million dead and another half incarcerated. "We do not know what the results would have been had America applied Iraqi democracy in a smaller country than Iraq. Perhaps that country would have been entirely wiped out, with ballot boxes empty because no one would be left to cast votes in them," contended a piece in *Al-Arab Al-Yawm*. It described the American democracy strategy as a "cheap project" to break up the Arab East under the pretext of promoting human rights.[41]

The United States has been exercising pressure on Arab governments to embrace democracy, its own flawed form of democracy, according to *Al-Hayat*. Washington does not truly want to spread democracy in the Arab world, added the Saudi paper.[42] It is determined to form an American-Arab government alliance to counter national Muslim resistance movements, particularly in Lebanon and Palestine, which pose a threat to U.S.-Zionist hegemony, alleged an article on the Qatari-owned Islamonline.net. In doing so, it shows that it mainly cares about its interests and not the sponsorship of democracy.[43] This deadly "American drug for democracy" is plaguing the region, contended Karam Gabr of Egypt's *Rose El-Yossef* magazine. "America sides with the devil and makes him a friend if that serves its interests," he added.[44]

In Arabs' view, there is no shared definition of what democracy is and whether it can be planted in the culture of all societies and at all times; nor do they believe, as mentioned earlier, that states that hold elections are free. Under the false slogan of spreading democracy, the "white man" invaded third-world nations, including Arab ones, to control their resources, proclaimed an article in the Egyptian newspaper *Nahdt Misr*. The United States has stolen their wealth under the claim of spreading American freedom.[45] It is pitiful that a land that holds thousands in its jails without trial preaches democracy, noted the Syrian paper *Tishreen*. "The Bush Administration did not, and will not, do any real thing for the sake of human rights in general and Arabs in particular. All its efforts are directed toward compelling Arabs to bend to Israel's desires and America's crooked politics," it stated in early 2008.[46]

America's slogans of democracy and political reform erupted following 9/11, said Mustapha Al-Fiqi, chairman of the Egyptian People's Assembly

Foreign Affairs Committee, in an interview with Al-Jazeera.[47] Following a trip he made to Washington early in 2008, Al-Fiqi cautioned in an article he wrote for *Al-Hayat* that these slogans cannot stand alone against future challenges without practical programs. He called on American policymakers to realize that the "reform process is tied to each society's culture and method of thinking."[48] Al-Sayed Yassin, one of the Arab world's most distinguished media and political observers, wondered in a piece in *Al-Ittihad* which norm of democracy should Arabs embrace and whether Arab societies with traditions deeply rooted in Islam can embrace a Western model of democracy.[49]

Arabs want reform, but they do not want U.S. involvement in their countries' internal affairs, according to the Saudi paper *Al-Watan*. They believe that America does not want democracy established in their countries and that its rhetoric on democracy is designed to coerce them into making more concessions.[50] The democracy that the United States is preaching in the Arab world is a false democracy; it is one of "invasion and destruction. It is the democracy of Guantánamo and Abu Ghraib prisons, destruction of Afghanistan and creation of crises in the Muslim and Arab world," said an editorial in the Bahraini paper *Akhbar Al-Khaleej*. This is the democracy that America prophesizes for the Arabs, added the editorial, which also accused some Arab regimes of working as puppets for the United States in order to remain in power.[51] Writing in the Egyptian paper *Al-Masry Al-Youm*, Hussein Ahmed Amin contended that America and other colonial states prefer to deal with "autocratic regimes" rather than democratic ones because on top of an autocratic regime is an individual or a few individuals, making the government easier to direct. It would be difficult to do the same thing with an elected parliament founded on the grounds of plurality and change of power, he added. When the United States occupied Iraq and pushed for democracy in the region, Arab leaders willingly or unwillingly welcomed America's demand as long as they remained in power. But after America's campaign for democracy in Iraq failed, these leaders turned their backs on the United States and started mocking American democracy.[52]

The United States, said political analyst Ahmed Asfahani, does not necessarily want secularist states in the Arab world; it wants systems that succumb to it—be they dictatorial or not. He made his comment in an interview with ANB, a privately owned TV channel with offices in London and Arab countries.[53] The goal of imposing democracy on the Muslim world is to offer chances to those who wish to tarnish Islamic law under the claim that freedom of speech protects their acts, remarked the Yemeni paper *Al-Thowrah*. "This reminds us of the freedom established in Iraq under the moguls' occupation, where many tricks appeared to the extent that one individual claimed that his poetry was better than the verses of the Quran."[54] Without a doubt, America's campaign for democracy is essentially orchestrated to exploit oppressive regimes and frighten them into submission, observed the United Arab Emirates paper *Al-Bayan*.[55]

In a commentary titled "American Democracy in the Shadow of Killing and Starvation," Laila Al-Hammoud admonished the United States for endeavoring to impose its notion of freedom and democracy on the Arabs. This, she cautioned, has resulted in an increase in the mistrust of America in the Middle East. She added, in her article in the Jordanian paper *Al-Rai*, that America's proclamations about freedom and democracy are "merely shining slogans to buttress its occupation of Iraq" and potential actions against Iran, Lebanon, and Darfur.[56] Those who vie for American democracy, remarked the Egyptian paper *Al-Osboa*, need to have a look at the democracy of Iraq, Afghanistan, Guantánamo, and Abu Ghraib.[57] Yehia Ali grieved over America's acts, which he said contradict what constitutes a true democracy. He wrote in *Al-Gomhuria* in 2007:

> I do not think that anyone in the entire world pays attention to what America says, especially about human rights and democracy, because all the acts of the Bush government are against human rights and democracy. . . . We do not know what human rights, freedoms or democracies are those that America speaks about. Is it the democracy of oppression and ignominy that it is practicing in Iraq or the democracy of human rights violations and perpetration of the most horrible crimes against humanity in Abu Ghraib or Guantánamo detention camps? Or is it the democracy of genocide and destruction of homes over their inhabitants' heads and the robbing of treasures, monuments, money and oil which it is practicing in Iraq? What democracy is that which permits a state to intervene in the affairs of another and impose its orders on it? What freedom is America talking about when Americans of African, Arab or Latino descent are themselves suffering abhorrent discrimination? The stories of discrimination and oppression cited by Americans of those ethnic backgrounds are varied and numerous.[58]

Democracy cannot and will not be fulfilled by holding a conference or two, declared Mohamed Kaoush in *Al-Arab Al-Yawm*. "It is not a commodity that merchants import from the USA at hard times or in the face of crises."

America has employed democracy, freedom, and human rights as an umbrella for its occupation of Iraq, he added. During its invasion of Iraq, Washington launched a media campaign calling on developing nations—Arab ones at the forefront—to embrace political, social, and economic reform. The United States claimed that it was coming to play the role of a reformer and not a colonialist. This campaign ended following the invasion, for Washington felt in need of Arab support to save it from its crisis in Iraq.[59]

In an interview with Egypt's Nile News television channel, Egyptian politician and journalist Mustapha Bakri accused the Western media of introducing American slaughters in Iraq as a model for establishing democracy.[60] The Bushian project of making Iraq a model for democracy in the Arab world failed, taking with it the integrity and reputation of the world's superpower, posited *Al-Thowrah*. This was due to Washington's "political stupidity."[61] Because the Bush administration failed in its wars in Iraq and Afghanistan, argued Hafez in *Al-Ahram* in 2007, it "is now employing a new phase of a 'war of ideas' founded on marketing American democracy as a model that our nations must imitate and pursue its values and ideas."[62] Hamrouch of *Sabah El-Kheir* perceived the 2007 U.S. arms deals to Israel and Arab states as an example of how the United States "imposes its hegemony on some regions and reveals the truth behind American democracy."[63]

Despite the Arab Gulf states' increased dependence on the United States for security, particularly with rising U.S.-Iranian tension, there is a mounting sense of discomfort with American politics in the Middle East in general and the Gulf region in particular. *Al-Ittihad* stressed that what the United States cares about in the Arab Gulf region is not the establishment of democracy but the accomplishment of its strategic goals: securing the flow of oil, protecting Israel, and continuing its campaign against terrorism.[64] Likewise, an *Al-Qabas* commentary was critical of U.S. political acts in the Arab Gulf, citing how Washington was overlooking the Kuwaiti government's attempt to dissolve parliament in return for possible Kuwaiti support for future American sanctions or war against Iran. "It is not peculiar to say that Americans are new in the region and ignorant of the domestic politics which governs its people. Therefore, when drawing their political map in the region, they have depended mostly, and still do, on Great Britain's past colonial experience."[65]

No one can dispute that the United States has failed in promoting its democratic system abroad and has instead become preoccupied with spreading military and political conflicts in parts of the world, observed the Palestinian paper *Al-Quds Al-Arabi*.[66] The puzzling question now, according to *Al-Ahram*, is this: What grants the United States the right to evaluate the state of democracy around the world?[67] In the same vein, *Akher Saa* asked in 2007, "From where does George Bush come up with this deceitful pomposity when talking about his 'democracy' and 'freedom,' which he declares and prophesies to the entire world?" The Egyptian magazine reasoned that he picked it up from the process of a "superior European mind," which denounces Oriental culture.[68] When Bush uses the words "democracy" and "freedom," the two words that symbolize the "noble dream of humanity" lose their meaning, contended the Saudi paper *Asharq Al-Awsat*.[69] American democracy will not be of "any use to us," and "George Bush is not qualified to speak about democracy," cried Bakri in a 2007 interview with the Egyptian television channel Al-Oula.[70]

American politics lacks ethics, many Arabs believe. The United States that is now pushing for democracy in the Middle East is the same United States whose main concern is the promotion of its own interests, qualified *Asharq Al-Awsat*. Hence, when the results of implementing a democratic system abroad do not suit American interests, Washington does not tolerate them.[71] Those in the Arab world who speak about democracy today are just holding some passing thoughts, wrote Said Al-Hamad in the Bahraini paper *Al-Ayam*.[72] The editor in chief of *Rose El-Yossef*, Abdullah Kamal, mockingly said in an interview with Al-Oula that he had tried to read as many books as possible on democracy to understand President Bush's notion of it but always ended up in failure.[73] "Democracy cannot be carried on tanks and planes as we are seeing in Iraq today," argued one Libyan political analyst in a program on the Libyan television channel Al-Jamahiriya.[74] The United States will continue to play the symphony of democracy for years to come, but this will prove, as it has in the past, to be ineffective and will cause conflicts, said *Al-Ahram*.[75] In that sense, elaborated the Yemeni paper *Al-Sahwa*, the Arab world today "seems to be saying that any land that America steps on never knows peace, stability or justice."[76] On the humorous side, *Al-Ahram* ran a caricature on June 30, 2007, of Bush holding a dagger in one hand and saying, "We must impose democracy through dictatorship."

Human Rights Violations

Arabs see Washington as the great promoter and patron of those who commit colossal violations of human rights worldwide. The American personality is full of contradictions, wrote Khafagi. In spite of the United States' human rights violations in many parts of the world, Americans believe deep in their hearts that their country protects human rights. Under the pretext of promoting human rights globally, a "racist culture" has been blossoming in America with a desire for power and money.[77] A professor of theology at Al-Azhar University, Mohamed Said Ahmed Al-Maceer, claimed: "The United States has been filling the world with its screams about human rights, yet the country is founded on horrible racism. It has eradicated the Red Indians while it continues the politics of racial oppression against blacks. It interferes in the affairs of developing nations to impose control under the claim that it is protecting human rights. It uses the right of veto to keep Zionist colonialism over the chests of Arabs and Muslims."[78] The few Native Americans remaining in the United States today live in isolated communities, merely as a "living human museum," wrote Zakaria.[79] Arabs also cannot forget that America was the first to use atomic bombs, resulting in the death of a quarter of a million people in two seconds.[80]

Criticism of the United States and its notion of democracy continues. Al-Saddani argued that the United States creates false claims when it wants to invade or punish other nations without right, as it did in Panama and Cuba. The United States, he wrote, "sheds tears for lost human rights" in some countries but never for the damaged human rights of Palestinians in Israel.[81] America's history must start with a blank page on which "killing the other" forms the beginning of the first sentence, said the Arab world's most distinguished journalist, Mohamed Hasseinein Heikel, who served as former chief editor of *Al-Ahram* newspaper and advisor to Egyptian president Gamal Abdel Nasser.[82] America is not an example to be followed when it comes to human rights, said Abdullah Al-Sinnawi, chief editor of *Al-Arabi*, in an interview with Al-Jazeera.[83] Americans are smart at creating enemies, proclaimed *Asharq Al-Awsat*.[84] This "American madness" has driven Washington to commit many atrocities in several parts of the world, according to the Yemeni news website Al-sahwa-yemen.net.[85]

The United States makes a travesty of the Arab mind when the country speaks of its kindness and caring for the weak and those who lose their life unjustly, argued one commentator in *Al-Ahram*. Citing the suffering of Palestinians, Mohamed Saleh questioned America's sense of humanity and justice, accusing Americans of violating the rights of Arabs: "Where are the rights of an Arab human being while living on his own land?" He added, "Where were America's humanitarianism and kind and loving heart when considering what it did in Iraq, Pakistan . . . and the destruction and chaos it has inflicted on the region?"[86] If Congress is supportive of religious freedom, why did it not condemn Israel for prohibiting Palestinians from performing their Friday prayer at Al-Aqsa mosque, wrote Farida Al-Shoubashi in *Al-Masry Al-Youm*. "I wish for any believer in American democracy to refer me to a U.S. condemnation of this cowardly and ugly atrocity on religious freedom in occupied Arab Jerusalem," she added.[87]

If we evaluate the United States' record on human rights over the past decade, we will find it full of violations, said Bakri in his Al-Oula interview.[88] How could America claim to be a promoter of human rights when it tortures prisoners, let alone ones who have not yet received a trial? From Vietnam to the McCarthy era to Iraq and Afghanistan, the United States has committed colossal human rights violations, *Al-Qabas* articulated.[89] America's antiterrorist laws largely resemble the emergency laws applied in third-world nations, stressed the Jordanian paper *Al-Arai*. These laws are founded on the suppression of civil rights.[90] Because of them, pointed out *Al-Ittihad*, the role of the media in America as the fourth estate has been damaged; the U.S. media no longer serve as protectors of democracy but as mouthpieces of government.[91]

In conclusion, when the United States speaks of bad human rights in the Middle East, Arabs see that as an intrusion on their internal affairs. In Prague on June 5, 2007, ahead of the G-8 Summit, President Bush called on countries he described as "U.S. allies"—particularly Egypt, Saudi Arabia, and Pakistan—to make more progress toward democracy and to release political dissidents. Assim Hanafi, an Egyptian journalist at *Rose El-Yossef*, found it a "strange matter" that "America in particular speaks of human rights and claims that it cares much for the principles of justice and democracy."[92] Muslims were used as proxies against Communism, alleged one commentator on Lebanon, a Lebanese television channel.[93] Washington has "supported dictatorships in the Arab world" and manufactured Muslim movements in Iran "in the hope that they would spread in other countries in the neighborhood" and help in the fight against the Soviet Union, concluded *Rose El-Yossef*. "Most terrorists were bred and blossomed under the protection of U.S. agencies."[94] Americans trained many of the terrorists that are now operating in Iraq, remarked one Iraqi in an interview with Al-Jazeera.[95]

Abu Ghraib and Guantánamo Prison Scandals

The Abu Ghraib and Guantánamo prison scandals have asserted in the Arab consciousness that America is not a bastion of freedom, with numerous Arab media channels often reporting on Muslims undergoing aggressive interrogations, including sleep deprivation, waterboarding, and forced nudity. Author

Nahed Hatr asked readers to consider the lessons to be learned from Washington's acts in Abu Ghraib and Guantánamo. His answer: "Lies, deception, lack of ethics, conspiracies and suppression of domestic and international public opinion."[96] The United States has a dark human rights record that goes back decades, according to Mohamed Ali Ibrahim, chief editor of *Al-Gomhuria*. "Thirty years ago, blacks and dogs were forbidden from entering restaurants." The Guantánamo and Abu Ghraib prisons are "good witness that Americans still do not respect human rights."[97]

After the Abu Ghraib and Guantánamo prison scandals, Arab governments became worried about growing resentment of the United States on the Arab street; they began rejecting political reform projects coming from abroad, replacing them with local ones. They started retreating from the promises they made to embrace democracy, with some declaring that their democracy was better than the American democracy Bush imposed on the Iraqis. The United States, according to Kamal of *Rose El-Yossef*, claims that it protects human rights, but one need only look at "Afghanistan, Pakistan, Guantánamo and Abu Ghraib" to realize that that is not the case. "American prison rectors at the Abu Ghraib prison relished watching prisoners run in front of prison dogs, and victims dancing on the voltage of electrical wire," he added.[98] The United States should be the last country in the world to talk about democracy and human rights, screamed one speaker on Al-Oula. "Just look at what they did in Guantánamo!"[99] Hundreds of Muslims have been held there without trial or access to lawyers, stated *Al-Bayan*. "If the rule of law is at the heart of democratic values, what type of democracy is that then that the U.S. Administration is practicing?"[100]

America in particular should not issue "fatwa" on the question of human rights, wrote Hanafi in *Rose El-Yossef*, because it "runs the Guantánamo prison for torturing, insulting, dehumanizing and violating the rights of people. It merely jails whomever it views as posing danger to it and then ships them to Guantánamo. It believes it is clever because this Hitler-style prison is held outside its border."[101] Bush is in no position to defend human rights, for he has the Guantánamo prison scandal on his record, contended Al-Fiqi on Al-Jazeera in 2007.[102] In an interview with the Egyptian newspaper *El-Dostour*, Al-Fiqi made similar remarks, in which he admonished Bush's human rights record.[103] "When I run across the word Guantánamo, there immediately comes to mind the pictures of those held captive in their orange clothes and sitting on the floor," wrote Waheed Gwad, a journalist with the Saudi-owned Al-Arabiya satellite television channel.[104] The head of the Algerian Association for Human

Rights called on Washington to shut down the "horrendous prison" and send those imprisoned back to their homes. A Moroccan human rights activist argued in an interview with Al-Jazeera that the United States is trying to get rid of the prison "dilemma," but this should not happen without the Bush administration being held accountable for all the atrocities it committed.[105] If the United States wants to preach a sermon on human rights, Bush should stand trial for his crimes in Guantánamo and Iraq, noted Bakri in his interview with Al-Oula.[106]

It might be of value to sum up by citing a program that Al-Arabiya broadcast on March 14, 2008, on the dreadful treatment of detainees in Iraqi jails. Titled *Who Is Ruling America's Prisons in Iraq?* the program showed horrible scenes of torture that took place in an Iraqi prison in October 2007. These shocking scenes raised a lot of uproar among Arab viewers, with many claiming that U.S. soldiers were behind the cruel acts. The Al-Arabiya program, wrote Reema Saleha, brought back to the Arab mind the crimes that Iraqi prisoners endured in Abu Ghraib. Americans must recognize that Iraqis held are not prisoners and should be treated with respect. They should receive all the legal rights granted to them under the umbrella of international law.[107]

6   THE LAND OF DREAMS

The American phenomenon is unique and incapable of being repeated. It is the result of grouping a number of circumstances that are impossible to bring together again in another place or at another time. FOUAD ZAKARIA, Egyptian philosopher

The noblest energy that God grants to people is the energy of love. AL-TIAB AL-SALIH, Sudanese novelist

Accepting the other means accepting the self, as is denying the other means denying the self. HELMI SALIM, Egyptian poet

The first principle that terrorist groups depend upon is poverty, not religion. NAGUIB MAHFOUZ, 1988 Noble laureate for literature

Although America has "no history or ancient civilization," the country has been "a homeland for people drawn to it by the American Dream," said international affairs analyst and newspaper columnist Attif Al-Ghamri.[1] Yet many Arabs today no longer consider the United States to be the promised land where immigrants are welcomed and helped in overcoming their difficulties. This is the picture shown of America these days on Arab television screens, theater stages, and in the print media. Arab journalists and recent visitors to the United States have been asking Arabs, particularly Arab youths, to forget about their American Dream, which is all about getting rich and enjoying the land of the free. It must be noted that a fair number of Arab intellectuals who lived in the United States charge Hollywood of making the American Dream look very attractive to the Arabs. In reality, wrote Abdel Aziz Hammouda, the American Dream is "neither all too good, nor all too bad."[2] Mahmoud Al-Saddani, a political muckraker, lamented that his generation has lived in the "American century and fallen under the might of America's best." However, similar to Hammouda, Al-Saddani believes that America is neither all too good nor all too bad.[3]

The United States is a "lucky country" with lots of land, natural resources, and a short history, wrote the Arab world's most popular journalist, Mohamed Hasseinein Heikel, who worked as chief editor of Egypt's *Al-Ahram* newspaper and advisor to Egyptian president Gamal Abdel Nasser.[4] It was formed as a refuge, an open land for anyone who could cross the ocean or was forced to do so, no matter what the reasons were. It was the promised land for people who wanted to achieve their dreams, and the vast country had no outside threat until long-range missiles appeared on the scene.[5] In the last part of the nineteenth century, the U.S. economy grew enormously, enabling America to "cross the ocean and return to the old world to impose the American age" on Arabs, said Heikel. He predicted that the first quarter of the twenty-first century would also be an American one, with U.S. hegemony asserted on the world.[6] Hammouda, who served as cultural attaché at the Egyptian embassy in Washington in the late 1980s and early 1990s, defined the American Dream as the "success of a human being in achieving prosperity, justice and freedom."[7] He believes the American Dream "was the driving force" behind the founding and prosperity of the United States.[8] Hammouda continued, "It is no exaggeration to say that the 'American Dream' has represented a central period, if not a pivotal one, in the history of the United States. . . . The United States has been founded on the American Dream and tortured by it at the same time."[9]

Mustapha Amin (to whom I have referred in earlier chapters) is a distinguished Egyptian journalist and cofounder of the weekly paper *Akhbar El-Yom*, which began publishing in 1944; later he issued the daily *Al-Akhbar* paper. In the 1930s he worked for over a year as a Washington correspondent for two weekly Egyptian newspapers that are now out of print. In the 1980s he wrote a book, *The Laughing America*, which he called a "journalistic reportage of the laughing life" that America was living in before World War II. He compared that United States to the one he visited more than twenty-five times over the next half century.[10] He said he witnessed an America—an

American culture—that is changing constantly and rapidly. He cited the shift of America's image among Arabs from President Theodore Roosevelt (1901–9) to President Dwight Eisenhower (1953–61), from being a friend and a just player in the region to being a supporter of Israel. He referred to how, after World War I, demonstrators on the Egyptian street "were shouting in the name of Saad Zaghloul, leader of the [1919] Revolution, and Mr. [Woodrow] Wilson, the president of the United States," who called for nations' right for self-determination. There was similar support for President Wilson (1913–21) in Syria. But President Wilson later supported Britain and France, of which (respectively) Egypt and Syria were colonies, and that drove Egyptians and Syrians to denounce Wilson.[11]

Amin said that the reason the United States cancelled its economic support for the Egyptian High Dam was the Nasser government's recognition of Communist China in 1956. He mentioned other incidents that he said aroused criticism of the United States in the Arab world, such as how in the 1980s America claimed that it was coming to protect Lebanon but later proved to be the aggressor. Arabs also detested U.S. meddling in Iranian affairs after the 1979 Iranian revolution because Iran was once America's closest ally in the region. "This horrible picture of how America is dealing with an old friend has left bad feeling among Arabs who deeply care about friendship," noted Amin. "An American changes friends every year the way he changes cars."[12] He added that what he admired most of an American was "his love for work because he gives a lot to take a lot," and "he is ambitious and desires the most beautiful, biggest and richest in everything."[13]

Hammouda believes that U.S.-Arab relations passed through two stages that influenced the image of the American Dream in the Arab word. The first stage dates from the end of World War II to the Six-Day War in June 1967, or a few years before that. "The American Dream was attractive, illuminating and dazzling" because there was no gap, no contrast between how U.S. foreign policy was perceived and America's image in the Arab mind. He added, "At least until the early sixties, American politics did not take an 'antagonistic' stance toward Arabs nor was it entirely pro-Israeli."[14] He believes that President Harry Truman's recognition of Israel as a state, right after its declaration of independence, did not much affect the picture of the United States in the Arab mind because international Zionism had earlier prepared the world atmosphere for such a declaration. The second stage began following the 1967 Six-Day War when Arabs became convinced that the United States was heavily arming Israel to insure that it could defeat all Arab armies. A gap then began to appear between Arabs' admiration for the American Dream and their rejection of American policies in the Middle East. Nevertheless, admiration for the American Dream continued, with Arab youths' applications to study in the United States increasing. The number of Arab immigrants in the United States also increased dramatically over the years. Hammouda concluded,

> This undoubtedly confirms that Arab "rejection" of the American people and American way of life did not turn into real "hatred" at least until a recent period, beginning with the 9/11 incidents and ending with the barbaric Israeli invasion of the Palestinian Authority's land and America's full collaboration with Israel. This has strengthened the burden upon the Arab mind to continue to just reject [America], for the line between "rejection" and "hatred" has became thin and weak, and thus it cannot stand long. Perhaps the next few months or years could prove that the latest American position was not merely an ethical plunge but the biggest American mistake in the region until now.[15]

Following the 9/11 attacks on the United States, the U.S. regime "raised the stick in the face of those who criticized its politics," with many U.S. voices connecting Islam with terrorism, said Turki Al-Hamd in the Saudi paper *Asharq Al-Awsat*. It is possible that there might have been some previous hatred among some Arabs toward the United States for one reason or another, but after 9/11 such hatred became a "general phenomenon."[16] Americans entered a "new phase of strategic thinking," stemming from fear of international terrorism and the need to strengthen U.S. power in order to "expand their control over the Middle East and concentrate their world leadership," noted the Qatari magazine *Al-Doha*.[17] With this, Arabs began to move from a state of anger to hatred—hatred directed predominately at American politics and cultural values, which Arabs denounced as purely materialistic.

This sense of the rise and fall of the American Dream in the Arab mind is well echoed in Arab movies and plays. Prior to the mid-1970s, most Arab movies tended to mirror the cultural differences between Arabs and Americans, but Arab heroes always achieved and enjoyed their American Dream at the end. From the mid-1970s on, Arab movies began to reflect Arabs' ideological clash with the United States. The 1978 assault on Lebanon by Israel and its later invasion of the Arab state awakened Arab movie directors to the "reality that part of that war may have been manufactured by American politics," claimed *Al-Doha*.[18] Lebanese movie director Randa Al-Shahaal introduced *Step By Step*, a movie that tries to link the scandals of the Lebanese war to the step-by-step politics of Secretary of State Henry Kissinger. In the 1979 *Alexandria Why* by popular movie director Youssef Shaheen, the hero is in his early twenties and arrives to New York on board a ship after a long struggle to get to the United States. As the ship approaches the Statue of Liberty, a smile dances on the young man's face as he feels he has won his battle to pursue his American Dream. Suddenly the Statue of Liberty interacts with him, with a fierce and antagonistic smile. Whether such an angry smile on the face of the Statue of Liberty mirrors the hero's fear of failure or his worry about American life and culture is not clearly known. What is known is that it has carved in the minds of the millions of Arabs who have watched the movie negative feelings toward America's stance when dealing with Arabs.

The 1994 movie *Mr. President's Visit* is about an Egyptian village whose people hear that the U.S. president will stop by for a short time during his visit to Egypt. Motivated by the economic liberalization of the time and the Egyptian press's glorification of Egyptian-American relations and how that could bring billions of dollars to their country, the American Dream of getting rich spreads in the village. To the village dwellers, life all of a sudden just seems beautiful, with many of them dressed American style. They beautify their village and prepare requests to present to the U.S. president, but the movie ends with the train passing and not stopping in their village. The 1998 movie *Se'adi at the American University* by Sudanese director Saed Hamed is about an Egyptian professor who advocates and promotes anything that is American but is fiercely met with criticism from his students.[19] A year later Shaheen introduced *The Other*, a movie about a successful Egyptian businessman who comes with his American wife to live in Egypt. In one popular scene, he condemns his wife's American roots and society. Angered by her husband's behavior, she hires terrorists to kill the Egyptian girl her son married. The terrorists end up mistakenly killing both her son and the Egyptian girl. Two years later, in 2001, Shaheen launched *The Tempest*, which forms a powerful criticism of the first Iraq War and how it has divided Iraqis.

What all these movies show is that there was a sense of anger among Arabs toward America during that pre-9/11 period but no hatred. There are certainly a few Arab movies produced during that time that portray the United States with a not-too-negative approach; for example, an Arab will go to America and achieve his or her dream, or an American will come to the Arab world and melt into Arab traditions. In these movies, there are definitely cultural shocks at the beginning but not deep anger; after all, many are derivatives or founded on American movie themes.[20] Hatred toward the United States did not emerge in Arab movies until after the U.S. invasion and occupation of Iraq. Shaheen's 2004 movie *Alexandria New York*, which is, in a way, a continuation of *Alexandria Why*, criticizes America's colonial ambitions. The movie throws its hero, who studied in the United States in the past, into a feeling of disorientation; he dreams of the good old days of America—the land of dreams—before it betrayed its values and pushed on to dominate the world. The movie concludes that the America that once represented people's hopes and dreams has now become their enemy.

Prior to the U.S. invasion and occupation of Iraq, some theatrical plays took a pure comedy approach, catering to an Arab obsession with American political scandals, particularly during Monica Lewinsky's fame. In 2000 Egypt introduced two plays: *Kimo and the Blue Dress* and *Monica, My Wife and I*. The first play is the story of a young American nurse who goes to work as a psychiatrist in Egypt and falls in love with her boss. Although her tricks of wearing tight clothes and blue dresses work at seducing him, she fails in getting him to marry her. She then turns on him, doing all she can to wreck his life. Her war on her lover attracts the press's attention, with the tabloids placing her picture on their cover pages. The second play tells the story of an Egyptian doctor about to go bankrupt. To rescue his failing career, he fabricates a scientific discovery and becomes a celebrity. No sooner does he marry a young and rich woman who loves him than Monica—an American lover whom he met at Disneyland—arrives to ruin his life. Motivated by a craving for money, Monica tries to sell his research in America and have him kidnapped and brought to the United States. When she discovers his fabrication, the Egyptian doctor is thrown out on the streets of New York, begging for food and money.

"Al-Khawaga" Uncle Sam

"Al-Khawaga" is a slang Arabic word meaning "foreigner," and it often refers to people of Western descent. It was coined during European colonial role in the Arab world to refer to the British, French, Portuguese, Italian, or German. In criticizing the U.S. government and America, the Arab media at times utilized the words "Al-Khawaga" and "Uncle Sam" to mockingly allude to America as the new colonial power in the Arab world. The behavior of Uncle Sam shows irrationality and injustice, wrote Said Al-Lawandi, an international relations expert.[21] Its justice "means supporting the strong over the weak," alleged Al-Saddani. "It is like the law of the jungle."[22] Nazzar Basheer, a foreign affairs analyst, dedicated his book *Culture of Blood: Chapters of the History of*

American Terrorism to "all victims of American terrorism and all those who were buried under the bombs of Uncle Sam."[23]

Unlike "old and shrewd Britain," wrote Ahmed Shaheen in the Egyptian magazine *October*, "Uncle Sam came [to Iraq] from a continent, from a semi-isolated island that does not know anything about the ancient world—with all its unseen and unknown—to fall in a trap which he created by himself for himself."[24] In a commentary titled "With Deep Sorrows for Al-Khawaga," Assim Hanafi mocked America and its principles of equality, human rights, and democracy. A journalist at the Egyptian magazine *Rose El-Yossef*, Hanafi ridiculed the "children of Uncle Sam" and stressed that Cairo is not in need of their advice. He viewed the United States merely as a foreign invader and a violator of all the principles of justice and democracy.[25]

The scolding of Uncle Sam went on, even beyond politics and culture, with *October* carrying in its January 13, 2008, issue an article on the deteriorating situation of the American economy headlined, "The Unemployment of Uncle Sam." On the declining value of the U.S. dollar against the Egyptian pound, popular caricaturist Mustapha Hussein published a caricature in Egypt's *Al-Akhbar* newspaper in which President Bush is asked by one of his officials what the United States should do about that. Bush replies, "'Change all our dollars into Egyptian pounds.'"[26] Two days after President Obama's speech to the Muslim world from Cairo University on June 4, 2009, and his visit to the pyramids, *Al-Ahram* published a caricature showing the sphinx and Obama, with a smile dancing over the U.S. president's face. Alluding to Napoleon Bonaparte, who destroyed its nose during the French invasion and occupation of Egypt (1798–1801), the sphinx says to Obama: "The last Khawaga who stood in front of me was 200 years ago. He was white, wicked and spoke French. His face lacked a smile. But it seems this Khawaga has a different look."

September 11 and U.S. Policy on Terrorism

The tragedies of September 11 have exhibited in a terrifying manner that willing groups do not need sophisticated weapons to cause agony and devastation. They have changed everything, with America vying to punish any country that harbors terrorists or is part of what President George W. Bush called the "axis of evil": Iraq, Iran, North Korea, and other states considered a threat to America and its interests abroad (such as Syria, Cuba, or Libya). Yet Arabs believe that terrorism cannot be eradicated via a third world war and consider terrorism the product of political crises and social upheaval. In their opinion, the 9/11 attacks have turned the world into a mess. In this international disorder, the Middle East lies at the midpoint.

To this day, the majority of Arabs continue to perceive America's antiterrorism policy as flawed and catastrophic, and they often accuse Washington of employing the tragedies as a tool to dominate them. The lesson to be learned from 9/11 is that the American empire is facing a crisis in leadership; it is an empire that does not want to shoulder the cost of being an empire.[27] The United States, noted one U.S. policy analyst, has dealt with terrorism from the surface without digging deep into its causes so as to be able to uproot it.[28] When the incidents of 9/11 took place, it was "evident that a new phase was beginning in relations between the United States and the Arab and Muslim world," wrote Waheed Abdel Mageed, a political science expert.[29] The Arab region was the "biggest loser politically" from the 9/11 acts, observed Ibrahim Nafie, former board chair of Egypt's Al-Ahram Press Group. Since then, the United States has been working to impose its political model, with all its various forms, on the Arab world, added Nafie. This has raised fears of Americans controlling the Arab economy, causing tension in U.S.-Arab ties.[30]

Wars never come to America; Americans go to wars outside their country. Hence, the amount of "nervousness—which almost reached the degree of hysteria—that materialized following September 11, 2001," can be understood, Heikel pointed out.[31] The war against terrorism is against an enemy without an address, and the current U.S. policy in the Middle East will result in an increase of terrorist cells. While the United States is the only superpower, it continues to deal with the Middle East with a Cold War mentality in which Islam has replaced Communism, wrote Ahmed Al-Mossali, a professor of political science and Islamic studies at the American University in Beirut. According to him, the United States has formed undesirable alliances with governments, mainly to "serve American interests. . . . Yet, it continues its negative avoidance of, or direct opposition to, regional Muslim movements, strong transitional movements, and national states." Al-Mossali added that in the absence of a just U.S. policy in the Middle East and an end to the ongoing crisis in Iraq, extremism will increase.[32] It is a grave mistake to blame Arabs and Muslims for the acts of a few fanatics and compare the war on terrorism to that against Communism. "It seems that the West will not rest until it exterminates Islam."[33]

Some Arabs claimed that the perpetrators of the 9/11 attacks were not Arabs. "Strangely," noted Abdel Moneim Said, "almost all Arabs put the blame on the U.S. because it was the one who created Osama bin Laden and his followers during the war of liberating the Afghans from the Soviet Union."[34] Since 9/11, the United States has been hastily taking actions without calculating their results.[35] The bloodshed in Iraq and Afghanistan has made the world less secure than it was before 9/11. By globalizing its antiterrorism propaganda and establishing military bases worldwide, the United States wants to exercise influence on all regions of the world. The "U.S. media, or the Americanized media, describe terrorism as devilish plants that appear in every place and without prior warning," said Al-Lawandi. He added, "If the Middle East, as America claims, is the main sanctuary for terrorists, the United States is itself the factory that manufactures and promotes them. Al-Qaeda is nothing but one of the products that Washington has invented to tighten its grip on the world."[36]

America's post-9/11 inept propaganda war is resulting in the eruption of conflicts in parts of the world, according to Said, who wrote a number of books on the 9/11 acts and their repercussions in the Arab world. In *Arabs and September 11*, Said expressed a belief that the world has witnessed three wars: World War I, World War II, and the Cold War. After 9/11, a "fourth world war has suddenly imposed itself on the international relations sphere." He added, "Certainly, the crisis has uncovered a lot about the United States and its Western allies, be they inside or outside of the North Atlantic Alliance."[37] The United States has defined this "fourth world war" as a "war on terrorism" but has stopped short of identifying what terrorism is, remarked Al-Ghamri, who headed the *Al-Ahram* news bureau in the United States from 1995 to 2000.[38] He added that the Bush government declared a war on an "unseen enemy without a single address, border, flag or national anthem. Its members do not share a single citizenship or common traditions and customs."[39]

The majority of Arabs believe that it was from the ruins of the Twin Towers of the World Trade Center in New York that a more assertive ideological U.S. foreign policy emerged, with President Bush declaring a new doctrine of preemptive strike. Arabs saw the Bush doctrine as a ploy for justifying a U.S. invasion of Afghanistan and Iraq. "It could be said that the American war on terrorism is a declared route for undeclared politics," observed the Egyptian paper *Al-Masry Al-Youm*. "This war is essentially a cover-up for the motives and inclinations of the ruling administration."[40] It is an American invention driven by neoconservatives in Washington, said one Middle East expert in a 2007 interview with the Egyptian radio station Sout Al-Arab.[41]

The rise in global terrorism is the result of oppressive rule, lack of human rights, and U.S. colonial aggression against Arabs and Muslims following the

9/11 attacks, observed the Jordanian paper *Ad-Dustour*.[42] Since then, noted *October*, "the U.S. has publicly been practicing terrorism in the Middle East region—in Iraq, Lebanon, Sudan, Iran and Syria."[43] Regrettably, the 9/11 terrorist attacks have given the United States a carte blanche to rule the Arab world, alleged Karam Gabr, board chair of the Cairo-based Rose El-Yossef Press Group. Americans, he cautioned, ignore that "what they are doing, whether directly or indirectly, supports, promotes and firmly establishes terrorism; it produces generations of haters. After all, can flowers grow in blood? Can skulls decorate a bar of sweet? Can orphans one day abandon their feelings of hatred which Washington is inflaming in different ways?"[44]

The 9/11 tragedies have changed the traditional, bilateral relations between the United States and the Arabs. In "Changes in American-Arab Relations" Al-Ghamri said, "Tensions rise from time to time in Arabs' relations with the U.S., and this is expected because of the essential changes that have made America after September 11, 2001, different from the one before. The Arab world has itself also changed," with its ties with world powers no longer the same as they were before 9/11. Al-Ghamri continued in his *Al-Ahram* commentary, "If it is expected that vital changes will generally take place in the foreign policy of the government that succeeds Bush, it is also anticipated that the outcomes of September 11 will meddle in the decision-making process of its policy. This is because Americans will continue to hold to their strong views on how to fight terrorism and counter anything that threatens their national security."[45]

Alas, the 9/11 attacks have affected the U.S. mentality in dealing with the Arab world, with Americans today preoccupied with the Arab and Muslim world in a way that "cannot be imagined," wrote Mustapha Al-Fiqi, an author and chair of the Egyptian People's Assembly Foreign Affairs Committee, in a piece in the Saudi paper *Al-Hayat*. He added that the attacks "are deeply engraved in the American mind and the nation's mentality, hence the task of manufacturing an enemy was not a difficult one. And Americans have chosen Arabs and Islam as the new foe, on whom they can practice all forms of challenge, confrontation and rejection."[46] The United States is leading the world toward a "holocaust of civilizations, in which it will be the first victim and the party most hurt," remarked Taha Al-Amri in the Yemeni paper *Al-Thowrah*.[47] In a piece in *Asharq Al-Awsat*, Bouthaina Shabaan contemplated, "How could the Zionist lobby donate millions of dollars to candidates of the U.S. presidency, Congress and European parliaments while an Arab or a Muslim cannot transfer money for his son or brother to study in another country?" She believes that many of the Middle East's problems "are the product of the United States' dependence on Israeli information that aims essentially to strengthen Israel's occupation of Palestine by settling Jews there and killing more Arabs and pushing them to camps like what happed to the Red Indians."[48]

With terrorists hitting the Twin Towers and Pentagon, the legend of America's wealth and power collapsed in front of Americans and the world, maintained the United Arab Emirates paper *Al-Bayan*. No sooner did that happen than the United States rushed to link Islam with terrorism and fell in the Iraq and Afghanistan quagmire.[49] All Arabs and Muslims condemn the horrible attacks on America by bin Laden's followers, said *Al-Ahram*. But America's war on terrorism has sadly hurt the Arab and Muslim world, which is often portrayed as harboring terrorism.[50] This anti-Arab sentiment has flourished in the United States since the 9/11 attacks, particularly among right-wing groups, claimed Mohamed Wahbi in an article in the Egyptian magazine *Almussawar*. He said that evangelists in America—who number roughly seventy million—view "Arabs after 9/11, and after all that has taken place in Iraq, as terrorists and killers."[51]

In the view of *Al-Hayat*, President Bush's war on terrorism has proved to be a motive for "radicalism" and "turned the agreed-upon principles of international relations and ethical values upside down."[52] Because the American president failed in achieving economic stability for his people, he "decided to busy his citizens with two issues: terrorism and democracy," noted the Egyptian paper *Al-Gomhuria*. "He stressed to them that the message of Uncle Sam in this direction must be supported by the world, for the terror they faced on 9/11 was due to the absence of democracy in developing nations and Arab states in particular."[53] Furthermore, when speaking of U.S. atrocities and the struggle to dominate the Arab world after 9/11, references were made at times to Britain and Israel. Some Arabs mockingly referred to the three nations as the "axis of evil." For example, Jordanian writer Hassan Ayesh wrote, "The blind bombings have empowered the triangle of evil in the world: Sharon (and later Olmert) in Israel, Bush in America and Blair (before leaving the premiership) in Britain." Ayesh's *Rose El-Yossef* article was titled "We Refuse to Be Driven in Chains Even to Heaven."[54]

According to Nile News, many changes have taken place in the world and the Middle East since 9/11, with state policies altered and America launching its "so-called war on terror." The Egyptian television channel pondered, "Has the U.S. accomplished the desired results of this war? Do the American people feel safer after this war or have they become imprisoned in their own country?"[55] These "hostile practices that stretch worldwide today under the slogan of fighting global terrorism" are "diffusing terrorism all over" the globe, said the Egyptian newspaper *Al-Arabi*.[56] Within this perspective, Arabs believe the problem of terrorism is one of political injustice and that it cannot be solved through force. As one guest on the Saudi-owned Al-Arabiya television channel put it, what generates extremism is injustice.[57] Arabs, said one Libyan political affairs analyst, do not export terrorism to the United States; they export some of their finest brains. He made this comment in an interview with the Libyan television channel Al-Jamahiriya.[58]

In short, the argument Arabs have raised is that the United States has failed in winning its war on terrorism, and it is possible that the country will continue to face terrorist threats unless it embraces a drastic change of its foreign policy. Almost all Arabs have stressed that constructing a successful policy to fight terrorism requires a strong international alliance that includes them. They said it is the lack of such an alliance that is behind America's failure in its war on terror. "Since Washington declared war on terrorism, Al-Qaeda's activities have increased, with its followers spreading around the globe," lamented Essam Abdel Aziz in *Rose El-Yossef*.[59] The United States has not gained anything from its propaganda war on terrorism, alleged *Asharq Al-Awsat*.[60] "Extremist activities will not stop as long as the USA continues its wars in the Muslim and Arab world. America's actions are offering groups of political Islam a pretext to enlist more youth," contended *Almussawar*.[61] It is then true to say that America's "World War III on terrorism" has turned al Qaeda into a "role model for extremism" worldwide, maintained Sout Al-Arab.[62]

Animosity toward Arabs and Muslims

In the opinion of Arab intellectuals, negative stereotypes of Arabs and Muslims in the United States go back decades. Writing in the mid-1950s, after teaching for a year at two American universities, philosophy professor Zaki Naguib Mahmoud observed that Americans are very friendly and humorous people, but their views are antagonistic toward Islam.[63] After 9/11 this vision of Americans as anti-Muslim has been reinforced. Khaled Abu Bakr, an editor at Islamonline.net, portrayed Americans as not antiterror but anti-Islam. He wrote:

> The Arab and Muslim people have been exposed to numerous campaigns aimed at tarnishing their image, harming their religion and attaching terrorism to every one of them. This took place via a fierce war

that U.S. President George W. Bush called the "war on terror." It began with the destruction of Afghanistan and later occupation of Iraq and the plunging of its people into cycles of division and civil strife, all the way through to American intervention in the internal affairs of Arab and Muslim states under the claim of political reform.[64]

Numerous references have been made to Samuel Huntington's controversial 1993 article (later published as a book).[65] Huntington warned that a "clash of civilizations will dominate global politics" in the post-Soviet era.[66] His thesis was that cultural division between "Western Christianity" and "Orthodox Christianity and Islam" will form a new fault line for conflict. According to him, the Muslim world lacks the core political values on which representative democracies—similar to those in the West—can be erected. These values, he pointed out, include the separation of religion from the state, parliamentary institutions, social pluralism, and the protection of individual rights and civil liberties. Arab intellectuals and Islamic scholars were very critical of Huntington's thesis, which they perceived as an attempt to tarnish Islam and the Muslim world. They argued that if such a clash of civilizations exists, the way out is by obliterating its roots: U.S. overdependence on Middle Eastern oil, the presence of U.S. soldiers in Arab states, lack of a viable solution for a Palestinian homeland, and bad human rights records. Others said that any clash of civilizations between the United States and Islamists should not take place on Arab soil.

Criticism of Huntington was severe among ordinary Arabs and public officials. Referring to Edward Said's *Orientalism*, political analyst Fawaz Sharf remarked that the West wrote history from a colonial perspective with a "hatred of Islam." He accused Huntington of inflaming racial discrimination against Arabs and Muslims.[67] Al-Ghamri stated that the 9/11 terrorist attacks revived Huntington's theory of the clash of civilizations on the world stage.[68] Nafie, on the other hand, believes that following the U.S. war in Afghanistan, it was right-wing Republican groups in America that "revived Huntington's 'clash of civilizations,' portraying the War as a clash between Western culture and Islamic culture."[69] There is no doubt today that "Western civilization is far away from being forthrightly humanistic; it is a colonial and racist civilization that lacks ethics," said Mohamed Said Ahmed Al-Maceer, a professor of theology at Al-Azher University in Cairo.[70] Huntington's clash of civilizations is a Western theory promoted by "Zionist media that work laboriously to tarnish anything that is Islamic."[71] The Western press "plants hatred in the hearts of

Westerners toward Islam and refers to Islamic movements as worse than the Leninist-Marxist movements," said Al-Mossali. This picture, which insinuates confrontation between Islam and the West, is more prevalent in Washington today than at any time before.[72] Americans must not forget that Islamists were allies of the United States in its war against Communism. Within this context, the "West's stand today against 'Islam' is similar to yesterday's stand against 'Arab nationalism.'"[73]

After the 9/11 tragedies, President Bush and some members of his cabinet tried to show that U.S. hostilities were toward terrorism and not Islam. He apologized for the early use of the terms "crusade" and "infinite justice." The Arab media picked up the story, claiming that the Bush administration was exploiting the 9/11 terrorist attacks to benefit its true intentions: invading Iraq and launching a "crusade" against Islam. "We believe terrorism is an American-European creation," stated Al-Maceer.[74] "American terrorism wants a new Islam without faith, strength or honor. It vies to control the curricula in order to raise a generation without Islamic identity."[75] Salaheddine Hafez, vice chief editor of *Al-Ahram* and general secretary of the Federation of Arab Journalists, argued that after its failure in Iraq and Afghanistan, the United States reconsidered its plan and began approaching moderate Islamists. It employed them to destabilize current Arab regimes on one side and establish a moderate Islam, similar to that in Turkey, on the other.[76]

Galal Amin, a popular political commentator and a professor of economics at the American University in Cairo, examined the various angles and campaigns used to defame Arabs and Muslims, particularly those that emerged after September 11. He argued that in today's age of secularism and a powerful Israel, Arabs and Muslims face a campaign of smear and defamation. "I do not," he said, "think they ever faced something like this in their long history."[77] Professor Amin disapproved of Huntington's theory as being artificial and weak and blamed members of the developing world, especially Arabs and Muslims, for paying so much attention to "such strange sayings about the end of history and clash of civilizations." He added, "It was clear from the beginning that that 'end of history' was similar to a 'celebration of ideas' for America's victory in the Cold War and the collapse of Communism."[78] Furthermore, Professor Amin fiercely criticized Bernard Lewis's *The Crisis of Islam: Holy War and Unholy Terror*, published in 2003.[79] The Princeton University professor's book, according to Professor Amin, echoed the "official story which the U.S. Administration broadcast: the master-minder is bin Laden, and the tapes which he broadcasts from time to time on the Qatari station are true and not fake, and the executers are either Saudis or Egyptians." Lewis's book, he added, tried to convince Americans of the "criminal tendencies of Muslims. . . . The picture that the reader gets about Muslims has to be very ugly."[80] Professor Amin criticized Arabs and Muslims who claim they are going to the Western world to improve the image of Muslims after 9/11. He cautioned:

> Some of those going to the West with the aim of "improving the image of Islam" after the September 11 incidents think they act well by saying that the real reason behind the incidents is American politics' extreme favoritism of Israel. Such saying may seem of little harm at the very beginning. But in fact, it harms Islam and Muslims without knowing. The saying first includes readiness on the part of its declarer to admit that it is we who committed the crime of September 11 while no final evidence has proved that yet.[81]

If the image of Arabs and Muslims is to be improved in America, U.S. curricula need to be rewritten, because Americans are ignorant about the Arab and Muslim world, observed one Arab scholar. "School books and curricula speak briefly of Arabs and their civilization and show no interest in Islamic civilization."[82] Terrorism began with the establishment of the United States and the eradication of Native Americans, claimed Basheer. "Still Americans now are more violent and nothing will quench their thirst but our blood, Arabs' blood," he added. "I swear that unless we stand united, face the tempest and defend our land, there will come a day in which we weep like the Red Indians did, that is if the cowboy shows some mercy and leaves some of us alive."[83] Arabs must not surrender to American tyranny and fight for their survival, as the "enemy is now standing by the door."[84]

The United States has never introduced to the world a "humanist philosopher" who advocates peace and love but rather capitalist ones who speak of a clash of civilizations, mourned the Jordanian paper *Al-Arab Al-Yawm*.[85] In the aftermath of Huntington's suggestions and 9/11, the United States began to see the Islamic world as an enemy, wrote Amr Moussa, secretary general of the Arab League, in the league's magazine *Arab Affairs*. Since then, issues have been characterized as battles or wars, sometimes called a "clash of civilizations," a "war against terrorism," or a "clash between moderates and extremists."[86] The Egyptian paper *Al-Ahali* argued that although Huntington believed in the "victory of capitalism, he did not accept that history had an end."[87] What Huntington truly desired was to raise animosity against Muslims in the West, stated *Al-Hilal*. According to the Egyptian magazine, he erroneously grouped religion and culture in one frame. It is hatred and greed, and not religion, that are behind the break out of conflicts and wars among nations.[88] In another *Al-Hilal* article, Mohsen Khadr, an academic, likened Muslims' call for dialogue with Americans and Westerners to an Arab tale in which a monkey aspires to cleanse a lion's heart of violence and the thirst for blood. The monkey starts to sing for the lion in a soft voice, but to his bad luck the lion is deaf and immediately attacks and gobbles him up. "This is what our call for dialogue among cultures . . . sounds like: singing for a deaf American lion." Khadr added that Huntington's "poor" theory has raised a "sea of hatred" against Arabs and Muslims.[89]

What America craves is to "fight Islamic civilization and tarnish its image," contended the Kuwaiti magazine *Al-Waei*. "The war of civilizations between Islam and the West exists and is blazing, no matter how America and Western nations try to deny that."[90] America's war "is not a war against terrorism but a cover-up for the neocons. It is a war against Islam," asserted an article on the Qatari-owned Aljazeera.net.[91] Today, Muslims are portrayed as if they were "caricatures and symbols of fascism, evil and cruel," noted Ghada Hamdi in a piece in *Al-Masry Al-Youm*. The propaganda of "Muslim fascism" is the newest tool that the American empire is employing in its so-called antiterrorism war, Hamdi asserted in her article titled "Tarnishing the Image of the Other: A Dirty Game America Excels At."[92] In a piece in *Arab Affairs*, former diplomat Mustapha Abdel Aziz Morsi blamed Arab states that deal with the United States as a friend and reminded them that the country continues to be a "crucial partner in all regional wars against Arabs."[93] America's first goal is to control the Arab and Muslim region, pointed out *Ad-Dustour*. It believes it can change the shape and structure of that region, but so far, it has failed.[94]

In his mind, Bush mixed terrorism with political Islam, according to the Lebanese paper *As-Safir*.[95] In a 2007 commentary titled "World Becoming Aware That the Great Danger Is America and Not Muslims," Nafissa Al-Sabagh alleged that the right-wing government of Bush employed 9/11 to put blame on Muslims. Many have begun to realize that the "biggest danger is not Islam or Muslims, but the Bush Administration and its policy which provokes anger and incites division in the world," she added.[96] "Certainly, coexistence between ethnic and religious groups and sects was more fruitful before the [Western] colonial periods, under Arab and Muslim rule and until the end of the Ottoman Empire. These waves of colonialism led to the eruption of differences and conflicts," wrote Soliman Taqi Al-Deen in *As-Safir*.[97] Arabs all support resisting the occupation of their land, whether the occupiers are Americans or Zionists, wrote Abdullah Al-Haddad in the Bahraini paper *Al-Ayam*. Yet they too all condemn the killing of the innocent as took place in New York and Washington.[98] You cannot be a Muslim if you do not denounce these terrorist acts, because what they essentially do is tarnish the image of Islam and Muslims, proclaimed the Jordanian paper *Al-Rai*.[99]

One of the negative consequences of 9/11, in the view of Morsi Attallah, board chair of Al-Ahram Press Group, is the awakening of "racist calls" in the United States to stop the influx of foreign immigrants, "particularly those coming from Arab and Islamic countries."[100] American politics in the Middle East is dead set against Arabs and Muslims, observed *Al-Arab Al-Yawm*.[101] Americans of all colors and races should not be treated badly because of the heinous acts of a few fanatics, cautioned the chief editor of *Rose El-Yossef*, Abdullah Kamal. Americans, he argued, "never stop, get full or quench their thirst. They forget that the nation is not responsible for what some of its members have committed." Kamal maintained, "If the number of casualties of Arab Muslims in the last five years is meant to be a revenge for the 9/11 victims, they have been avenged several times. That is enough."[102] In the same vein, the director of the Arab Center for Development and Futuristic Research, Gamil Matar, called for just treatment of Arab and Muslim Americans. He added that due to fear of terrorism, the Bush administration managed to issue an "arsenal of laws that restrict an American individual's freedom and invade his privacy. This makes him or her in the end like a chess piece played by a ruling elitist group whose propensity is in reality undemocratic, if not close to fascism."[103]

On the other hand, there are those Arabs who believe that America's hostility toward them and Islam originated before 9/11, with the collapse of the Soviet Union in 1991. Theories arguing that the Arab and Muslim world is the enemy of the West first emerged in that year but died down thereafter, according to a commentary by Al-Ghamri in the United Arab Emirates paper *Al-Khaleej*. The idea reappeared in 1996, with the rise to power of Benjamin Netanyahu in Israel. Netanyahu led a wide and organized campaign in the United States to convince Americans that Muslim terrorism was replacing the Soviet enemy and that America needed Israel to counter that enemy.[104] In an *Al-Masry Al-Youm* article titled "Hollywood: Lots of Lies and Little Truth," Sammr Al-Naggar noted that hatred of Arabs is evident in Hollywood movies produced before 9/11, such as *Arabesque*, *Gallipoli*, *True Lies*, and *The Peacemaker*. However, she admitted that there are a few movies produced before and after 9/11 that defend Arabs, such as *Kingdom of Heaven*, *Guilt 9-11*,

In Plane Site, Loose Change, and *Civic Duty.* "Thus it is clear that Hollywood's relationship with the Arabs is a mixture of facts and lies, although lies regularly outweigh truth. The September 11 disaster almost did not change anything in that relationship."[105]

Everything considered, it has been an *idée reçue* in the American psyche that Arabs and Muslims are terrorists. In "It Is the American Century: If You Are Not With Us You Are With Terrorism," Al-Shayeb claimed that animosity toward Muslims would have emerged even if the 9/11 attacks did not take place, citing how U.S. president Richard Nixon spoke of Islam as posing a danger for Western culture. Al-Shayeb added in his *Al-Ahali* article that animosity toward Muslims emanated a decade and a half before the 9/11 attacks. The United States "cannot live without an enemy," and since the demise of the Soviet Union, we have witnessed a rise in racist and far-right groups in the United States, with Islam becoming America's first enemy. This, he stated, "was coupled with the spread of ideas about the final victory of the capitalist, liberal model," with some Western thinkers speaking of the "end of history."[106]

Like Al-Shayeb, Eideh Qanah of *Ad-Dustour* insisted that the United States was not in need of 9/11 to unveil its aspiration to dominate other nations and spread hatred and division in the Middle East. She said that that was America's policy in the region long before 9/11. She added, "And after all that, [Americans] ask: Why do they hate us?"[107] In another *Ad-Dustour* article, Mohamed Abdel Aziz Rabee expressed a belief that Bush's question of "Why do they hate us?" was a "mean beginning for introducing a smart media campaign against Muslims in general, and Arabs in particular, in order to gain support for the launching of a military campaign to invade Iraq and control Arab oil," among other goals.[108] Even before 9/11 it has been the case that any U.S. politician who takes an antagonistic position toward Arabs and Muslims will gain politically, argued Khalid Al-Dakhil in the United Arab Emirates paper *Al-Ittihad.* He pondered, "Does this mean that there is a deep-rooted hatred against Arabs in the Western culture?" He answered with "not really," attributing such antagonism to a desire for exploitation on the part of Western politicians and to an Arab weakness that increases over time.[109]

What may sound strange to many in the West is how some Arabs believe that the terrorist Osama bin Laden is merely an agent of the United States. Essam Abdel Aziz of *Rose El-Yossef* is one of them. He called bin Laden an ally of the United States, an "American general who never misses carrying out the missions of American interests." He described him as a "millionaire who has mastered exploding bombs and running his money from the caves of Pakistan.

Men commit suicide in obedience to his orders, and all his moves serve, by accident, American interests." He said when bin Laden bought a farm in Sudan, the United States bombed a pharmaceutical factory, and when he formed an alliance with the Taliban, there was the U.S. invasion of Afghanistan.[110] On April 21, 2007, *As-Safir* ran a caricature of Uncle Sam but with a long beard. Next to it is written: "Uncle Sam bin Laden."

To some extent, the Arab media perceived the war in Afghanistan as a prelude for the Bush administration's portrayal of Arabs and Muslims as actual or potential terrorists targeting America. Arabs viewed the U.S. war on terrorism as a preface for the Iraq War. America, according to them, is a querulous nation that has no qualm about hurling lethal weapons on Arab children. It enjoys killing Arabs and has gotten used to justifying its colonial expansion in the Arab and Islamic world through its "civilized mission," which mandates picturing Arab and Muslim societies as backward and cruel. With this perception, many Islamic and legal thinkers, such as Mahmoud Ismail, a professor of Islamic history, have vehemently criticized America's attempts to restructure education at schools in the Arab and Islamic world.[111]

America wants Arabs to stand divided, away from economic and technological progress, suggested some commentators. Pro-Israeli think tanks in America, such as the American Israeli Public Affairs Committee, have skillfully benefited from the 9/11 attacks by advocating that Israel and America "face a joint enemy, namely 'Muslim-Arab terrorism,'" wrote Assad Abdel Rahman in *Al-Ittihad*.[112] According to a piece in the Egyptian paper *Al-Wafd* by legal consultant Mohamed Hamed Al-Gamel, "One of the most dangerous strategic goals of imperialism, American Zionism or evangelism is the damaging and hindering of Islamic and Arab thinking" in order for it not to become technologically and militarily advanced.[113] *October*'s Shaheen wrote that these "vicious Western campaigns" against Arabs and Muslims are a "repetition of the old and rejuvenated Crusaders' campaigns against the Arab and Muslim world."[114]

In short, Arabs accuse the American media and Western scholars of Middle Eastern and Islamic studies of never introducing the positive aspects of Islam, such as equality between rich and poor and respect for people of other religions. The United States uses its war on terrorism as a tool to fight Islam, cried Nassr Al-Dean Qaseem, chief editor of the Algerian paper *Al-Hiwar,* in an interview with Nile News.[115] Americans have described Muslim groups that follow the path of political reform in their countries as terrorist groups, noted an article posted on Almotomar.net.[116] There is a side of Islam and Muslims other than the terrorist one often propagandized by the U.S. media, noted Safi Nazkazim in *Al-Hilal.* "Islam is a religion of civilizations and peaceful coexistence, and Arabs bestowed upon European civilizations merits that cannot be forgotten," he added.[117] In an *Al-Hayat* article, Mahmoud Al-Mubarak asked, "When will the time come that an Arab or a Muslim parliament dares to ask that America be tried for its crimes in Palestine, Afghanistan, Iraq, Somalia and the other nations that it destroyed militarily, politically and economically?"[118]

End of the American Dream

In the view of many Arabs, the 9/11 terrorist attacks produced an atmosphere in America in which all the principles and values that the country was founded on are violated.[119] Heikel contended that America's asymmetrical wars in Afghanistan and Iraq have thrown it and the "American dream in a cage filled with fear."[120] The American Dream has become purely materialistic and based on the dollar, observed Professor Amin.[121] Within this purely capitalist atmosphere, the American people live in a state of brainwashing by the elites and under a false Hollywood picture that the American lifestyle is the finest in the world, said Raji Inayet, an expert on American affairs.[122]

With President Woodrow Wilson and President Franklin D. Roosevelt (1933–45) in power, the American Dream (which Hollywood promoted relentlessly) became the world's dream. Everyone aspired to go and live in the land of dreams. In the 1950s U.S. secretary of state John Foster Dulles visited the Middle East in an attempt to lure Arabs away from the Soviet Union. America's image then, as it continued to be until September 11, 2001, was full of optimism; the United States of America was the land of dreams. Under the unilateralist policy of the younger Bush, that dream turned into a nightmare, said *Asharq Al-Awsat,* with the United States becoming a symbol of tyranny.[123] The Bush administration "turned the 'American Dream' into a deep nightmare," reiterated *Al-Bayan.*[124] Bush and his government stole optimism from the American people, and the American Dream has become "just a dream," mourned *Al-Hayat.*[125]

America's mistreatment of Arabs and its invasion of Iraq have put an end to the American Dream, which was once vibrant in the minds of Arab youths. Since the events of 9/11, Arab commentators and journalists have cautioned their readers and viewers not to travel to America in pursuit of the American Dream, drawing their attention to the risks they could face when there. "The American Dream and model that America presents to the world are in reality nothing but fake models" because "they are not founded on the law of equality among people," claimed *Al-Arabi*.[126] After the events of 9/11, wrote Raouf Tawfiq of *Sabah El-Kheir*, "America is no longer the land of dreams, particularly for those coming to it from the Middle East."[127] "The Manhattan attacks have eliminated the puritanical American dream, leaving Americans to face their great past, painful present and gloomy future," noted a Tunisian writer in the Palestinian paper *Al-Quds Al-Arabi*. It might not be far from the truth, the writer mused, to argue that the 9/11 attacks awakened American society from its "false dream" and brought it back to its real history, to an American history filled with tyranny and exploitation of other nations.[128]

Not long ago, the American Dream captured the world imagination, according to an article by Emil Eamen in *Al-Khaleej*. Eastern Europe listened to Radio Free Europe, and Chinese students erected a copy of the Statute of Liberty in Tiananmen Square. Eamen argued that nations that in the past had admired the American Dream have now lost that admiration. He wondered whether the United States has fallen in the "imperialist experience," causing the world to turn away from its "utopian model of freedom, democracy and human rights." He continued, "The United States has wasted more than one chance in the second half of the past century to be the city on a hill capable of illuminating the world with the optimism of human progress and . . . the spirit of justice, supremacy of the values of equality and advancement of the ethics of friendship. . . . The American model [could] have been an icon for a true vision that many would aspire to."[129]

In denouncing the American Dream, Arabs often criticize the American political structure, including its electoral system. When one scrutinizes the 2008 U.S. presidential election, noted *As-Safir*, one sees a "political circus" that shows that "America is losing its greatness."[130] There is a general impression among Americans today that the world fascination with the American way of life, as exhibited over generations, contradicts the rejection of its foreign policy in many parts of the world, wrote Al-Fiqi in *Al-Hayat*.[131] Anger at U.S. foreign policy has "damaged the traditional image of the American Dream"; America is no longer viewed as the "city on the hill" that people can admire and pursue as a model, wrote Mohamed Khaled Al-Azzar, a Palestinian academic, in *Al-Bayan*.[132]

Because of the war in Iraq, Matar emphasized in a piece in *Al-Hilal*, the United States has "lost many of the assets it collected in the nineties, reaching its highest losses following the Twin Towers blast in New York. The U.S. lost its asset of veneration and respect." It lost its honesty and integrity as a state and as a "preacher of democracy and respect for human rights."[133] In "An Empire Burning in Itself: America on the Burning Edge," Ibrahim Qaod of *Akher Saa*, an Egyptian magazine, expressed his belief that the social fabric of America is under the threat of fragmentation because of racism and hatred lurking inside it. He added that the United States is a giant that will turn into a dwarf, with challenges to the unipolar world political system coming from Russia, China, India, Japan, and Iran. Qaod made the following comment:

> The factors of America's strength are the same points of its weakness. The American Empire possesses elements of disintegration similar to those that the Roman Empire held. American hegemony on the world has begun its countdown in the face of the rise of a new power on the world center stage. The economic situation is in threat of a sudden and dramatic crush. American ethical values have retreated only to be replaced by the laws of the jungle and the prehistoric age. Blood is starting not to sufficiently flow as to reach the limbs of the American giant. This is hastening its demise.[134]

Besides caricatures, photographs are used at times in the Arab media to ridicule America. For example, on August 15, 2007, *Almussawar*, which regularly features a two-page photograph with a comment, ran a photograph of a large number of U.S. soldiers standing in lines with their right hands raised, pledging to serve their country. On top of the photograph there was the headline, "The Price of the American Dream." On the right side of the photograph there was the following comment:

> The photograph below was taken at the 4th of July Independence Day celebration of the United States of America. The place is Al-Nasr camp located at the heart of Baghdad. This crowd of soldiers is pledging allegiance to serve the interests of America. Until this date, the roots of these soldiers were Mexican, Lebanese or Haitian. But from this date on, they all have become Americans. To "relish" this new residency, they have joined the army and become part of the 157,000 American soldiers in Iraq. Some of them have always dreamt of achieving this dream; others have accomplished it due to necessity. This photo shot shows the price of the American Dream.

7 WHAT DO ARABS WANT FROM OBAMA?

We cannot change the present unless we understand it. MOHAMED GABER AL-ANSARY, Bahraini writer

There is no despair with life and no life with despair. AHMED SHAWQI, Egyptian poet

With the above title, the Egyptian paper *Al-Akhbar* headlined one of its articles on December 31, 2008. It added, "What do [Arabs] expect as far as their causes are concerned from the first black American President with African roots?" Will he play a more active role in the Middle East? Will he call for withdrawal of U.S. troops from Iraq and the establishment of an independent Palestinian state? These questions have busied the minds of Arabs since the victory of Barack Hussein Obama in the 2008 U.S. presidential election, with some cautioning against too much optimism and arguing that he has shown strong support for Israel. Others have been far more optimistic and greatly welcome Obama's success, contending that he has made resolving the Arab-Israeli struggle and withdrawal of U.S. troops from Iraq main themes of his presidency. But there are also those who stress that the economic and political challenges he faces are huge and likely to preoccupy his administration and divert his attention from the problems in the Middle East.

America's First Black President

Historic Event

As in many parts of the globe, the Arab world praised the election of Obama and described it as a historic event. Arabs of all sects of society watched the U.S. presidential election closely, as if it belonged not just to the American people but also to them. They were unable to believe that a young black man of African descent could win. Hence, the amount of coverage the Arab press placed on the issue of race and ethnicity was enormous, with almost every article of the dozens analyzed in this chapter raising the issue of color. Obama's election is a historic event showing that change for the rights of African Americans is possible, said the Lebanese paper *As-Safir* in an editorial on January 23, 2009.

To the surprise of many, contended the Kuwaiti paper *Al-Qabas*, the most powerful nation on earth did not choose a president of European descent but a man whose father was African and named Hussein.[1] "Obama elected President! America sure has changed," declared the Egyptian paper *Al-Ahram*.[2] Even Dr. Martin Luther King Jr. would not have imagined that his dream would come true in such a short time, noted the popular Egyptian journalist Salaheddine Hafez, who offered his sympathy to blacks and other minority groups in America for being deprived of such right for over two hundred years.[3] Similarly, the Jordanian newspaper *Ad-Dustour* described it as a historic election and an "official end to racial discrimination" in America. It proves that the United States is capable of change and that the ideals of Dr. Martin Luther King Jr. did not vanish, it said.[4]

According to Abdullah Al-Etabi, antiblack sentiment has mainly been confined to America, and hence Obama's election is historic. But, he added, "Obama is undoubtedly not the first leader in history with a dark skin, for if we examine the history of other nations and that of Arab and Muslim ones we will find many black rulers. But within the Western and global sphere in which he was elected this is a major historic event," with America demonstrating that it remains the "carrier of the torch of freedom and equality around the world." Al-Etabi made these points in a commentary he wrote for the United Arab Emirates paper *Al-Ittihad*.[5] Indeed, this is a moment in which America overcomes obstacles, argued Attif Abdel Gawad in the Omani newspaper *Al-Watan*.[6] "Having a black man in the White House says a lot about Obama. But it says a lot more about the changes that are taking place in a society in which slavery had remained for long periods of time." Gawad prognosticated that fifty years from now, Obama will be remembered for reasons other than his color—for his political achievements.[7]

Racial Justice

In an article in the Saudi paper *Al-Iktisadia* titled "How Did America Vote for a Black President?" Saudi writer Ammar Bakkar indicated that Arabs witnessed a big change in America. It was not merely the getting rid of Bush but the election of the country's first black president. Americans, he wrote, believe in the value of ending discrimination because they realize the importance of working as one nation. "To some, Obama is a symbol of individual achievement, of a man who made history; but to me, he is a symbol of an amazing story of change, of people who once prohibited blacks from any form of decent life to people who elected a black leader in the White House. This is a rare story in the history of humanity."[8]

Salah Montasir pointed out in *Al-Ahram* that Obama's election did not come easy, for if he had not won, it would have been "100 more years" before another black American considered running for the White House.[9] Indeed, January 20, 2009, was a great day for the "victory of democracy and equality between blacks and whites," declared the Qatari paper *Al-Watan*.[10] By electing Obama, noted *Ad-Dustour*, America regained its spirit and values, which were exposed to "destruction at the hands of the Zionist, right-wing, conservative gang."[11] Even hard-line Arab states, such as Syria, offered their applause. The Syrian paper *Al-Thawara* congratulated Americans on overcoming racism in their society and electing a black man as president.[12]

In the Qatari *Al-Watan*, Ahmed Ali wrote of his respect for American democracy, despite his contempt for American policy in the Middle East. "The entry of a 'black President' to the 'White House' is the biggest proof of American democracy."[13] America has, undoubtedly, succeeded in its "democracy test," said *Ad-Dustour*; Arabs never thought that Anglo-Saxon, white Americans would allow for a black man to become president of the most powerful nation on earth.[14] The success of Obama shows that the "distance between a dream and fulfilling it is a long one," according to political commentator Abu Bakr Al-Saqaf, and that justice might arrive late, but it does arrive. Titling his article "Long Live the Arab Dream," which he published in the Yemeni paper *Al-Ayam*, Al-Saqaf urged Arabs to also work toward achieving their dream of ending the oppression imposed on them by their governments.[15] Everyone, and every nation, must have a dream, he added.[16] (One caricature in the Saudi paper *Asharq Al-Awsat* showed Obama racing out of a book—which also has a door knob—with the following sentence written on its cover: "I have a Dream: Martin Luther King."[17])

African Arabs Taking Pride in Obama

As mentioned earlier, Obama is not only America's first black president but also its first leader of African roots, of Kenyan descent. Once his victory was announced, festivities spread in many parts of Africa, and not just in Kenya. Even Sudan claimed that Obama's ancestors were Sudanese, with celebrations being held in the south of the country. Obama's heritage provoked pride among some Arabs whose states are located in Africa, namely Morocco, Algeria, Tunisia, Libya, Egypt, and Sudan. For example, the Sudanese paper *Alnilin* applauded a Sudanese couple for naming their child "Obama" before the U.S. presidential election was even held. The commentary was titled "Congratulations to the 'Sudanese Obama.'"[18]

When the Kenyan soccer team came to play with Egypt in a final for the African tournament on January 23, 2009, a journalist at the Egyptian paper *Al-Masaa* welcomed the Kenyan players and characterized them as the "brothers of Obama."[19] As an "African, Arab and Egyptian citizen," offered another Egyptian journalist in a piece in *Al-Ahram*, "I congratulate you Mr. Obama on being the first black man to occupy the White House."[20] It is possible, claimed the Moroccan paper *Attajdid*, that Obama's African heritage will encourage members of Congress with similar African backgrounds to work toward resolving African conflicts, particularly the Moroccan-Algerian dispute over the Western Sahara.[21] Optimism that Obama might play a more constructive role in solving Africa's problems was also echoed in non-African Arab states, such as the Gulf ones. It would be unwise, stressed the United Arab Emirates paper *Al-Bayan*, to think that the U.S. leader will view the situation in Africa in the same manner as a European leader. "He is the son of that environment, one which is filled with conflicts. Obama will employ his personal expertise . . . to sympathize with Africa's troubles."[22]

End of Bush's "Tyranny": A Major Triumph

Other Africans glorified Obama's political agenda and the end of Bush's rule rather than the issue of ethnicity. They characterized his victory as a major triumph and a return of the American Dream. When Arabs celebrate Obama's victory today, they do not do so because part of his ethnic roots are African but because he has revived in them the "human dream" and not just the "American

Dream," observed Noureddin Madni in *Alnilin* in 2008.[23] Finally, said Al-Etabi in *Al-Ittihad*, the American political system "has triumphed over itself and corrected its mistakes." Bush's years of "political tyranny" have ended and the "role of reason" has begun.[24] The world has turned its back on the "miserable past" of Bush's governance and is now looking forward to a "new dawn with a new President who knows how to move the public conscience," stressed the Lebanese paper *Al-Anwar*.[25]

In the view of the Palestinian paper *Al-Ayyam*, the whole world in general, and the Arab one in particular, will be better off after Bush, a man who ignited wars during his two terms in office.[26] His faults have hurt the vision of American democracy and placed a lot of "filth" on the Statue of Liberty so that it needs to be "repainted," *Ad-Dustour* lamented.[27] After eight years of discrimination, Arabs and Muslims can now feel a sense of hope, asserted Mazen Hammad in the Qatari *Al-Watan*. The moment of Obama's inauguration did not just mean the "death and burial of the presidency of George W. Bush" but also the extermination of right-wing thought in America. His inaugural speech was in many ways a condemnation of Bush and his administration's failure in "distinguishing between security and high values," added Hammad.[28] Gladly, observed *Al-Ahram* in 2008, Obama's triumph marks the end of a "dark stage in America's modern history" and the beginning of a "new phase characterized by realism and justice."[29]

Al-Baath mockingly saw a resemblance between the "insanity" of King George III of England and that of George W. Bush, with one clear distinction: The madness of the latter caused a lot of destruction on the global level.[30] In another article, the Syrian paper stated that Bush left the White House after he had occupied Iraq and put it fifty years behind. He disregarded the Palestinian cause for seven years, only to wake up in the eighth and hold the Annapolis conference at the end of 2007—a conference that brought no positive results.[31] He even launched a war on the Arab media, terrorizing journalists and offering Arab rulers an excuse to tighten their grip on free speech, according to *Ad-Dustour*. He established American television and radio channels, namely Al-Hurra and Sawa, to spread his propaganda in the Arab world. *Ad-Dustour* asked that Obama end all that and allow for Arab public opinion to be expressed freely.[32] Mahmoud Al-Hayan urged Obama, in a piece in *Ad-Dustour*, to place a sign on the entrance of the White House that reads, "Bush and his friends are not allowed in."[33] Farewell to the White House staff, from George Bush to Dick Cheney and Condoleezza Rice, cried the Omani *Al-Watan*. America can lead the world in a way that is different from that of the neocons, it declared.[34]

Return of the American Dream

On the day of Obama's inauguration, a young Arab told me in Cairo that the new U.S. president offered his people the chance to dream again—dream of a better future and even of "going to America to pursue their American Dream." It must be said, stated *Asharq Al-Awsat*, that nobody symbolizes the American Dream as much as Obama does. His ascendance to the White House has revived the American Dream in the hearts and minds of many Arabs.[35] It has shown that America is a land in which dreams can be accomplished, according to the Omani *Al-Watan*.[36] His election certainly forms a "crucial moment" of the rise of the American Dream, commented *Al-Baath*. The Syrian paper wondered, nonetheless, whether Obama would truly succeed in revitalizing the American Dream after eight years of erosion under Bush.[37]

In electing its first black president, and the first black president in the Western world, America has truly regained its "moral values and demonstrated that it is the country in which any human being can achieve his dreams and ambitions via hard work," noted *Asharq Al-Awsat*.[38] In another commentary, the Saudi paper compared Obama to John F. Kennedy, arguing that both men carried an optimistic view of liberating America from fear and regaining the world's trust.[39] The U.S. president genuinely exemplifies the rise of the American Dream and hopes for better Arab-American relations, said the Saudi paper *Al-Hayat*.[40]

Prospect for Change

The Arab press praised Obama as a charismatic president with great leadership skills, a man who sees the goodness of America in its respect for international law rather than the use of military power. "In electing Obama," wrote Ellias Murad in *Al-Baath*, "the American people have demonstrated a strong desire for change. A change that is not based on the color, shape or belief of the President but on his politics and ability to exit America out of its plights in Iraq, Afghanistan and the complex problems it has with many of the world's nations in the West and East."[41] Indeed, Arabs found hope and inspiration once news of Obama's victory was announced, with cheers and shouts erupting on Arab streets. Both Arabs and Arab Americans wanted Obama to win, argued the Omani paper *Al-Watan*. It added:

> Undoubtedly, Obama's victory will carry changes toward regaining some of the glamour that America's image has lost abroad. But the change on the national level will be very profound, for the America that chose Obama as President is not the same America that selected

George W. Bush four years ago. America has changed, but it is in need of carrying such change to the world—away from unipolarity, axis of good and evil, preemptive wars, isolation, hegemony, violating nations' sovereignty, confiscating people's freedoms and double standards.[42]

In the view of *Ad-Dustour*, Obama's victory was not merely the result of the economic crisis but of other important factors, such as a desire by the American people to renew their traditional form of democracy and put an end to "a long period and a heavy inheritance of racial discrimination." Adding to this was the new leader's desire to secure for his people affordable health care and education systems and the abolishment of poverty. The Jordanian paper continued, "The reality is that Obama's amazing intelligence, deep eloquence and extraordinary courage in placing his fingers on America's wounds, together with his fierce criticism of the politics of Republicans, are what pushed the American people to sense the seriousness of that man and his desire to change America's shaky image, which is threatened of deterioration around the globe."[43]

Obama is a unique and courageous leader, claimed *Asharq Al-Awsat*, the first to call for structuring the American social system on the path of the Western European model of democracy.[44] He is a man who understands the world as it is because he has lived it the way it is, noted the Omani *Al-Watan*.[45] His presence in the White House has moved America from fear to hope, stressed *Asharq Al-Awsat* in another commentary.[46] It does not just mean an improvement of America's relations with the world but an enhancement of America's relations with itself, suggested *Al-Baath*.[47] Such an accomplishment exhibits that the United States is capable of changing itself by replacing its officials with new ones; in the Arab world, sadly, "our leaders try to save their systems by changing their 'people' via deluding them that they are the ones who are wrong," mourned *As-Safir*.[48] What is taking place in the United States today is an entire change in the American consciousness, thinking, and practice, stated Ahmed Gomaa in the Bahraini paper *Al-Ayam*. It shows to the world that the United States has achieved all its progress via continuous change. "It is the secret of the greatness and power of that nation," and Arabs should learn from that, learn to accept change.[49] Like Gomaa, Algerian journalist Khaled Amr bin Qaqa called on Arabs to embrace change and scolded Arab rulers for staying in power for decades. Qaqa's article in the Omani *Al-Watan* was titled "Obama's Victory and the State of Muslims in the American Age."[50]

Obama's America has a golden chance of opening a new chapter with the world, wrote Madni in *Alnilin* in 2008, and Arabs "congratulate the American people, both Democrats and Republicans, for such victory, which carries with it more than one humanitarian, economic and political connotation. We say to them that the victory of the will for change is the beginning of the long path toward a better future for the American people and the world altogether."[51] *Al-Hayat* praised Obama for taking some constructive steps toward change during his first week in office, particularly his call for closure of the Guantánamo prison, withdrawal of U.S. troops from Iraq within sixteen months, and initiation of a peaceful dialogue with the Muslim world. This, added the Saudi paper, shows that the U.S. leader might be placed high on the list of America's fine presidents. "Observers might differ on where to rank him on the list of fine presidents, but they will not differ on placing George Bush on top of the list of America's failed presidents."[52]

Americans "Not Our Enemies"
In welcoming Obama and celebrating the departure of Bush, there was less criticism directed at America in the Arab press. It could be said that Arab journalists are beginning to use a more friendly language when referring to Americans. Take, for example, this excerpt from a piece in *Alnilin*: "The changes that you [President Obama] desire for America, we too desire for your people."[53] The Saudi paper *Al-Jazira* carried an article emphasizing that Obama is serious about dialogue with Arabs and has proved that the United States is not an "enemy of Islam." Titled "Americans Are Not Our Enemies," the article commended the American president for offering his first interview since taking office to an Arab satellite station and called on Arabs and Muslims to work jointly with the Obama administration to overcome past obstacles caused by the Iraq War.[54] Today, suggested Hashem Al-Khaledi of *Ad-Dustour*, "let us Arabs open a new chapter with America and the American people, believing to some extent in the notion of change that Obama proposed."[55]

Americans should realize that the goodness and morality of their nation are much more powerful than its military, and only through them can the United States bring the world closer to it, observed the Omani *Al-Watan*.[56] The American people's desire for change and their election of Obama should be greeted by the world's nations, wrote Nawaf Abul Haija, a Palestinian, in *Ad-Dustour*. He added that all he asks from Obama is for him to "clean the dirt which the Bush administration has swarmed the world streets with, hurting America and its people. I wish from now on that the man—the black man who will govern the White House—will work in accordance with the determination of the American people and the unprecedented world welcome for change to the best."[57] What Arabs desire from the White House, declared the Omani *Al-Watan*, is for it to "clean the dark picture which Bush has left behind, for no one wants to target the United States when it is good with all the people."[58]

No Likelihood for Change

Arguments were also made that there was no good reason to assume that Obama's rule would be much different from his predecessor's, stressing that the U.S. political process is generally not run by an individual but by corporations and think thanks. "The ascendance of Obama to power will not change American politics as Arabs imagine," noted the Kuwaiti paper *Al-Anbaa*. America is run by organizations and think thanks, not an individual or two, not even by one party, and Obama represents merely a part of that entire process, added the paper. True that part has a big influence on the American political process, but it is still just a part of it.[59]

The focus of the new U.S. president will be on America's internal affairs and not on Washington's relations with the world, claimed one Iraqi writer in the Omani *Al-Watan* in early 2009.[60] American politics is, anyway, a "game of interests, be it Bush, Obama or any other individual who occupies the White House," argued the Palestinian paper *Al-Ayyam*.[61] No American president can escape from certain requirements, emphasized *Ad-Dustour*, mainly adherence to the capitalist system, support for Israel, and the use of absolute power and the dispatching of U.S. troops abroad, even when there is no war.[62] After all, said the Bahraini paper *Al-Ayam*, the American president is a "person tied in to the power of capitalism that governs his country."[63]

A Sudanese writer spoke in a piece in *Alnilin* of how he felt a sense of happiness among Sudanese when Obama was elected. He attributed that to an "emotional reaction" among his people. He argued, however, that there would be no change in U.S. policy "toward Sudan or other nations in months or in a year's time," stressing that an America under a black president would not differ from an America under a white president. In spite of that, he said he still held hope for change in U.S. policy under the new U.S. leader.[64] This position was reinforced by another commentary in the Qatari paper *Al-Arab*, titled "Obama and Africa: The Hoped and Expected." In it, Hamdi Abdel Rahman argued that he does not anticipate any essential difference in American politics in Africa under Obama. The problems of Africa can only be solved by its people, he stressed. Yet, he added, "having a black President in the White

House can form a means of ethical and moral pressure on African leaders, pushing them to learn from the American democratic lesson."[65]

As-Safir carried a piece under the headline, "Black Arabs and White Arabs." Citing what he called the "suffering" of Palestinians, Iraqis, and Lebanese, columnist Hossam Ettani classified "white Arabs" as those who escaped gun shells and could "enjoy the pleasure" of expressing their feeling of sympathy for those three "tormented" Arab groups of people, be that while sitting in front of their television screens, walking in demonstrations, donating money, or shedding tears. Stressing that his comparison was not founded on any racial prejudice, Ettani described "black Arabs" as those who "met death carried to them on the gun machines of their occupiers and subordinates without being offered real choices and convincing alternatives." He wondered if the solution for the Arab status quo is for black Arabs, who directly pay the price of mounting conflicts in the Arab world, to take hold of power and authority. He grieved that whenever such a chance emerges, it soon becomes a source of "fear, discrimination, and oppression." Ettani then cleverly moved to pose the question: "Will Barack Obama be in that category?" He answered with no, arguing that the world, including Obama's America, will continue to support the oppressor and condemn the oppressed.[66]

It might also be of importance to cite here that the majority of radical Muslim groups have echoed a "not welcome" signal to the election of Obama, describing him as merely a "snake with dark skin," according to *Al-Ittihad.*[67] Furthermore, on the civil rights issue and the abolition of antiblack sentiment in America, some Arabs held doubts that the new U.S. leader would succeed. "Barack Obama is not Dr. Martin Luther King who motivated the American civil rights movement and moved the world conscience, for he was raised in a white family," observed Osama Al-Mirghani in a column in *Asharq Al-Awsat.*[68]

Middle East Conflict

Hope for Solution

During his first week in office, President Obama showed positive moves toward resolving the Palestinian-Israeli conflict by dispatching former Senate majority leader George Mitchell, his new special Middle East envoy, to the region. He called for dialogue with Iran, engaged in talks with Syria, and gave his first interview as president to the Arab satellite television station Al-Arabiya. He spoke of how he was raised in the Islamic state of Indonesia and of the need for Americans to strengthen their relations with the Muslim world. "My job to the Muslim world is to communicate that the Americans are not your enemy," the U.S. president told the Dubai-based Al-Arabiya on January 27, 2009. He repeated a pledge he made during his presidential campaign, in which he promised to offer a speech in a Muslim capital in his first one hundred days in office. In the interview, Obama showed a radical break in tone and policy from Bush and urged Israelis and Palestinians to resume talks. "I think it is possible for us to see a Palestinian state—I'm not going to put a time frame on it—that is contiguous," he said.

By electing Obama, elucidated the Yemeni paper *Al-Thowrah*, Americans have revealed a strong desire for change and for resolving conflicts worldwide. It added, "What Arabs wish from the new U.S. Administration is for it to exert more efforts in order to initiate a just and comprehensive peace and establish a Palestinian state in accordance with international laws and signed agreements, particularly when considering that it was the new American President who promised during his election campaign to work constructively toward achieving this peaceful mission—one that has become at the center of many of the aggravating crises in the region."[69]

We have seen some good intentions on the part of the new president toward engaging in talks, not just with Syria and Iran but also with Hamas and Hezbollah, said the Qatari *Al-Watan*.[70] His inaugural speech offered a lot of hope toward engagement, commented the Palestinian *Al-Ayyam*. After all, "major disputes in modern history have been settled via dialogue."[71] Obama, unlike his predecessor, is a man who desires dialogue rather than the use of force, noted *Ad-Dustour*. He is not a man who will shake hands with autocratic regimes but who will work toward establishing the principles of democracy worldwide.[72] Sooner or later, predicted *As-Safir*, Obama will engage in dialogue with Lebanon, and he will immediately realize that the Lebanese people are ready for talk; however, they "cannot wait for long."[73]

When Arabs celebrate Obama's victory, said *Alnilin*, they also celebrate the victory of democracy and the will of change. His success has fulfilled the "dreams of nations, particularly those which suffered from the previous U.S. administration's policy in Afghanistan, Palestine, Iraq, Iran and Syria."[74] In "We and Obama," the editor in chief of the Syrian paper *Al-Thawara* said that Syrians feel content with the election of Obama and the end of "Bush's politics and hatred of the region, its peoples and nations." He described the Bush administration's policy toward Syria as "political stupidity," adding that his country has an open mind for dialogue and will be waiting for change in American politics. "Here is Syria's hand extended," he said in 2008, "waiting for the American hand, waiting for the hand of the President-elect Barack Obama."[75]

Arabs agree with many of Obama's political, economic, and security measures, particularly the closure of the Guantánamo prison and his prophecy for a just and peaceful world, said Madni in *Alnilin*. He added that the U.S. leader has learned a practical lesson from his predecessor, that of not involving America in more conflicts. Arabs hope that he will also realize that confining the war on terror to the Arab and Muslim people is unjust and needs reexamining, Madni continued.[76] Obama's inauguration speech carried huge promises, and the Muslim world will be watching. The new American president should realize that without a relationship founded on "mutual respect and shared interest," it will be impossible to write a new chapter between the Muslim world and the United States, stressed *Attajdid*.[77] After eight years of tension, we hope that peace will return to the world, concluded the Omani *Al-Watan* in November 2008.[78]

More of the Same

When Israel attacked Gaza late in December 2008, Obama—who had not assumed office yet—remained silent, and that led to criticism of the president-elect in the Arab press and reinforced the argument of those who prognosticated no dramatic change in U.S. policy in the Middle East. "Obama's speech did not refer to a major change in American foreign policy that in our region focuses on a 'war on terrorism,' which targets the present, future and history of the Arab world," declared *As-Safir* in early 2009. The Israeli war on Arabs will continue, and the Arab world will remain submitted to the tyranny of American imperialism.[79] On his second day in office, the Tunisian paper *Al-Sabah* wrote: "Sorry Obama we cannot join your celebration" while the children of Gaza "continue to bleed."[80] In spite of the good intentions Obama has shown toward resolving the Arab-Israeli conflict, he has not offered any promise for shifting his Middle East policy, which is exclusively pro-Israel, accused *As-Safir*. "In short, the new U.S. President, on whom Americans place a lot of hope, and perhaps they are right, may not find the suitable tools to break the ice that is crippling all peace efforts" in the Middle East, the paper said.[81] But that does not mean that Arabs should ignore Obama's desire for change, particularly in his country's relations with the world, argued *Al-Ahram*.[82]

Although Obama took some very positive steps toward solving the Arab-Israeli conflict during his first week in office, Arabs should realize that Americans did not elect him to solve the Middle East conflict, contemplated *Al-Hayat*.[83] "It does not matter much to Arabs if the occupier of the White House and his staff are republicans or democrats, for American administrations over the past 60 years have been pro-Israeli," *Al-Ahram* reasoned. "Madrid, Oslo and Annapolis did not achieve Palestinians' ambitions for establishing a statehood, with Jerusalem as its capital, and the right of return of refugees."[84] Samir Karam mockingly wondered, "What makes the Arab citizen think that there can be a change in U.S. politics toward the Arab-Israeli conflict because of the arrival of a new President of African roots and a father named Hussein, while that same Arab citizen cannot change the politics of his rulers toward that conflict or any other conflict?"[85]

It would be immature to judge the president of a mighty nation such as the United States, which is governed by organizations and think thanks, based on a decision or two, stated *Al-Baath*.[86] The new American president speaks with "a new and softer tone about Arabs and Muslims, but the American language remains the same," and he will, in the end, play in the same manner that his predecessors did to win all of America's games in the Middle East, wrote *As-Safir*.[87] Arabs should not be overly optimistic, because Obama will be pro-Israeli like his predecessors, maintained *Al-Ahram*.[88] They should not expect much change or a dramatic change in American politics in the Middle East, particularly when it comes to the establishment of a Palestinian state side by side with Israel, said *Al-Akhbar*.[89]

Tough Challenges Ahead

Obama has many tough challenges ahead, and the biggest mistake that Arabs can commit when dealing with the "Obama phenomena" is to look at it from an optimistic or a pessimistic approach, commented *Al-Hayat* in early 2009.[90] What Obama has inherited from the Bush administration are the toughest tasks ever in the history of American presidents, according to the Omani *Al-Watan*.[91] The victory of a black man of African background and a middle-class family was an "internal American revolution," proclaimed the Palestinian *Al-Ayyam*, but that does not mean Obama will undertake revolutionary decisions in America's foreign and national policies. All he can do is "change America's horrible and hostile picture in the world."[92]

Arabs, in the view of Al-Etabi of *Al-Ittihad*, will be busy watching Obama's handling of the principal issues in the Middle East, from Iranian intimidation of the Gulf states to the Arab-Israeli conflict and the situations in Iraq and

Afghanistan.[93] "When Obama enters the White House on January 20, 2009, he will begin his term with a heavy inheritance of regional conflicts by Bush in Iraq, Iran, Afghanistan, Somalia, Sudan, Palestine and others," stressed popular *Al-Ahram* columnist Attif Al-Ghamhri in December 2008.[94] The changes that the new leader has called for will help in improving America's image, for Bush left the Arab region suffering from conflicts that resulted in the rise of extremism, *Al-Baath* suggested. The Obama administration must prove that it is capable of changing the Middle East for the better, because that is in its interest and the interest of the world.[95]

It must be stressed yet again that one of the challenges Obama faces is how to deal with Israel's tough policy toward Hamas. The Israeli attack on Gaza late in December 2008 hurt the image of the then newly elected president. While Arabs welcome Obama's call for mending relations with the Muslim world, said Mustapha Al-Khalify in *Attajdid*, the Israeli attack on Gaza might make it difficult for the U.S. president to achieve such a mission. Obama must realize that any solution to the Palestinian cause that does not ensure the establishment of an independent Palestinian state with Jerusalem as its capital is a "failed solution."[96]

In an article in *Asharq Al-Awsat* titled "Messenger without a Message," Waleed Abi Morsheed wondered which deserves celebration: Obama's nomination as president or Bush's departure from the White House. He cautioned that the "problem of Obama will not be the 'future' of his Administration as much as it will be the 'past' of the Bush administration."[97] *Ad-Dustour* noted in early 2009 that there were fears Obama's victory could prolong the period of "American fascism" instituted by his predecessor.[98] The new president is optimistic about the possibility of solving the Arab-Israeli conflict, argued *Al-Ittihad*, yet some Arab intellectuals believe that pulling America from the tough economic situation it is facing will be Obama's biggest challenge and will consume most of his time.[99]

There is no doubt that a feeling of injustice pushes the Arab and Muslim world to wait and see what will come from the new U.S. president and his administration, observed *Al-Thowrah*. The way for America to improve its image in the Arab and Islamic world is for the country to work toward rescuing the Middle East peace process and push Israel to comply with past signed agreements. The notion of change that Obama carried with him to the White House will remain lacking unless he seeks a solution to the Arab-Israeli conflict that does not "equate justice with injustice, legitimate resistance with terrorism, and hegemony and supremacy with the right of self-defense," added the Yemeni paper. Unless that is achieved, the Middle East will remain buried in a state of instability, violence, and extremism.[100]

Summary

No Arab has doubted the nobility and courage of the new American president. Nonetheless, Arab public opinion is divided between those who believe that having an American president with African and Islamic roots can help Arab causes and those who argue that there will be no change because a "hidden hand" rules American national and international interests. Some rebel against this conspiracy theory because a change has actually happened in American politics; others stress that America has certain key interests that do not change over time and must always be defended.[101] But in general, Arabs are comfortable with the election of Obama and the end of a regime that, according to them, exhibited deep hatred toward Arabs and Muslims.

Under Obama's rule, hopes for resolving the Arab-Israeli conflict and reaching a peace arrangement between Palestinians and Israelis have risen, although such optimism remains limited among some. Arabs certainly expect better U.S. policies in the Middle East, suggested a commentary in the Palestinian paper *As-Sabeel*, but Obama's America will remain supportive of Israel.[102] Finding a solution to the Palestinian cause may not be placed high on Obama's list of priorities, wrote Al-Ghamhri in *Al-Ahram*, yet Arabs still hold some hope.[103] The new president should assist the embattled Palestinian people in their struggle for a homeland by putting an end to the "longest colonial, terrorist occupation that modern history has witnessed," asserted *Ad-Dustour*.[104]

Even though changes in American politics under the new U.S. leader are "mainly in style and shape, we welcome all endeavors to improve the image of American politics in the world, particularly in our region," suggested *Ad-Dustour*. The Obama administration is striving to change the means of achieving U.S. goals by using "soft power" instead of "military power."[105] The new president, according to *Al-Anbaa*, "has arrived at an age of crises to solve problems and dilemmas as if he were carrying a magic stick," but that is not how American politics is run.[106] If Arabs truly want change in U.S. foreign policy in the Middle East, they should—after years of weakness and submissiveness to Bush—use their economic and political weight to influence the American political decision, contended *Al-Akhbar*.[107]

Change or no change, one thing is certain: All Arabs were genuinely happy for Bush's departure. We are glad that Bush is gone, wrote journalist Ahmed

Novell in *As-Sabeel,* but he has left behind him a bundle of economic and political problems. The American people elected a young, civilized, and energetic
black man to "reconstruct what the white and the stupid Bush has destroyed."
Novell feared that white Americans' election of a black man in these tough economic times carried with it a "racist sentiment." Whites, he said, wanted to say
to the world: look, we gave blacks their chance, but they failed. He prayed that
Obama would succeed in his mission.[108] Nabil Al-Sherif took a similar stance
in a piece in *Ad-Dustour.* If Bush's record was not filled with deadly mistakes,
Obama might not have won the election, he contended.[109] Sympathy for
Obama was echoed in a caricature in *Al-Anbaa* in which Bush is standing in
front of the White House entrance, about to depart, handing to a bewildered
Obama waiting outside a sheet of paper on which is written: "economic prob-
lems, Iraq, Iran, Afghanistan, peace, Korea, terrorism, etc."[110]

With evidence continuing to reveal that Bush's policy "has resulted in Abu
Ghraib," criticism and ridicule of the Bush team will certainly continue in the
Arab media for years to come. Bush is a "dull person" and him "leaving office
is a victory for us," even though Arabs should not expect much change in
American policy in the Middle East, said Ammar Al-Sherai, a famous Egyptian
musician, in a television interview on New Year's Eve of 2008. Known for his
deep sense of humor, Al-Sherai added in his interview with Egypt's Dream II
that Egyptians do not know such a thing as discrimination against people of
color and that the "issue of black and white is merely an American one and
does not concern us." What matters is that "Bush has left, gone."[111] A column
in *Al-Qabas* sarcastically called on Bush to head back to Texas and "enjoy making coffee for his wife."[112]

Referring to the 1958 novel *The Ugly American* (which is discussed in the
introduction of this book), Al-Sherif argued that Arabs greatly suffered under
Bush and that they should celebrate the end of the rule of a man who for eight
years "embodied the character of the ugly American." He added that although
Arabs do not place a lot of hope on Obama when it comes to their causes, the
"reality is that the age of 'the ugly American' has passed . . . despite the fact that
Bush's legacy will chase us for years to come."[113] Abi Morsheed took a similar
stand in a piece in *Asharq Al-Awsat,* arguing that Obama's election might not
bring much change in the Middle East, but the end of the rule of Bush, the first
"evangelist" president in Washington, aroused comfort in the hearts and minds
of Arabs. He cheered: "Oh, how wonderful the world will be without Bush."[114]

8 TOWARD A BETTER FUTURE

It is our duty to proceed from what is near to what is distant, from what is known to that which is less known, to gather the traditions from those who have reported them, to correct them as much as possible and to leave the rest as it is, in order to make our work help anyone who seeks truth and loves wisdom.
ABUL RAYHAN AL-BIRUNI, Arab scientist (AD 973–1050)

Arabism is a state of love with Arab culture. NIZZAR KABBANY, Syrian poet

If this book shows anything it is that Arabs have been alarmed by the rise of a right-wing, neoconservative mind-set in American politics and the increase of an anti-Arab, anti-Muslim sentiment in America. The United States should be deeply worried about this rising anti-Americanism among Arabs. In world politics, Arabs view themselves as the abused, not the abusers. They are victims; hence, the conspiracy theory is placed high in the Arab mind. The democracy that the Bush administration predicted for Iraq has turned into a battlefield, with Iraqi blood carrying names: Shiite, Sunni, Kurdish. America's involvement in Iraq was a disastrous imperialist adventure, and unless the United States pulls all its troops from Iraq (and Afghanistan) and plays a fair role in resolving the Arab-Israeli conflict, all of Washington's efforts to win the hearts and minds of Arabs will fail. Indeed, Iraq proved to be America's new Vietnam, and had public support for the U.S. military presence there not waned, it is possible Barack Obama might not have won the presidency.

Dialogue demands knowledge about ourselves and about the "other." If Americans hold stereotypes of Arabs as violent, Arabs too retain negative images of Americans. Neoconservative politics has cultivated hurtful images of Americans in the Arab consciousness, making it much harder for Arabs to understand the U.S. cultural and political life. Among these negative images are views of Americans as violent, as cowboys, and as gold diggers with a vast land full of natural resources. Rarely did I read in today's Arab press about the reasons behind America's success—hardworking American individuals and their ability to utilize their country's natural resources in the most productive manner. Arabs and Americans have been making a mockery of each other. However, as Abdel Aziz Hammouda argued, more Americans are growing interested in knowing about that "other," the Arab, with new courses being taught at U.S. universities about Islam, Arab culture and media, and the Arab-Israeli conflict. The former Egyptian cultural attaché to the United States added:

> We too are more desperate to understand that "other American," to know the cultural forces which move him and shape his view of the "other Arab." The day we truly succeed in knowing about that other American—particularly since the USA has become, and will continue to be for some time, the sole world power and hegemon—will we be able to influence his vision of us. His mental picture of us is what shapes the nature of the key judgment and final decision he takes toward us.[1]

Western scholars have often argued that Arab rulers promote hatred of America in their societies to hide failure of their political regimes. Nevertheless, anyone who lives in the Arab world today can easily sense that anti-Americanism stems from ordinary Arabs themselves. The anger I felt among Arabs at Bush's America was more than any I had sensed during the visits I paid to the region during the two decades I lived in the Western world. The resentment and suspicion that Arabs hold of the United States are founded on five main factors: (1) America's emergence as a world hegemon and its pure capitalist intentions when conducting its foreign policy, (2) the rise of ultraconservatives and religiosity in U.S. politics, (3) Washington's pro-Israeli policy, (4) its invasion of Iraq, and (5) neocons' "fake" campaign for democracy in the region. Furthermore, Arabs claim that bin Laden and those at the center of al Qaeda are creatures of a flawed U.S. policy, and they dismiss two of the most frequent boasts of the Bush administration: that bin Laden and al

Qaeda are "on the run" and that the Iraq invasion has made America safer. They believe that unless U.S. leaders recognize this fact and adjust their policies abroad accordingly, America's enemies will grow and even moderate Arabs and Muslims might join the bin Laden camp. It must also be said here that there is fear among Arabs of a nuclear Iran penetrating their region, but their fear of the United States controlling their resources is much more.

Alas, the view of America from the Arab world looks grim, with Arabs muttering within themselves and in public: We will not surrender that easily to the logic and delusive politics of the world's superpower and its "canteen" culture. Even moderate Arab voices that used to speak out in defense of American democracy and technological advancement now keep silent, as they are experiencing a sense of alienation and discomfort toward American politics in the Middle East. Many of those who pioneered this neoliberalism in the Arab world are now calling for the nationalization of liberalism in a way that appeases their autocratic governments and satisfies citizens' growing resentment of the United States. Such deterioration in ties has extended even to Arab states that hold good relations with the United States. Today, very few Arab governments still feel secure about their alliance with the United States, for threats to internal stability have increased due to "Bush's faults" in the Middle East. The United States has lost the moral conscience needed to win Arab support.

Undoubtedly, Arab-American relations have never passed through a worse time than under Bush's rule, and it all began following the 9/11 tragedies and America's invasion of Afghanistan and Iraq. Since 9/11, Arab media portrayal of the United States has become an issue of great magnitude. If the tragedies of 9/11 have hurt the image of Arabs in the United States, they have also damaged the way Arabs view America and their pursuit of the American Dream. To many Arabs, particularly Arab youths, America is no longer the city on the hill that they once dreamed of migrating to. American policymakers must realize that spreading U.S. propaganda in the Arab world via media channels, such as the U.S.-owned Al-Hurra television channel and Radio Sawa, will not help in improving America's image in the Arab world; what is needed is for them to exert more public diplomacy efforts in the region. Settling the Arab-Israeli conflict and withdrawing U.S. troops from Iraq and Afghanistan should be America's main priorities. The United States, according to Said Rafaat, editor of the Arab League's magazine *Arab Affairs*, has invaded and occupied Iraq and Afghanistan through "false claims."[2] Unless and until Washington withdraws its troops from the Middle East and plays a balanced role in resolving the Arab-Israeli conflict, one could anticipate anti-Americanism growing in the Arab world.

In no way are Arabs an American-phobic people. However, American policymakers should be aware that Arabs' experiences of colonial interventions have made them very distrustful and skeptical of any foreign intrusion in their region. Arabs easily mix emotions with politics, and that has increased their resentment of the United States. They strongly believe that Americans hate them and their culture, and hence they denounce the United States as the "evil empire." They accuse the "devilish policies" of neocons of being behind their increased hatred of America. On top of being flamboyant, Arabs see America as dangerous, hauling its allies into violent spots. It is true, at least from what I have felt while in Egypt, that the United States cares only about the oil-rich Arab states. To win Arab support, the United States should strengthen its relations with economically embattled Arab states. Furthermore, the United States should try to nurture a more balanced relationship with the Arabs, reaching out not just to Arab regimes but also to Arabs on the street. It must begin by convincing ordinary Arabs that its foreign policy in the Middle East is not dictated by Israel. To show that it is a friend of the Arabs, the United States must withdraw its troops from Iraq and Afghanistan and persistently work to solve the Arab-Israeli conflict and save Palestinians from what Arab journalists often label as the "barbarism of Israeli war machines."

Most Arabs believe that as long as America is powerful militarily and remains the world's single superpower, it will continue its invasions of other nations in order to gain financially and protect its markets worldwide, which are the soul of its capitalist system. America's desire for capital—its ethical imperialism in the post–Cold War era—has sadly demolished faith in the United Nations as a moral agency. Talk to any citizen in the Arab world today about his or her view of the UN and the answer will always be negative, with some labeling it the "United Nations of America," as I have discussed in chapter 3. Unfortunately, I anticipate this condemnation of America and its policy in the Middle East to continue in the Arab world unless some positive steps are taken toward resolving Middle East conflicts. Arabs do take issue with what they see as Washington's insistence on dominating Arab countries and Americans' lack of knowledge of the people of the Middle East. Certainly it is of benefit to both Arabs and Americans to avoid this misunderstanding and instigate good relations that are crucial for future stability in the Middle East. Unless a constructive dialogue is initiated between Arabs and Americans, Arabs will continue to question America's role as a promoter of justice, peace, and equality in the world. If justice and the bonding of peoples of diverse cultures and backgrounds worked, we would produce the best for humanity. It is my-opic to speak of this "clash of civilizations" nonsense; what we should be pro-moting is dialogue among different peoples, for world violence is the product of a desire to have everything, of a growing capitalist culture and not religion.

America's vision of a "New Middle East" was founded on getting rid of dictatorial regimes in the region and imposing an American-style democracy. But that vision has been met with obstacles, the most prominent of which are the rise of Islamists and an increased U.S. backing of Israel. This has raised doubts among Arabs of an objective American role in the Middle East. In this complex world of a New Middle East, Washington has lost its authority; it is no longer able to distinguish between friends and enemies. Although many Arabs have called for political reform in their countries in the past, distrust of Washington, which began when the younger Bush assumed power, has now weakened their voices and given credit to those against reform. Pro-reform Arabs, advocates of an American-style democracy in the Arab world, are now denounced as "puppets" of the United States; in the opinion of their detrac-tors, they strive for the extermination of Arab culture. I must stress that crit-icism and condemnation of U.S. democracy in the Arab world is less a repudiation of Americans in general than a condemnation of Washington and its politicians' belief that American democracy is the best model in the world, and that it should be enforced on other nations. At least, that is how I feel the debate on democracy is reiterated among Arab intellectuals, who often claim that too much freedom can also have its own consequences and that even the richest and most democratic society in the world has its own flaws.

To take the discussion a bit further, one can argue that when the founding fathers drafted the U.S. Constitution, they could not have imagined such rapid technological advancements and the influence of images (as manifested in ad-vertisements) on a society and its culture. For instance, they could not have en-visioned the health hazards of tobacco, let alone realize that many of the tobacco industry's victims would be America's youths. If the marketplace of ideas, as envisioned by Thomas Jefferson and his followers, offers these cor-porate, capitalist-driven giants a carte blanche to damage the health of America's youths, then we need to redefine freedom of speech. After all, the First Amendment's definition of free speech is open to interpretation. What I am advocating here is not the removal of our freedom or the embrace of au-thoritarian rules (common enough these days in parts of the developing world) but rather that freedom should also have its limits. I commend President

Obama for having the courage to raise this issue in the speech he gave at Cairo University. He is the first U.S. president to admit that an American-style democracy should not be imposed on other nations due to cultural differences. I also give a round of applause to President Obama for taking the first steps toward a national health care system in America, for a true democracy means that every American has the right to be treated.

Some Arabs believe that it would be impossible for a new administration to shift politics quickly due to the influence of neocons, an influence that they anticipate will continue in Washington. Anti-Americanism in the Arab world will not end with the arrival of President Obama in the White House, although his election raises some hope among many Arabs of a more just U.S. policy in the Middle East. How his administration will implement that is what matters now, and Arabs will be watching closely. Indeed, since Obama assumed the presidency Arabs have seen positive moves in American foreign policy; the new U.S. leader has called for dialogue with Tehran and Damascus, withdrawal of U.S. troops from Iraq, and closure of the Guantánamo prison camp. "It is possible that he can bring some change, or give peace in the Middle East a push, or else what is the point of being the president of the most powerful state in the world," a sixty-nine-year-old Arab woman told me following Obama's election. But if Arabs want better and warmer relations with the Obama government, they too should get their house in order and allow for political reform and more media freedom. Nevertheless, fear of American politics will remain in the Arab consciousness for some time. As Sadaqa Fadel, a member of the Saudi Shura (Consultative) Council, said in an interview with the Saudi television channel Al-Arabiya: What threatens the Arab region the most is American policy.[3] "Yes, American stupidity in dealing with political events is unmovable," noted the Kuwaiti paper *Al-Anbaa*.[4]

Why Do Arabs Resent America?

Do Arabs and Muslims really hate the United States? The majority of Arabs and Muslims do not, but they resent many aspects of its foreign policy. This is a view held by many Arab intellectuals and public figures, the most prominent of whom is the secretary general of the Arab League, Amr Moussa. In a commentary in *Arab Affairs*, Moussa wondered how Arabs can agree with a completely pro-Israeli American policy in the Middle East and whether relations between the United States and the Muslim world will continue to deteriorate. He cautioned neocons not to be imprudent and think that they could defeat the Muslim world. Likewise, he called on Arabs not to hang all of their problems on the United States, for it is not to their benefit to instigate conflicts with America.[5]

While in the past there have been tensions in relations between Arab states and America due to Washington's support of Israel, the Iranian hostage crisis, stationing of U.S. troops in the Arab Gulf, and the attack on Libya, there was no resentment of American culture and life as there is today—so I sensed while conducting my research in the region. While many Arabs praised and supported America for liberating Kuwait from Iraq in 1991, almost all Arabs have been against Washington's invasion of Iraq in 2003. With its invasion of Iraq and Afghanistan, the United States has lost the moral compass that guides its foreign policy in the Middle East. Prior to that, many Arabs respected America, showing an admiration for the American way of life and notion of freedom— a freedom that they saw as lacking in their homelands. Any negative mentions of Americans then were due to Washington's pro-Israeli policy and incidents of discrimination against Arabs, Muslims, or Africans in the United States. I well recall my late father, who would have been eighty-two years old by the time this book goes to print, speaking highly of President Dwight Eisenhower for insisting that British, French, and Israeli soldiers withdraw from the Suez Canal zone, which they seized in September 1956.[6] He often also spoke highly of Woodrow Wilson and how he, after the First World War (1914–18), called for nations' independence and self-determination. He said that Wilson's ideals were a motivation for the Egyptians in their 1919 revolution against British occupation. Eighty-two-year-old Mohamed Hasseinein Heikel echoed a similar opinion: "The U.S. was once a promise to [the Arabs]. I sit with young people and try to differentiate between American policies and Americans. But the enemies of the Americans are not only the Taliban, Hamas, Hezbollah, but a wide sea of ordinary people who hate them because the Americans created polarizations in their lives."[7] In short, there was refusal then of America's pro-Israeli policy, but in no way did the Arab media show any sense of detestation of America and its culture.

Arab resentment and condemnation of America is something new; it has emerged since the younger Bush and his neoconservative government assumed power, particularly following his invasion of Iraq and speech in 2003 that called for political change in the Arab world. From that time on, Arabs have grown fearful of America and its Greater Middle East project, which they believe aims at further imposing U.S. hegemony on the region under the false umbrella of democracy and human rights. The younger Bush, unlike his father, lent a blind eye to the Palestinian-Israeli conflict and offered no hope for peace in the region—at least until the last phase of his term in office. During his rule, U.S. politics exhibited an antagonistic stance toward Arabs and became more pro-Israeli. Under the regimes of the older Bush and Bill Clinton in the 1990s, and earlier during the Jimmy Carter administration, that glimpse of hope for peace in the Middle East was alive and well. Their initiatives overrode the tension that characterized U.S.-Arab relations in the late 1960s during Egyptian president Gamal Abdel Nasser's time in office. From the late 1960s to 2001, there was refusal of U.S. politics in the Middle East but no antagonism against Americans or American values. Most Arab youths at the time continued to dream of traveling to and living in America; the American Dream remained attractive in the Arab mind.

Bush's "war on terror" speech, invasion of Afghanistan and Iraq, failure in easing violence between Palestinians and Israelis, and use of phrases such as "you're either with us or against us" and "axis of evil" have all raised negative representations of America in the hearts and minds of Arabs—something I was told is new in Arab culture. American soldiers' acts in these wars and in detention camps have tested America's benchmark on human rights. Instead of declaring a war on "state terrorism," observed *Arab Affairs*, America has waged its war on "Muslim terrorism," causing it to be seen as a racist act.[8] Since 9/11, Arabs have watched on their TV screens the torture of Arabs detained in U.S. prisons and the killing of innocent Palestinians and Iraqi children, women, and men. They have shouted that Americans and Israelis are murdering Arabs and Muslims. Arabs have persistently ridiculed U.S. efforts to link Saddam Hussein to 9/11, with the Arab media constantly describing them as unconvincing. His ignominious capture and later execution have definitely intensified Arabs' resentment of America. Within this distorted atmosphere, many Arabs and Muslims are exhausted; they see death lurking for them in the air. They perceive America as trying to take away their homes, obliterate their religion, and dominate their culture.

Arabs were fearful of Bush's America, stated Al-Sharqiya, a Dubai-based Iraqi TV station,[9] for his administration was "hesitant to solve the Palestinian cause," noted Al-Arabiya.[10] History shows that Arabs love America, said Mohamed Abdel Aziz Rabee; at times they have stood in long lines in front of U.S. embassies, seeking visas to study, travel, migrate, or get medical treatment. "They have every right to despise American politics, which is pro-Israeli and entirely against the Palestinians," wrote Rabia in the Jordanian paper *Ad-Dustour*. He claimed that instead it is America that hates Arabs, and he asked his readers to remember Iraq and the torture of prisoners in Abu Ghraib. "This American stance, which is antagonistic toward our people, and the silence of Europeans on Israeli crimes against us, makes us wonder: 'Why do they hate us?'"[11] If America wants an answer to the question "Why do they hate us?" said political science professor Ali Edeen Hilal in an interview with the Egyptian television channel Al-Oula, it is simple: it is because of the "works and policies of George Bush."[12]

During Bush's presidency, there were those Arabs, although few in number, who said they were not against the United States; they said their hands were open for all those who wanted to initiate a dialogue with them.[13] Abdullah Al-Ayoubi believes that Arabs resent American politics and politicians but hold great respect for Americans. He argued that different U.S. administrations have consistently worked to convince Americans that the world hates them because of their country's scientific and economic achievements, which have made it the most powerful nation. He asserted that many Americans believe such propaganda, and that has helped different U.S. administrations to keep the American voter away from world affairs and granted them a carte blanche to spread corruption and destruction in many parts of the world. Al-Ayoubi stressed, "There is not one nation on the face of this earth which denies the great role that American people have played in the advancement and development of humanity." He praised Americans for never endorsing any of their "governments' crimes" and asked Arabs to remember how they demonstrated on American streets in the 1970s in opposition to the Vietnam War. "Our people, like other nations of the world that have suffered under the gunfire of direct U.S. aggression, like Iraq, and indirectly, like Palestine, hold great love and respect for the American people," concluded Al-Ayoubi in the Bahraini paper *Akhbar Al-Khaleej*. His article was titled "We Hate You Sir but Respect Your People."[14]

Mahgoub Al-Zaweri took a somewhat similar stance. "The U.S. does not see the picture as people observe it here in the Middle East. It always tries to view facts from within one prism, which goes in harmony with the big goals of American politics in the region," he commented in *Ad-Dustour* in 2007. After all, it was neocons and their stick-and-carrot policy and arm-twisting tactics that enfeebled the representations of Americans in the Arab media and aroused Arabs' hatred toward the United States, added Al-Zaweri.[15] As Emil Eamen bluntly put it in the United Arab Emirates newspaper *Al-Khaleej*, "American diplomacy and the politics of preemptive wars have inflamed a wave of hatred that truly threatens America." Sadly, he lamented, the Arab media failed on a number of occasions in distinguishing between the American people and the Bush administration.[16]

Undoubtedly, the Arab region was the biggest loser politically from the 9/11 attacks, which empowered neocons in America to revive Samuel Huntington's so-called clash of civilizations argument. Just mention the word "Guantánamo" in the Arab world today, and you will see a flood of anger rising on people's faces, with many shoutings of "American injustice" and that the United States is fighting terrorism but promulgating its stereotypes of Arabs and Muslims. Furthermore, when it comes to solving the Palestinian cause, Arabs complain of a chasm between what American politicians say and do. Such cryptic and abstruse Middle East policy by Washington has polarized initiatives for solving the Arab-Israeli conflict, they argue. They insist that there exists a collusion between America and Israel and that "Zionist Jews and right-wing Christians" signed a covenant—a reciprocal agreement against the Arabs. Following the 1956 British-French-Israeli attack on the Suez Canal, in which the United States sided with Egypt, "Zionist Jews began to infiltrate the American society," and that enabled them to control "decision-making institutions beginning with Congress," wrote Waheed Abdel Mageed, an academic and author of numerous books on international affairs.[17] Arabs too must work toward influencing American public opinion by supporting Arab and Islamic organizations, which have begun to flourish in the United States, he emphasized. "The U.S. is not an enemy of the Arabs, regardless of disagreement over its support of Israel and the overlooking of the rights of Palestinians," added Mageed. He cautioned that it is not in the interest of Arabs to turn the United States into an enemy.[18]

Writing in *Ad-Dustour*, Kamal Rasheed did not deny that many Muslims were happy following the 9/11 tragedies, not because they are "advocates of murder, blood and destruction" but because "they underwent a lot of Western and American oppression in their own homelands. They felt happy because the oppressor experienced some of the repression he had committed against others, as if they were saying to Americans test, feel and estimate your crimes in our countries and to our peoples." The attacks have created a new concept known as terrorism, making it justifiable to occupy and destroy any nation, added Rasheed. "If the attacks ended the lives of 3,000 civilians in America, they also cost the lives of hundreds of thousands of Arabs and Muslims, in addition to the thousands held in American, Arab, and Muslim jails, or secret prisons in other nations."[19] In short, Arabs cry that they need new and objective U.S. policies in the Middle East and a better portrayal of Arabs and

Muslims in the American media. As the Yemeni paper *Al-Thowrah* commented in 2007:

> Arabs fought in defense of the United States in more than one place, and they fought each other on behalf of that same country. The reward for them was more support and backing of the aggressor and conqueror, the Zionist entity. The reward has also entailed the destruction of Iraq, slaughter of hundreds of thousands of its children and the attempt to transfer that horrible experience to neighboring Arab states. The big question reiterated daily in all parts of the world today is this: Does the U.S. no longer have great men that can tell the President and his entourage of extremist conservatives enough of blood? That they are pushing their nation in losing battles without justification or clear goals.[20]

In "Do We Really Hate the West?" Cherif Al-Choubachy, a foreign correspondent for the Egyptian paper *Al-Ahram*, saw Arabs' relations with the West as "complex and complicated . . . a product of a heritage of conflicts, wars, clashes, admiration, hatred, and mutual attraction and repulsion."[21] In another *Al-Ahram* article, Al-Choubachy claimed that it is not only Arabs who resent America but almost all nations of the world; many people view America as a "complex" nation. He saw a deep contrast when considering America's relation with the world over the second half of the twentieth century. He wrote that while the United States holds good relations with most world governments, people feel an "amount of hatred toward America, which they view as a symbol of political hegemony and haughtiness." Stressing his criticism of a U.S. move that hindered a UN Security Council decision demanding that Israel stop its attack on Gaza, Al-Choubachy asked, "How could Americans not understand that they are stirring up feelings of hatred toward them in the Arab world" by these unjust acts? He saw a "peculiar contrast between this declared hatred and a desire by hundreds of millions of world youths to immigrate to and live in America."[22]

As I mentioned earlier, the reasons for the ongoing Arab alienation from America are its pro-Israeli policy in the Middle East, wars in Iraq and Afghanistan, and the grandiosity of the policies of the former U.S. president George W. Bush and neocons in Washington. Arabs believe the United States and Israel are "conspiring" against them. In the past, most Arabs snubbed America for its biased policies in the Middle East; now there are some who reject American values and culture, describing them as capitalistic, violent, and hateful of Arabs. This should be alarming for all Americans who vie for better understanding among nations. "No one should be bothered by how other people live their lives," I once said to an Egyptian youth who, in my view, was critical of the American way of life even though he had never been to the United States. He quickly rebuffed me and said, "We are not troubled by how Americans live their lives but rather by how Americans impact our lives." He waited for a couple of seconds and then burst at me, "We do not hate Americans." An Egyptian foreign policy expert made a similar comment in an interview with Egypt's Nile News TV channel: "We are not against the American people, but we are against the U.S. government and its politics."[23]

Heikel believes Arab countries are tied to the American empire but are divided in their relations with themselves. Arabs' relationship with the United States is "similar to a Greek tragedy; if left to chance it will end in blood, either by the hero being killed or committing suicide," he wrote in his masterpiece *The American Empire and Its War on Iraq*.[24] For the Arab and Muslim world to succeed in defending its causes, it has to hold ties with the United States, affirmed Bassem Khafagi, a Saudi thinker. The American personality is neither all good nor all bad, and understanding it is an endeavor to comprehend the whole world we live in. He urged Arabs not to stand waiting for the downfall of the United States but to try to understand its "personality and deal with it intelligently to benefit from its positive aspects and avoid its negative ones."[25]

There are those Arabs who view the United States as posing a dangerous threat to their culture and religion and ask that U.S. troops withdraw from their region. From my point of view, the problem of the United States is that it looks at Arabs through its own prism, and most Americans are not at all prepared to put themselves in the place of Arabs to feel how they think and behave. Indeed, the behavior of neocons promulgates that the world is America and America is the world. My fellow Americans and Arabs: We live in one world to which we all contribute. If Americans do not hate Arabs, Arabs' perception of America is then based on stereotypes. There is an urgent need for the establishment of American studies centers in the Arab world to help Arabs better understand how the political process and public opinion are shaped and constructed in the United States. Arabs have sent many of their children to study in the United States, and it is time that all Arab students learn more about the world's most technologically advanced nation.

Understanding the Arab

Americans need to break their cultural isolationism and endeavor to understand Arabs better. Arabs are emotional people who feel angry at times, but they have an incredible capacity to not only forgive but also to forget. This is manifested in how, since Obama's inauguration, the Arab media have begun to use a rather friendly language when talking about America (discussed in chapter 7). However, for a constructive and productive dialogue to be initiated between Arab states and the United States, Americans need to understand the Arab people—their history, culture, and traditions. Some Americans still cannot distinguish between Arabs and Muslims, viewing them as representing "another" culture, often with negative connotation. Prior to the arrival of Islam in the seventh century, Arabs were divided into tribes, though there was a sense of cultural awareness among them. Today, over three hundred million people around the globe define themselves as Arabs. Arabs are bonded by one language, and most of them embrace one religion: Islam. But there are also Arab Christians and Arab Jews. The word "Arab" refers to inhabitants of the Arab world, to Semitic people who speak Arabic and share Arab culture, history, and civilization without regard to their religion. Furthermore, not all Arabs are white; there are also black Arabs, such as the Sudanese.

Since their liberation from European colonialism, Arabs have been very suspicious of any Western intervention in their internal affairs. Denouncing attempts aimed at dividing Arabs, columnist Rageb Al-Banna contemplated in a piece in the Egyptian magazine *October*:

> Arabs are one nation, even if haters despise to see that. They speak one language and have one culture. They have the same ethical and social values, a joint history and live on one land separated only by borders manufactured by colonialism. They face the same challenges and share mutual interests. . . . How could some call on Arabs to split while the world's nations work toward unification in large entities in order to be able to achieve development, prosperity and security for their people?[26]

Yet Arabs (in opposition to Al-Banna's view) do not live in a monolithic society, for social, cultural, and political differences exist among them. For almost a century, particularly following the end of European colonialism in their region by the early 1970s, Arabs have been troubled by whether they should apply a strictly Islamic Shura political system or embrace a Western-style democracy. If the latter is accepted, which form of democracy should they apply: an American or a European model? It would be a mistake for American politicians and policymakers to continue to treat the Arab world as if it is one state, for there are wide cultural and political differences among Arabs. American policymakers should realize that there are Arab countries that have experienced democracy in the past and those that have not.

Due to strict rule in parts of the Arab world, the majority of Arabs tend to escape politics, often taking sanctuary in humor. In Egypt, for example, a country of almost eighty million inhabitants, only 27 percent of registered voters balloted on the constitutional amendment referendum in March 2007. But there is also the problem of a high illiteracy rate in countries such as Sudan, Morocco, and Egypt. Adult illiteracy rates in the Arab world are projected at 43 percent, higher than the average in developing countries.[27] For instance, it is estimated that up to 60 percent of Egyptians cannot read and write. This high illiteracy rate has made Arabs more attached to the broadcast media, to the spoken word, rather than the print press. As I mentioned in chapter 2, those who own the broadcast media in today's Arab world hold great influence on shaping Arab public opinion.

As most cultures do, Arabs see the world through their own lenses. When negotiating issues with Arabs, Americans should understand that the past and the present are strongly tied in the Arab conscience. For example, whenever an Arab negotiator sits with his American counterpart, trying to explain the Palestinian cause, the American asks that he or she be saved from debating historical facts, for the present we live in is what is important. Heikel noted how this was reflected in a meeting he held with former secretary of state Henry Kissinger in November 1973 at the Nile Hilton hotel in Cairo; Kissinger asked Heikel not to talk about the past. Once again, American peace negotiators must understand that the past, that history, is of great importance to Arabs, just as technology is to Americans.

To sum up, it is important to stress that, as one Arab noted, "Arab nations do not deride . . . America and Israel from a religious standpoint but because of their colonial practices in the region."[28] Arabs feel they are victims of an American-Israeli conspiracy to dominate them and tend to take an emotional stand when observing American politics and international relations. They resent an "imperialist America" and what they describe as its politics of arrogance and injustice. Yet they still watch Hollywood movies and enjoy American arts and technological advancements. The American Dream is not dead in the Arab soul; there are still those *Wikas*, or flamboyant Arabs, who dream of going to the United States and living the American Dream.

Improving America's Image in the Eyes of Arabs

I anticipate the Middle East will continue to be mired in this state of convolution and that anti-Americanism will keep rising in the social fabric of Arab society. America's image in the Arab world will remain bleak unless the Obama administration not only withdraws all U.S. troops from Iraq and Afghanistan but laboriously works toward finding a solution to the Arab-Israeli conflict. To dismantle this ongoing distrust between Americans and Arabs, the Obama government should also reach more to young Arab leaders (such as Morocco's Mohamed, Jordan's Abdullah, Syria's Bashar, and Bahrain's Hamad) and help— without intervening in nations' internal affairs—in implementing a wider system of democracy (not necessarily one modeled on the U.S. system), where all citizens are treated equally, and a mass media system that operates freely.

An Egyptian American now in my early forties, I am fortunate to have lived half of my life in the Western world, including thirteen years in America, three years in England, one year in Holland, and almost two years in New Zealand. Having lived in both Arab and Western cultures, I can say that Islam and Arab traditions can be interpreted in ways that are compatible with Western democracy. (Whether this is true or not is debatable, of course, and in no way am I advocating mixing politics with religion.) The problem lies in America promoting autocratic regimes in the Arab world; it leads to a belief that what Washington wants in the Arab world is not democracy and reform but to further an interest in oil and in ensuring Israel's security and its Zionist ambitions. It is also important to stress here that many of the conflicts that the world has witnessed, such as Darfur, Rwanda, Bosnia, and Kosovo, were not founded on religious factors, as the Western media often advocate, but rather on socio-political and economic ones.

The clash between Muslims and the West is not a clash of civilizations. It is a product of many issues, with roots going back to Islamic states' struggle for freedom from Western imperialism. It emerged following the Anglo-French-Israeli attack on Egypt in 1956, the 1967 Arab-Israeli War (during which America supported Israel), the 1979 Iranian revolution, and Israel's invasion of Lebanon in 1982. It further escalated following the U.S. invasion of Iraq in 2003 and Israel's war on Lebanon in 2006. In today's technologically advanced and real-time world, there is one civilization and many cultures. Every now and then, there exists a clash among these cultures, but all live under the umbrella of one civilization. Hence, I find Huntington's thesis disappointing, and it ignites an atmosphere of distrust between Islam and the West. While using religion in his definition, Huntington overlooked the conflicts that have taken place in Western European states with Christian values, such as hostilities in sixteenth-century Europe and World Wars I and II. He gave a blind eye to the good relationship between Western Christian societies and Islamic ones such as Egypt, Turkey, Morocco, Saudi Arabia, and Kuwait, which distanced themselves from nations such as Libya and Iran. I should also stress that in a world submerged in materialism and individualism, like our present one, conflicts are likely to arise.

To accelerate momentum for better relations between Arabs and Americans and improve its image in the Arab world, the United States should:

1. End its occupation of Iraq and Afghanistan, withdraw its troops and military bases from the Middle East, and work more diligently toward reaching a solution to the Arab-Israeli conflict.

2. Fulfill its moral obligation toward the Iraqi people by arousing in their hearts and minds a sense of real hope for a better future. It can do so by planting optimism that a democratic system of government can be established in Iraq. The way for the United States to do that is by linking with educated Iraqis—writers and researchers who were pushed out of public life by U.S.-backed autocratic Iraqi politicians.

3. Stop promoting dictatorial regimes in the Arab and Islamic world.

4. Maintain its strong economic ties with moderate Arab states.

5. Employ America's technological advancement more effectively to address Arab cultures and traditions.

6. Establish American research centers in the Arab world and encourage Arabs to establish think tanks in the United States.

7. Initiate dialogue with the Arab League with the aim of improving the current Arab-American discussion.

8. Use the media more positively and shut down Al-Hurra TV and Radio Sawa or radically reform their programs so that they become acceptable to Arabs. They should offer Arabs a sense of pride by reporting stories on successful Arabs inside and outside the Arab world. By focusing on the positive in the Arab world, the U.S. media can help in winning the trust of Arabs.

9. Work more extensively with Arab and Muslim groups and organizations in the United States and call for an end to laws and acts that discriminate against Arabs and Muslims.

10. Entice American scholars to study the history and politics of the
    Arab world not through their own prism but by travelling, living,
    and indulging in Arab cultures.

It is time that American policymakers consider these points of view, which
I gathered from numerous works by Arab intellectuals, many of whom were
educated in the "land of dreams." But Arabs too need to view today's America
from a different perspective rather than the Pax Americana one, argued popular media commentator Mustapha Al-Fiqi in a piece in the Saudi paper *Al-
Hayat* titled "Arabs and America: A New Vision." The United States is
changing and realizing that its "policy of dual containment, military invasion
and media distortion" cannot succeed.[29]

Without a doubt, a clash between Arabs and Americans, between Muslims
and the West, is ultimately preventable. There are scientific facts that support
such a viewpoint. According to a 2008 report by the World Economic Forum,
the majority of populations surveyed from over two dozen Muslim and Western
nations believe that conflict between the Muslim world and the West is avoid-
able.[30] Through my experience of living in the United States, I can say to my
fellow Arabs that the American people are generally kind and sociable. They are
victims of a system dominated by corporate greed and a culture of consumption, which at times distances them from the outside world. Like me, Arabs
who visit or live in the United States often come back with a better picture of
the American society than they once held. Consider this opinion, for example:
Writing in the Saudi paper *Asharq Al-Awsat*, Fatma Saad Al-Deen, a Sudanese
writer and researcher, highly praised the friendship, kindness, helpfulness, and
generosity of the "senior women" who hosted her during her stay in the state
of Virginia. She stressed that her dialogue with them unveiled the humanity and
good ethics of the American people and that it "completely changed her thinking about the American society."[31] Al-Deen's words are right; I witnessed it in
the five U.S. locations I lived in. Arabs must differentiate in their criticism between ordinary American citizens and American politicians whose unwise policies in the Middle East were the propeller of much of today's anti-Americanism
in the Arab world. The American people have an educated class that is deeply
interested in learning about Arabs and Muslims, away from the extremist hysteria that dominates the minds of neocons and right-wing groups.
Consequently, it is incumbent upon Arab intellectuals to make a link with that
educated American class for the benefit of all of us—Arabs and Americans.

One can also argue that Arab television networks, particularly Al-Jazeera and
Al-Arabiya, have exploited crises to further inflame the anti-American sentiment

in the Arab world, similar to their Western counterparts, which Arabs accuse of being anti-Arab and anti-Muslim. Sadly, on numerous occasions the Arab media failed to distinguish between the American people and the U.S. administration, resulting in an intensification of anti-American sentiment on the Arab street. There is no doubt that much of this misunderstanding began following the 9/11 attacks and attempts by the Bush administration and some right-wing U.S. media to link the words "terrorist" and "terrorism" to Arabs and Muslims. By avoiding using those words in his speech, President Obama has initiated a new beginning with the Arab and Muslim world based on mutual respect, a beginning that can truly counter violence and hatred, not just in the Middle East but throughout the entire globe. I have great hope that we can erect a world in which we can all—Arabs and Americans, Muslims and Christians and Jews, believers and disbelievers—live in peace.

Obama's Speech to the Muslim World: A Glimpse of Hope

In the beating heart of Cairo and at the Arab world's oldest educational institution, Cairo University, President Obama delivered a remarkable, intelligent, and emotionally moving speech to the Muslim world on June 4, 2009. Arabs waited anxiously for Obama's arrival. Never before in history had Arabs and Muslims waited for a speech by an American president as they did with Obama, wrote Osama Saraya, editor in chief of *Al-Ahram*, six days before the arrival of the U.S. president to the Egyptian capital. "His speech to one-sixth of the world's population is a unique chance in history."[32] Obama came to make America's relations with the world better, and we wish him success, said former Egyptian minister of foreign affairs Ahmed Maher in a debate on Al-Oula. For his peace initiatives in the Middle East to succeed, Obama needs to break the barriers between the West and East, stressed Mohamed Kamal, a political science professor at Cairo University, on the same Egyptian television channel.[33]

Obama's well-crafted speech did not just receive the Arab and Muslim world's attention but that of many of the world's nations. After all, it was the first speech in history by a Western leader delivered exclusively to the Muslim world. Broadcast by scores of Arab television channels, some historians referred to it as one of the most important speeches of modern times. The Arab media were inundated with commentaries, focusing on how the American president showed genuine respect for Muslims and the Quran, which he repeatedly referred to in his speech. Arab intellectuals and religious figures praised it as a positive change in America's Middle East policy. They characterized it as a "historic initiative," a new beginning toward improving America's image in the eyes of Arabs and Muslims. It was just too good to be true, said one Arab. The grand mufti of Egypt, Sheik Ali Gomaa, welcomed the speech and said that it laid the foundation for a new beginning in relations between the United States and the Arab and Muslim world based on respect. He added that the U.S. president should back his words with concrete actions, including the establishment of an independent Palestinian state, ending U.S. occupation of Afghanistan, and helping in the fight against negative stereotypes of Muslims.

No Arab can doubt the sincerity, passion, and charisma of the new American president, with many hoping that his words for dialogue among religions and a solution to the Middle East conflict can be "translated into action." Most of the Arab commentators who spoke of him favorably often attached the words "charismatic" or "charisma" to his name, with some likening his speech to that of President Anwar Sadat at the Knesset in 1977. Others spoke of an "Obama phenomenon," of the charm of a man of great intelligence and nuance in his thinking. The U.S. president tried to reach the soul of Muslims and succeeded in winning the moderate voices in the Arab world. He offered hope that a better relationship between Muslims and Americans can one day crystallize, after eight years of tension under Bush's aggressive rule. "It is as if Obama was saying, 'I am coming to clean Bush's dirt,'" a seventy-year-old Arab woman told me right after the speech. She wished "he would have stayed with us for a week or two because he is a nice man."

The American president began his speech by recognizing Islam's achievements and contributions to world science and culture, and the role played by the Muslim community in America. He said, "America is not—and never will be—at war with Islam." He changed course away from the "axis of evil" rhetoric and used terms such as "violent extremism" instead of "Muslim terrorists." He said he would join hands with Muslim communities to achieve security and isolate extremists. Referring to U.S. interference in the internal affairs of some countries, Obama admitted that his country is not always right. It was as if he were attempting to rescue America's declining popularity by shifting from unilateralism to multilateralism by use of "smart diplomacy."

Without a doubt, President Obama showed deep respect for his audience. Some said he stood in front of the Muslim world as a preacher, an imam, and a knight. He said he came to initiate a new beginning founded on mutual interest and respect, "one based upon the truth that America and Islam are not exclusive and need not be in competition. Instead, they overlap and share common principles, principles of justice and progress, tolerance and the dignity of all human beings." He said obstacles that the United States and Muslims face should be dealt with through partnership, with sources of tension addressed directly. "There must be a sustained effort to listen to each other; to learn from each other; to respect one another; and to seek common ground," Obama said. "So long as our relationship is defined by our differences, we will empower those who sow hatred rather than peace, those who promote conflict rather than cooperation that can help all of our people achieve justice and prosperity. This cycle of suspicion and discord must end."

The Arab discourse on Obama's extraordinary speech carried seismic dimensions. The speech was a "highly detailed" one with "lots of humility and realism," noted Waleed Shukir in *Al-Hayat*. The American president realizes that improving his country's image in the Muslim world necessitates a change in American foreign policy. He is trying to repair and define America's leadership in the world, beginning with the Middle East, Shukir said.[34] Arabs received a "kind, reconciliatory word" from him, wrote Rakan Al-Mgali in *Ad-Dustour*. Although it does not heal all of the "faults and sins" committed against us, our "caring spirit has received with comfort the noble axioms contained in the speech."[35] Obama has made us—"Muslims, Christians and Jews; Arabs, Americans, Israelis and Iranians—partners in solving the region's tough problems," argued Sami Al-Nesf in *Al-Anbaa*.[36] "It is strange that some Arabs are saying that they are waiting for actions and not words. For Obama's speech is in itself a leading action," contended Tariq Al-Hameed, editor of *Asharq Al-Awsat*. The American president compared Palestinian suffering to that of black Americans before they gained their rights. It would be foolish not to join hands with him, added Al-Hameed, for Arabs today have a "historic chance to found a Palestinian state, free occupied Arab land and embarrass Israel in front of Americans and the international community."[37]

Obama has the skills and charisma needed to revive in the world the "glamour of the American Dream," commented the Palestinian paper *Al-Quds Al-Arabi*.[38] The U.S. president has every right to enhance his country's hurt image in the eyes of the world, wrote Ali Al-Ghafli, head of the political sciences department at the United Arab Emirates University, in *Al-Khaleej*. He added that Obama has managed to "win the hearts in the Muslim world," but he has yet to win the minds of Muslims. To do so, he will need to employ the right policies on the long and tough road ahead. Al-Ghafli called on Arab and Muslim governments to back Obama's efforts in the process in order to achieve success. "Obama will not succeed if Arabs fail, and their success does not automatically mean that Obama will succeed," he added.[39]

Arabs also wondered if Obama could truly deliver, with some describing his speech as carrying a "strong message but poor stance." They added that Obama's "we can change" statement is great, but pure idealism cannot cause change; actions do. Others said that the United States is in deep economic trouble, and to pull out of it, it will need the Arab and Muslim world on its bandwagon. There were also those, such as Hezbollah leaders, who labeled the speech another American "public relations campaign," a "new language of an old world." Egypt's banned Muslim Brotherhood group issued a statement a couple of days after the speech, saying that Obama tried to play on the feelings of Muslims. It added that the speech focused on the Jewish Holocaust while overlooking Israeli "crimes" and acts of "ethnic cleansing" against Palestinians. Like Hezbollah, the group called the speech a "public relations exercise" aimed at improving America's image and isolating al Qaeda.

Obama specifically tackled over half a dozen issues, from violence and extremism and the situations in Iraq, Afghanistan, and Pakistan to the Palestinian-Israeli conflict; from the Iranian nuclear arms program to democracy and religious freedom; from women's rights to economic development. He spoke of the threat that violent extremists pose and what the United States has done in Iraq, Afghanistan, and Pakistan. He called for banning of torture and promised to close the Guantánamo detention center and withdraw U.S. troops from Iraq by 2012. He also promised to withdraw troops from Afghanistan if the country frees itself from terrorism. There was criticism from some Arabs that the U.S. president spoke a whole paragraph about the 9/11 tragedies and not a single word on the hundreds of Iraqis killed or made homeless because of U.S. occupation of the Arab state. Nevertheless, it must also be cited that the American president called the war in Iraq a "war of choice" that could and should have been avoided. Make no mistake, he said—the United States does not want to keep its troops in Afghanistan, but Americans will remain so long as there are "violent extremists in Afghanistan and Pakistan determined to kill as many Americans as they possibly can." He added that military power alone would not solve the conflicts in Afghanistan and Pakistan, and that is why Washington plans to invest $1.5 billion annually for five years to build roads, schools, hospitals, and businesses there.

President Obama also showed determination to restart Israeli-Palestinian peace negotiations, which stalled in 2008. He called for a two-state solution and demanded that Israel freeze its settlements on Palestinian land. He spoke of the sixty years of dislocation and suffering of the Palestinians in "pursuit of a homeland" and used the word "Palestine" instead of "Palestinian territories." He also acknowledged the suffering of Palestinians in refugee camps in Gaza and neighboring Arab states and did not characterize Hamas as a terrorist organization. "The continuing humanitarian crisis in Gaza does not serve Israel's security," he said. On the other hand, some Arabs stressed that Obama should have gotten tougher on Israel, particularly when addressing the nuclear arms issue in the Middle East. They said he was vague on his definition of a two-state solution, for he did not declare that East Jerusalem should be the capital of Palestine.

On Iran's nuclear ambitions, Obama pointed out that for many years, the United States and other nations in Europe and the Middle East have been working to encourage Iran to halt its nuclear arms program. Calling for a nuclear-free world, President Obama said a "decisive point" has been reached, and it is in no one's interest for a devastating nuclear arms race to develop that could lead the Middle East "down a hugely dangerous path." He contended that while it will be difficult to overcome decades of distrust, the United States, others, and Iran must carry on with tenacity to solve this crisis. On the democracy issue, Obama said that while no form of government should be imposed on any nation by another, he believes vigorously in a system of government that gives voice to the people and that respects the rule of law and the rights of all. "Governments that protect these rights are ultimately more stable, successful, and secure," he said. "Suppressing ideas never succeeds in making them go away." In supporting the role of democracy, the U.S. president called also for greater religious freedom as essential for peoples of the world to be able to live together. He also encouraged the advancement of rights for women and said that "a woman who is denied an education is denied equality. And it is no coincidence that countries where women are well educated are far more likely to be prosperous." He spoke of how women in some Muslim states have achieved progress in gaining equal rights with men, while the battle for women's rights in some aspects of American life continues unabated.

In conclusion, since Obama ascended to power Arabs have realized that they are dealing with a drastically different administration than its predecessor, one that promotes change and is trying to resolve conflicts between America and the outside world—the Muslim one in particular. Unlike his predecessor, the man now at 1600 Pennsylvania Avenue realizes that politics is not a profession but a humanitarian mission that never ends. It is because of this that I anticipate anti-Americanism to dwindle in the hearts and minds of Arabs. In fact, after Obama's inauguration and Cairo speech, I began to see less anti-Americanism and better representations of Americans in Arab public opinion and the Arab media. I wish to say this to President Obama: The stature and standing of America in the Arab world is getting better since your arrival. I expect for this reset in U.S.-Arab relations to get healthier, particularly if you continue to work laboriously on resolving the Arab-Israeli conflict and keeping your promise of withdrawing all U.S. troops from Iraq.

As Obama himself said, one speech cannot change years of distrust. Promising a solution to the Middle East conflict is easy; delivering it will be difficult without extensive diplomacy on all tracks. For peace to be established in the region, Washington must work simultaneously on all fronts: Palestinian refugee camps, Jerusalem, and the Golan Heights. The Middle East is no longer far away from America, as some of us used to think, and it should be placed high on the agenda of U.S. policymakers, be they Republicans or Democrats. We must exert all efforts to help Palestinians and Israelis—Arabs and Israelis—live in peace. Only then will relations between Arabs and Americans be truly strong and productive. If we do not make this effort, our children—Arab and American children—will one day scold us.

Undoubtedly, President Obama's policies have offered a glimpse of hope for better relations between Arabs and the United States and dismissed the myth of the clash of civilizations. This passion is vibrant on the Arab street today, with a Sudanese couple going so far as naming their child Obama. The new American president has been trying to forge ties with Arab states, demonstrated by his resumption of diplomatic relations with Syria. With his peaceful initiatives, the Arab media are now talking of dialogue among cultures. But whether the Obama administration will succeed in mending all of America's fences with the Arab and Muslim world remains to be seen, and Americans and Arabs should be watching closely. Watching—perhaps that is not the right word. They should all work collaboratively and contribute toward resolving conflicts and constructing new ties founded on mutual respect.

POSTSCRIPT

I began working on this book roughly from mid-2004 to mid-2009, examining Arab public opinion as echoed in the Arab media from President George W. Bush's second term in office until President Barack Obama delivered his speech at Cairo University on June 4, 2009. I stressed how the speech was well received by most Arabs and raised a spirit of hope for a shift toward a better perception of the United States in the Arab world. I ended the book there and submitted it to my publisher. As the book was about to go to print, my editor and I agreed in mid-June 2011 that I add a postscript. (I am very grateful for the support of all the staff at Potomac who helped in producing this book, including Senior Editor Hilary Claggett and Production Editor Kathryn Owens.) I found the idea genuine because many events had taken place during those two years (from mid-2009 to mid-2011), and I was sitting in Benha, my suburb of Cairo, watching them unfold. Watching is perhaps not the right word; I sat there documenting them and at times even tried to prognosticate: Will the picture of the "ugly American" evaporate from the Arab conscience and America be liberated from the "sins" of the era of the younger Bush? What is likely to happen in the Arab world after the Cairo speech in which Obama, unlike his predecessor, intelligently and without imposition encouraged Arabs to move toward political reform?

During those two years, President Obama vigorously continued his struggle to win the hearts and minds of Arabs and Muslims. From Jakarta to Arlington, Virginia, he defended the rights of Arabs and Muslims and called for better treatment and representations of them inside and outside the United States. And the Arab media were busy covering and recording, with commentaries often screaming in support of his stance. Yet, some Arabs were also suspicious and observed closely whether he would deliver on his promise of establishing an independent Palestinian state in one year.

Pentagon and Jakarta Speeches

In remarks at the Pentagon Memorial in Arlington on September 11, 2010, Obama defended the rights of Muslim Americans to have an Islamic cultural center near the Ground Zero area in New York City and criticized a Florida priest who called for burning copies of the Quran on that day. Two months later, on November 10, the U.S. president delivered a speech at the University of Indonesia in Jakarta. Described in a press release by the White House as a "follow-up" to the Cairo speech, Obama's Jakarta speech primarily addressed the issues of development, democracy, and religion. Some Arabs described it as an attempt to promote the issue of democracy, which they accused him of being soft on in his Cairo speech. Yet one can argue that by admitting in Cairo that an American-style democracy should not be imposed on other nations, Arabs got invigorated and began thinking and searching within themselves for a way to get rid of the dictatorial regimes that have been ruling them for decades.

On democracy, Obama said in Cairo that a "government of the people and by the people sets a single standard for all who would hold power: You must maintain your power through consent, not coercion; you must respect the rights of minorities, and participate with a spirit of tolerance and compromise; you must place the interests of your people and the legitimate workings of the political process above your party. Without these ingredients, elections alone do not make true democracy."[1] In Jakarta, the U.S. president's argument on the role of democracy was more assertive:

> Of course, democracy is messy. Not everyone likes the results of every election. You go through your ups and downs. But the journey is worthwhile, and it goes beyond casting a ballot. It takes strong institutions to check the power—the concentration of power. It takes open markets to allow individuals to thrive. It takes a free press and an independent justice system to root out abuses and excess, and to insist on accountability. It takes open society and active citizens to reject inequality and injustice.[2]

Arab Spring Uprisings

First, I wish to admit that I was wrong to say that pro-democracy voices in the Arab world would remain silent for some time. But I also want to stress that that does not in any way mean that Arabs would embrace an American-style democracy or grow less suspicious of Washington politicians and U.S. foreign policy. In a way, one can also argue that the 2008 victory of a man of African Muslim descent in the U.S. presidential elections—which one Arab paper described at the time as a "victory of democracy"[3]—has raised the hopes of Arabs that they too can change their political system and push for reform. If some Arabs have accused the American electoral system of being "racist" because no minority was elected to the White House until Obama's arrival, Arabs are now admitting that theirs are "dictatorial" political systems because only death has been able to remove an Arab leader from office—at least until the Tunisian revolution erupted in mid-December 2010. The United States has changed and so too has the Arab world. Welcome to the age of Arab Revolutions.

While intelligently keeping a clear distance from the internal affairs of the Arabs, Obama has shown support for the Arab uprising and "revolutions," which has been received mostly well in the Arab world. His applause of Egyptians and Tunisians following their successful revolutions was loud and clear—though it was louder for Egypt, perhaps because of the country's sheer size and strategic role. In his State of the Union address on January 27, 2011, Obama said that the United States backs Tunisia as a nation "where the will of the people proved more powerful than the writ of a dictator. And tonight, let us be clear: the United States of America stands with the people of Tunisia, and supports the democratic aspirations of all people." On February 11, the day President Hosni Mubarak stepped down, the U.S. president observed, "Egyptians have inspired us, and they have done so by putting the lie to the idea that justice is best gained through violence. . . . We must educate our children to become like young Egyptian people."[4]

Many Arabs remain cautious, nonetheless, of possible future U.S. meddling in their internal affairs. I witnessed that when I went to Tahrir Square on February 18—on the "Friday of Victory"—and spent the day observing the reactions of Egyptians a week after Mubarak's resignation. In one instance, I saw people carrying signs and distributing papers in which there were the words: "We do not want the Americans." Arabs were also questioning why the Obama administration supported a NATO intervention in Libya but not in Yemen and Bahrain—home of the U.S. Navy's Fifth Fleet—two nations in which government clampdown on protesters was brutal. As an Egyptian journalist told me, why should Washington care about the "poor Yemenis" and "upset the Saudis" by strongly criticizing the Bahraini government and Saudi military intervention in the tiny Arab Gulf state. This sense of cautiousness, or fear of American politics, continues in the Arab world, and I have seen it worsening following Osama bin Laden's death and his burial at sea following a U.S. raid in Pakistan on May 1, 2011. (Islamic rituals call for a body to be buried within twenty-four hours, and burial at sea is allowed only in very rare circumstances.) The picture of America among Arabs has further been tarnished after Obama's Middle East speech from the State Department on May 19 of the same year.

Bin Laden's Death and Mideast Speech

It is true that since the Cairo and Jakarta speeches we have begun to see less anti-Americanism and an inching toward better representation of the United States in the social fabric of Arab society, though Arabs remain skeptical of America's policy in the Middle East. Yet the way the Obama administration has handled the story of the death of bin Laden (whom most Arabs resent because of his killing of the innocent), and how the president tackled the Palestinian issue in his State Department speech, as well as the comments he later made at the American Israel Public Affairs Committee (AIPAC), has resonated poorly in the Arab world. Following his speech, and as seen in his conversation with Israeli prime minister Benjamin Netanyahu thereafter, Obama did not stand firm on the right of Palestinians to have an independent state based on the borders before the 1967 Arab-Israeli War in which Israel occupied East Jerusalem, Gaza, and the West Bank. (Obama supported a Palestinian-Israeli peace solution based on the pre-1967 borderline but "with mutually agreed swaps.") After the speech, Netanyahu said Israel could never withdraw to borders that he described as indefensible. This has aroused a new sense of Arab resentment toward Obama—something I have never seen since his assuming the presidency.

The reaction in the Arab world to the State Department speech was muted and icy, with many describing it as ballyhooed and disappointing. Some commentators argued that the speech's goal was to discourage Palestinians from pursuing the resolution for a Palestinian statehood in the United Nations in September. For Arabs, the speech nurtured the Arab Spring but fell flat on setting a formal timetable for advancing Palestinian-Israeli peace talks. They described it as another major speech that will deliver little, particularly on the promise to establish a Palestinian statehood by the September deadline. Yet, I believe Arabs should applaud Obama for approving billions of U.S. dollars in debt relief and loans to help Egypt and Tunisia boost their troubled economies, a step which I am sure the younger Bush and his neoconservative administration would never have approved.

Once again, one must stress that Arabs have often examined speeches by U.S. presidents in terms of the Arab-Israeli conflict. In the speech, Obama warned Palestinians to refrain from pursuing the resolution. "For the Palestinians, efforts to de-legitimize Israel will end in failure. Symbolic actions to isolate Israel at the United Nations in September won't create an independent state." Listen to how this prominent Arab journalist, Soliman Taqi El-Deen, has denounced America's Middle East policy: No U.S. president, including Obama, could ever upset Israel. "The world is changing but America's position toward Israel never does."[5]

Following the death of bin Laden, Obama has opted for a new beginning with the Arab and Muslim world. In his State Department speech, he spoke of how al Qaeda has lost ground and reached a dead end. "Bin Laden and his murderous vision won some adherents," observed Obama. "But even before his death, al Qaeda was losing its struggle for relevance, as the overwhelming majority of people saw that the slaughter of innocents did not answer their cries for a better life."[6] Despite Obama's statement that bin Laden's sea burial was handled in harmony with Islamic tradition, the U.S. decision to bury a body at sea drew admonition from some Muslim clerics. "They can say they buried him at sea, but they cannot say they did it according to Islam," stressed Dubai's Grand Mufti Mohammed Al-Qubaisi. "Sea burials are permissible for Muslims in extraordinary circumstances," he added. "This is not one of them."[7]

Short Note

One must caution that the Arab democratic movements, which have taken the United States by surprise, could also mean the ascendance of Islamism and rise of hardliners in politics. Six months after the Arab world erupted in a political firestorm, there now exists the wrong notion among some American foreign policymakers that the Arab uprisings and revolutions have led to favoritism of America and an American-style democracy among the Arabs. When Egyptians called for a new constitution and a Western-style democracy, I never heard anyone mention American democracy. In fact, many distinguished Egyptian thinkers and foreign policy analysts have favored a parliamentary system of government and a constitution modeled after the French system—not that of the United States. The rather friendly language that I observed rising in the Arab world after the Cairo and Jakarta speeches waned. The view of America from the Arab world still looks grim. Division of opinion of the United States and its policies remain. Despite that, I still see the American dream dancing on the faces and echoed in the language of some Arab youths— though not as strong as it was in the two years following Obama's popular Cairo speech. Only time will tell what the future image of America in the Arab psyche will be because of the heavy burden Obama and any future U.S. president must shoulder after Bush's eight-year rule.

As I noted in the book, Arabs are very passionate people just as their fellow Americans are. At times, they ask me (since I lived in the United States, studied journalism there, and wrote commentaries for the U.S. press) about how I perceive Americans. I tell them that Americans are just as passionate, kind, and friendly as you are. Their country is beautiful and full of good. They love company and have a sense of humor that demands wide imagination. Their life moves much faster than that of yours owing to the integration of advanced technology in every aspect of their lives. As I answer these questions, I see Arabs listening attentively, yet they often ask why Americans "come and occupy our land." An Egyptian woman in her early seventies told me right after bin Laden's death, "Look, son, if Iraq was left alone without America invading it, the Iraqis would have now been doing as their fellow Arabs are: revolting and bringing down Saddam's despotic regime as the Tunisians and Egyptians had done. Many lives would have been saved, and America's image in the Arab world would not have been as appalling as it is today." I found her words very touching and thought provoking, and I now ask myself and my fellow Americans, what if she is right? Who should carry the blame for the deaths of innocent Iraqi women and children? But we also cannot forget those who died in the September 11 terrorist attacks.

In Arab culture, courage demands the recognition of one's faults, and the faults of U.S. policy in the Middle East and those by Arab dictators (whom Washington has often endorsed) have been mammoth—if not altogether ugly. The "ugly American" and "ugly Arab" leaders are the ones to blame for today's wounds in U.S.-Arab relations. As the Arab youth continues its revolt against despotic leaders, Americans and Arabs stand today face to face, not in confrontation this time but in contemplation: Can we trust each other? What is likely to happen if we do or do not? The answers to these questions will all depend on how Washington reacts to the Arab Spring. My advice to U.S. policymakers is to assist but keep a distance, guide but not lead, help but without being driven by a capitalist desire to gain something in return. They should also continue working diligently toward finding a solution to the stalled Middle East peace process—one that ensures the establishment of an independent Palestinian state with East Jerusalem as its capital. America and Americans will then truly be the "friends" of the Arabs, and we will see an inching toward true reconciliation between the state of Israel and the state of Palestine, between Arabs and Israelis—among Muslims, Christians, and Jews—rather than these never-ending carnivals of peace and the thirty-second video clips of handshakes and signatures on dotted lines.

NOTES

1. How It All Began

1. Salwa Mohamed Yehia Al-Awadli, "Image of the United States among University Youth after September 11," *Egyptian Journal of Mass Communication Research* 14 (January–March 2002): 139–82.

2. Narmeen Zakaria Ismail, "The Picture of the United States of America among Egyptian Public" (master's thesis, Cairo University, 2001), 8. [In Arabic.]

3. President Mubarak, who in the past paid an annual trip to Washington, was scheduled to visit the United States on May 25, 2009, but the sudden death of his grandson forced him to cancel his trip. President Obama visited Egypt a week later, on June 4.

4. The margin of error in Egypt and Saudi Arabia was +/- 3.5 percent, and it was +/- 4.1 percent in Jordan, United Arab Emirates, and Lebanon.

5. To see the full results of the 2007 survey, please go to www.aaiusa.org.

6. The margin of error in Saudi Arabia and Morocco was +/- 3.7 percent, in Egypt it was +/- 3.5 percent, in Lebanon it was +/- 4.1 percent, and in Jordan it was +/- 4.7 percent.

7. For the full results of the 2006 survey, please go to www.aaiusa.org.

8. A poll conducted in 2008 by the University of Maryland and Zogby International showed similar results, with eight out of ten Arabs holding unfavorable views of the United States.

9. The poll did not mention how it was conducted or its margin of error. See Shawki Essam, "I Hate Israel and I Am Not in Need of America," *Rose El-Yossef,* April 21, 2007, 39–41. [In Arabic] Furthermore, I would like to stress here that young Egyptians tend to be more accepting than older ones, and hence it can be assumed they have a slightly more favorable attitude than older Egyptians toward America.

10. Eugene Burdick and William Lederer, *The Ugly American* (New York: Norton, 1958).

11. According to Dictionary.com, "ugly American" is a pejorative term for an American traveling or living abroad who remains ignorant of local culture and judges everything by American standards.

2. The Arab Media: A Brief Look

1. Jurgen Habermas, *Structural Transformation of the Public Sphere: An Inquiry into a Category of Bourgeois Society* (Cambridge: Massachusetts Institute of Technology, 1994).

2. Harold Lasswell, "The Structure and Function of Communication in Society," in *The Communication of Ideas*, ed. Lyman Bryson (New York: Cooper Square Publishers, 1948).

3. Gaye Tuchman, *Making News: A Study in the Construction of Reality* (New York: Free Press, 1978), 1.

4. Salama Ahmed Salama, *Press Over a Hot Tinplate* (Cairo: Al-Ain, 2009), 31. [In Arabic.]

5. Freedom House, *Freedom in the World 2008* (Washington, DC: Freedom House, 2008).

6. Lawrence Pintak, "Taking Stock," *Arab Media & Society* (January 2008), http://www.arabmediasociety.com (accessed December 25, 2008).

7. Jon B. Alterman, *New Media, New Politics? From Satellite Television to the Internet in the Arab World*, Policy Paper no. 48 (Washington, DC: Washington Institute for Near East Policy, 1998), 5.

8. Edward Ghareeb, "New Media and the Information Revolution in the Arab World: An Assessment," *Middle East Journal* 54, no. 3 (2000): 396–412.

9. Michael C. Hudson, "'Creative Destruction': Information Technology and the Political Culture Revolution in the Arab World" (revised version of a paper presented at the Conference on Transnationalism, Amman, Jordan, June 19–21, 2001); Jon W. Anderson, "Technology, Media, and the Next Generation in the Middle East" (paper delivered at the Middle East Institute, Columbia University, New York, September 28, 1999).

10. A number of the migrant Arab media have moved their operation centers. For instance, MBC and Orbit have moved from London and Rome to Dubai and Manama respectively. *Al-Hayat*'s London presence has also been diminishing, with some of its bureaus moving to operate from Lebanon and Saudi Arabia.

11. Interview with the Dubai-based Decision Makers TV channel, May 28, 2007.

12. Interview with Decision Makers, June 4, 2007.

13. *Al-Arabi*, July 29, 2007.

14. Al-Oula, December 9, 2007.

15. Pintak, "Taking Stock."

16. Egypt's Radio-Television Union employs some thirty-eight thousand people.

17. See, for example, Hassan Al-Rasheedi, "Money Warfare to Control Satellite TVs and Newspapers," *Al-Akhbar*, August 2, 2007, 9. [In Arabic.]

18. Hussein Y. Amin, "The Arab States Charter for Satellite Television: A Quest for Regulation," *Arab Media & Society* (March 2008), http://www.arabmediasociety.com (accessed January 12, 2009).

19. See Rania Salem and Nehal Balal, "From Dream to Mehwar, O.T.V., Life and C.T.V: Satellite TV Channels are a New Hobby for Businessmen," *Almussawar*, December 7, 2007, 20–21. [In Arabic.]

20. In a press conference given after the Arab Media Ministers meeting in Cairo on July 20, 2007, broadcast on Egypt's Al-Oula TV channel, Egyptian minister of media Annas Al-Fiqi said that in a few years there will be some five hundred satellite TV broadcast channels in the Arab world.

21. See Salem and Balal, "From Dream to Mehwar."

22. See Nua Surveys, "How Many Online," http://www.nua.ie/surveys (accessed June 8, 2002).

3. The American Empire

1. Mohamed Hasseinein Heikel, *The American Empire and Its War on Iraq*, 6th ed. (Cairo: Egyptian Company for Arab and International Publishing, 2006), 243. [In Arabic.]

2. Abdel Moneim Said, *Arabs and September 11* (Cairo: The General Egyptian Book Organization, 2003), 138. [In Arabic.]

3. Ashraf Gharbal, *Rise and Fall of Egyptian-American Relations: Secret Contacts with Abdel Nasser and Sadat* (Cairo: Al-Ahram, 2004). [In Arabic.]

4. Raji Inayet, *America to Where!* (Cairo: Nahdt Misr, 2006), 10. [In Arabic.]

5. Ahmed Thabit and Khalil Al-Anani, *Arabs and the American Imperial Inclination* (Cairo: The General Egyptian Book Organization, 2007). [In Arabic.]

6. Said Al-Lawandi, *The Greater Middle East: An American Conspiracy against Arabs* (Cairo: Nahdt Misr, 2005), 51. [In Arabic.]

7. Ibid., 7.

8. Ibid., 47.

9. Adel S. Bishtami, *Manifest Destiny of Imperial Decline: A History of American Injustice* (Beirut: Arab Institute for Studies and Publication, 2007). [In Arabic.]

10. Mahmoud Al-Saddani, *America Wika* (Cairo: Akhbar El-Yom, 1997), 5. [In Arabic.] *Wika* is a slang Egyptian Arabic word meaning "flamboyant" and "ostentatious."

11. Ibid., 7.

12. Ibid., 9.

13. Nazzar Basheer, *Culture of Blood: Chapters of the History of American Terrorism* (Cairo: Al-Zahra'a for Arab Media, 2003), 10. [In Arabic.]

14. Al-Saddani, *America Wika*, 27.

15. Ibid., 22.

16. Ibid., 23.

17. Ibid., 26.

18. Ibid., 25.

19. Al-Lawandi, *The Greater Middle East*, 30.

20. Attif Al-Ghamri, *Who Rules America: The Hawks Group and Their View of Arabs and Israelis* (Cairo: Al-Maktab Al-Masry Al-Hadith, 2002). [In Arabic.]

21. Heikel, *The American Empire*, 16.

22. Inayet, *America to Where!*, 10.

23. Thabit and Al-Anani, *Arabs and the American Imperial Inclination*, 22.

24. Waheed Abdel Mageed, *America's Wars from Bin Laden to Saddam Hussein* (Cairo: Dar Misr El-Mahrossa, 2003), 27. [In Arabic.]

25. *Al-Khaleej*, March 26, 2007.

26. *Al-Ahram*, October 3, 2007.

27. *Al-Hayat*, October 29, 2007.

28. *Al-Thawara*, November 14, 2007.

29. *Al-Hilal*, February 2005.

30. *Al-Rai*, April 1, 2007.

31. *Al-Ahram*, October 3, 2007.

32. *Al-Thowrah*, June 14, 2007.

33. *Al-Bayan*, January 15, 2008.

34. Al-Jamahiriya, June 16, 2007.

35. *Asharq Al-Awsat*, December 15, 2007.

36. *Al-Ahram*, December 27, 2007.

37. *Al-Hayat*, October 20, 2008.

38. *Al-Ahram*, August 1, 2007.

39. *Al-Hilal*, July 2004.

40. *As-Safir*, October 21, 2008.

41. Al-Jazeera, April 26, 2007.

42. *Al-Hilal*, July 2004.

43. *Al-Hayat*, October 25, 2008.

44. *Rose El-Yossef*, February 16, 2008.

45. *Almussawar*, August 17, 2007.

46. *Al-Ahram*, October 3, 2007.

47. *Al-Ittihad*, March 8, 2008.

48. *Al-Hayat*, November 13, 2007.

49. *Akher Saa*, August 22, 2007.

50. Al-Baghdadia, April 28, 2007.

51. *Weghat Nazar*, October 2007.

52. *Al-Thawara*, January 7, 2007.

53. *Almussawar*, October 26, 2007.

54. *Al-Quds Al-Arabi*, January 21, 2008.

55. *Rose El-Yossef*, July 29, 2006.

56. *October*, September 29, 2007.

57. *Asharq Al-Awsat*, April 1, 2005.

58. *Al-Baath*, December 2, 2008.

59. *Al-Ittihad*, March 8, 2008.

60. *Al-Ahram*, July 14, 2007.

61. Nile News, May 4, 2007.

62. Mohamed Said Ahmed Al-Maceer, *Earthquake of September 11 and Its Intellectual Consequences* (Cairo: Nahdt Misr, 2003), 33. [In Arabic.]

63. Samia Sadeq, *Kidnapping of a President* (Cairo: Arab Cultural Center, 2004). [In Arabic.]

64. *Rose El-Yossef*, June 6, 2007.

65. *Al-Arab Al-Yawm*, March 8, 2007.

66. *Al-Khaleej*, April 13, 2007.

67. *Al-Gomhuria*, September 29, 2007.

68. *Asharq Al-Awsat*, December 25, 2007.

69. Al-Jazeera, April 17, 2007.

70. *Al-Akhbar*, August 1, 2007.

71. *Al-Mawkef Al-Arabi*, September 25, 2007.

72. *Ad-Dustour*, October 31, 2006.

73. *Al-Gomhuria*, June 8, 2007.

74. *Asharq Al-Awsat*, December 3, 2007.

75. *Sabah El-Kheir*, July 7, 2007.

76. *Al-Chourouk*, December 4, 2007.

77. *Al-Hilal*, July 2004.

78. *Al-Nahda*, November 11, 2006.

79. *Al-Wafd*, December 29, 2007.

80. *Sabah El-Kheir*, January 15, 2008.

81. Alarabiya.net, November 15, 2008.

82. Al-Oula, October 13, 2007.

83. *Al-Arab Al-Yawm*, May 29, 2006.

84. *October*, August 5, 2007.

85. *Al-Ittihad*, May 20, 2008.

86. *Al-Gomhuria*, June 16, 2007.

87. *Ad-Dustour*, June 4, 2007.

88. Al-Jazeera, April 26, 2007.

89. *Al-Thawara*, August 29, 2007.

90. *Al-Ahram*, August 1, 2007.

91. *Asharq Al-Awsat*, December 3, 2007.

92. *As-Safir*, January 15, 2008.

93. Al-Jazeera, January 20, 2008.

94. *Al-Shabiba*, January 16, 2008.

95. *Akher Saa*, January 9, 2008.

96. *Tishreen*, January 10, 2008.

97. *Rose El-Yossef*, January 12, 2008.

98. *Al-Watan*, January 15, 2008.

99. *Akhbar Al-Khaleej*, January 10, 2008.

100. *Al-Bayan*, January 12, 2008.

101. *Al-Thawara*, January 11, 2008.

102. *Al-Akhbar*, January 18, 2008.

103. *Al-Watan*, January 12, 2008.

104. *Al-Ahram*, January 22, 2008.

105. *Ad-Dustour*, January 10, 2008.

106. *Al-Bayan*, January 12, 2008.

107. www.annabaa.org, accessed January 10, 2008.

108. *Almussawar*, January 18, 2008.

109. *Sabah El-Kheir*, January 15, 2008.

110. *As-Safir*, January 12, 2008.

111. Al-Iraqiya, January 14, 2008.

112. *Al-Ittihad*, January 24, 2008.

113. *Al-Ittihad*, January 14, 2008.

114. Al-Jazeera, January 20, 2008.

115. Al-Sharqiya, January 9, 2008.

116. *Al-Ahram*, January 18, 2008.

117. *Al-Quds Al-Arabi*, January 20, 2008.

118. *As-Safir*, January 19, 2008.

119. Nahed Hatr, *Iraqi Resistance and Crisis of American Imperial Project* (Cairo: Merit, 2004), 43. [In Arabic.]

120. Hatr, *Iraqi Resistance*, 128.

121. Galal Amin, *Age of Defaming Arabs and Muslims: We and the World after 11 September 2001* (Cairo: Dar El-Shorouk, 2004). [In Arabic.]

122. Al-Lawandi, *The Greater Middle East*, 49.

123. Ibid., 27, 49.

124. Rida Hilal, ed., *The American Empire: Pages from the Past and the Present* (Cairo: Al-Shorouk International, 2002). [In Arabic.]

125. Al-Maceer, *Earthquake of September 11*, 35.

126. Heikel, *The American Empire*, 39.

127. *Al-Ahram*, June 8, 2007.

128. *Sabah El-Kheir*, April 10, 2007.

129. Sout Al-Arab, April 7, 2007.

130. *Al-Hilal*, June 2005.

131. Bahaa Taher, *Sunset Oasis*, 3rd ed. (Cairo: Dar El-Shorouk, 2007). [In Arabic.] The novel has also been translated into English.

132. *Sabah El-Kheir*, May 15, 2007.

133. *Weghat Nazar*, September 2003.

134. *Al-Ittihad*, February 26, 2004.

135. *Akhbar Al-Khaleej*, January 14, 2008.

136. Al-Jazeera, April 26, 2007.

137. Jordan TV, June 11, 2007.

138. *Asharq Al-Awsat*, October 29, 2007.

139. *Al-Quds Al-Arabi*, January 5, 2008.

140. Nile News, August 9, 2007.

141. The party upholds liberal nationalist politics representing the upper strata of Egyptian society.

142. Al-Oula, June 17, 2007.

143. *Al-Osboa*, December 29, 2007.

144. *Akhbar Al-Khaleej*, January 11, 2008.

145. *Al-Hayat*, October 7, 2008.

146. *Al-Ittihad*, February 26, 2004.

147. *Al-Qabas*, November 10, 2006.

148. *Al-Bayan*, January 4, 2008.

149. *Al-Gomhuria*, November 24, 2007.

150. *Al-Wafd*, August 1, 2007.

151. *As-Safir*, January 15, 2008.

152. *Al-Ahram*, August 1, 2007.

153. *Al-Bayan*, January 14, 2008.

154. *Al-Gomhuria*, June 14, 2007.

155. *Al-Ahram*, July 31, 2006.

156. *Al-Masry Al-Youm*, April 11, 2007.

157. *Al-Thawara*, January 19, 2007.

158. Nile News, May 4, 2007.

159. Al-Oula, June 17, 2007.

160. *Al-Hilal*, July 2004.

161. *Al-Masry Al-Youm*, October 11, 2007.

162. *Akhbar Al-Khaleej*, June 5, 2007.

163. *October*, August 5, 2007.

164. *Sabah El-Kheir*, October 30, 2007.

165. *Al-Ahram*, December 27, 2007.

166. Al-Oula, June 20, 2007.

167. Jamahiriya, June 16, 2007.

168. Future, May 21, 2007.

169. Al-Lawandi, *The Greater Middle East*, 51.

170. Hilal, *The American Empire*.

171. Thabit and Al-Anani, *Arabs and the American Imperial Inclination*.

172. *Al-Hayat*, August 15, 2006.

173. *Akhbar Al-Khaleej*, January 12, 2008.

174. *Ad-Dustour*, November 16, 2006.

175. *Al-Bayan*, January 14, 2008.

176. Zaki Naguib Mahmoud, *Days in America*, 2nd ed. (1955; repr., Cairo: Angelo, 1957), 7. [In Arabic.]

177. Ibid., 277.

178. Ibid., 19.

179. Mustapha Amin, *The Laughing America* (Cairo: Akhbar El-Yom, 1996), 181. [In Arabic.]

180. Fouad Zakaria, *Arabs and the American Model* (Cairo: Egyptian Library, 1991), 41. [In Arabic.]

181. Mustapha Mahmoud, *The American Civilization* (Cairo: Al-Ghad Publishing, 1995). [In Arabic.]

182. Bassem Khafagi, *The American Personality* (Riyadh: Center for Humanities Studies, 2005), 90. [In Arabic.]

183. Ibid.

184. Al-Ghamri, *Who Rules America*, 7.

185. Al-Ghamri, *Who Rules America*, 8.

186. Khafagi, *The American Personality*, 18.

187. Khafagi, *The American Personality*, 56.

188. Al-Ghamri, *Who Rules America*, 7.

189. Al-Ghamri, *Who Rules America*, 218.

190. Khafagi, *The American Personality*, 92.

191. Nile News, August 9, 2007.

192. *Asharq Al-Awsat*, March 1, 2007.

193. *Almussawar*, August 3, 2007.

194. *Al-Arabi*, November 14, 2006.

195. *Al-Ahram*, April 5, 2007.

196. *Rose El-Yossef*, January 12, 2007.

197. www.annabaa.org, accessed January 8, 2008.

198. Al-Jamahiriya, June 16, 2007.

199. *Al-Masry Al-Youm*, April 5, 2007.

200. *Al-Hilal*, July 2004.

201. *Al-Ittihad*, October 6, 2008.

4. American Policy in the Middle East

1. Zakaria, *Arabs and the American Model*, 44.

2. Hatr, *Iraqi Resistance*, 42.

3. Al-Ghamri, *Who Rules America*.

4. *Al-Ahram*, August 7, 2006.

5. Robert Fisk, "Mohamed Hasseinein Heikel: The Wise Man of the Middle East," *The Independent*, April 9, 2007, http://news.independent.co.uk/world/fisk/article2434980.ece (accessed April 28, 2007).

6. Al-Jazeera, April 26, 2007.

7. Nile News, May 13, 2007.

8. *Al-Ahram*, July 31, 2006.

9. Sudan, May 17, 2007.

10. Nile News, May 4, 2007.

11. Al-Jamahiriya, August 1, 2007.

12. *Asharq Al-Awsat*, September 16, 2007.

13. *As-Sabeel*, January 20, 2007.

14. *Almussawar*, September 21, 2007.

15. *Rose El-Yossef*, July 29, 2006.

16. Al-Lawandi, *The Greater Middle East*, 28.

17. Ibid., 5–6.

18. Ibid., 16.

19. Thabit and Al-Anani, *Arabs and the American Imperial Inclination*.

20. Ibid.

21. Ibid.

22. Hatr, *Iraqi Resistance*, 286–87.

23. Edward Said, *Orientalism* (New York: Vintage, 1979).

24. *Asharq Al-Awsat*, July 31, 2006.

25. *Al-Ahram*, August 16, 2006.

26. *Al-Ahram*, August 7, 2006.

27. Quoted in Anwar Elshamy, "Annual Doha Dialogue of Islamic Sects Urged," *Gulf Times*, January 22, 2007, www.gulf-times.com (accessed January 28, 2007).

28. *Al-Ahram*, August 1, 2007.

29. *Akhbar Al-Khaleej*, June 5, 2007.

30. *Ad-Dustour*, November 16, 2006.

31. *Al-Ahram*, November 26, 2007.

32. Al-Jazeera, January 20, 2008.

33. *Akher Saa*, August 1, 2007.

34. Aljazeera.net, April 11, 2006.

35. *Akher Saa*, August 1, 2007.

36. *October*, August 5, 2007.

37. *Asharq Al-Awsat*, August 16, 2006.

38. *Al-Qabas*, January 12, 2008.

39. Inayet, *America to Where!*, 105.

40. Ibid., 119.

41. Abdullah Mohamed Al-Nasser, *America: The Armed Mentality* (Beirut: Dar Riyadh Al-Reece, 2007). [In Arabic.]

42. Al-Lawandi, *The Greater Middle East*, 8–9.

43. Galal Amin, *Egypt and Egyptians in the Mubarak Era (1980–2008)* (Cairo: Merit, 2009). [In Arabic.]

44. Mustapha Bakri, *Creative or Destructive Chaos: Egypt in America's Target* (Cairo: El-Shorouk International, 2005), 16. [In Arabic.]

45. *Al-Gomhuria*, June 14, 2007.

46. *Asharq Al-Awsat*, January 28, 2007.

47. Al-Jazeera, July 4, 2007.

48. *Al-Khaleej*, April 23, 2007.

49. Al-Oula, August 4, 2007.

50. *Ad-Dustour*, October 13, 2006.

51. *Al-Watan*, January 12, 2008.

52. Abu Dhabi, June 2, 2007.

53. *The Diplomat*, August 2007.

54. *Al-Osboa*, September 29, 2007.

55. *Al-Hilal*, July 2004.

56. *Al-Ittihad*, April 17, 2007.

57. Lebanon, June 3, 2007.

58. *Al-Gomhuria*, November 23, 2007.

59. *Al-Khaleej*, June 5, 2007.

60. *As-Safir*, January 12, 2008.

61. Al-Jamahiriya, June 16, 2007.

62. *Al-Akhbar*, January 18, 2008.

63. Ein, June 21, 2007.

64. Al-Adala, June 3, 2007.

65. Al-Jamahiriya, June 16, 2007.

66. Al-Jazeera, July 13, 2007.

67. *Al-Qabas*, November 10, 2006.

68. Al-Jazeera, April 26, 2007.

69. *Akher Saa*, August 1, 2007.

70. *Al-Hayat*, April 8, 2008.

71. *Al-Shabiba*, January 13, 2008.

72. Sudan, May 17, 2007.

73. *Al-Gomhuria*, September 29, 2007.

74. Al-Arabiya, October 4, 2005.

75. Al-Manar, May 4, 2007.

76. *Al-Bayan*, January 15, 2008.

77. Nile News. August 9, 2007.

78. *Al-Bayan*, January 14, 2008.

79. Al-Jazeera, November 30, 2007.

80. *Al-Masry Al-Youm*, December 1, 2007.

81. *Al-Gomhuria*, November 23, 2007.

82. *Al-Khaleej*, April 24, 2007.

83. *Al-Gomhuria*, November 23, 2007.

84. *Al-Gomhuria*, June 15, 2007.

85. Abdel Aziz Hammouda, *The American Dream* (Cairo: The General Egyptian Book Organization, 2002), 10. [In Arabic.]

86. Mageed, *America's Wars*, 146.

87. Fateen Ahmed Fareed Ali, *American-Egyptian Relations: Second Part from 23 November 1963 to 28 September 1970* (Cairo: Police Printing, 2002). [In Arabic.]

88. Al-Ghamri, *Who Rules America*, 51.

89. Zakaria, *Arabs and the American Model*.

90. Gharbal, *Rise and Fall of Egyptian-American Relations*, 176.

91. Heikel, *The American Empire*, 25.

92. *Al-Rayah*, January 10, 2008.

93. *As-Safir*, January 15, 2008.

94. *Akher Saa*, August 1, 2007.

95. *Al-Ahram*, July 25, 2007.

96. *Al-Baath*, January 10, 2008.

97. *Arab Affairs*, Fall 2007.

98. *Al-Rayah*, January 9, 2008.

99. *Akhbar Al-Khaleej*, January 11, 2008.

100. *As-Safir*, January 19, 2008.

101. *Al-Arabi*, July 2, 2007.

102. *October*, September 30, 2007.

103. Al-Oula, February 13, 2008.

104. *Al-Massa*, April 19, 2007.

105. Al-Jazeera Mubasher, June 11, 2007.

106. *Al-Hayat*, April 8, 2008.

107. *Akhbar Al-Khaleej*, June 5, 2007.

108. Al-Arabiya, January 24, 2008.

109. *Al-Watan*, January 15, 2008.

110. Al-Jazeera, April 26, 2007.

111. *El-Dostour*, May 9, 2007.

112. Al-Adala, June 3, 2007.

113. Al-Adala, April 30, 2007.

114. Al-Sharqiya, June 5, 2007.

115. Al-Manar, May 12, 2007.

116. Al-Jazeera, June 7, 2007.

117. *Asharq Al-Awsat*, January 18, 2008.

118. *Al-Ahram*, October 28, 2007.

119. Al-Sharja, July 12, 2007.

120. Future, June 21, 2007.

121. Jordan, June 11, 2007.

122. Al-Jazeera, May 29, 2007.

123. *Al-Ittihad*, June 28, 2008.

124. *Al-Arab Al-Yawm*, June 2, 2007.

125. Al-Arabiya, January 24, 2008.

126. *Arab Affairs*, Spring 2007.

127. Mustapha Al-Fiqi, *Renewal of National Thought* (Cairo: The General Egyptian Book Organization, 1996), 61. [In Arabic.]

128. Arab Thought Forum, *Arab Speech: Content and Style* (Amman: Almuntada, 2003). [In Arabic.]

129. *Al-Gomhuria*, September 29, 2007.

130. Radio Cairo, July 20, 2007.

131. *October*, August 5, 2007.

132. Al-Manar, June 17, 2007.

133. Al-Sharqiya, June 5, 2007.

134. Al-Sharja, July 4, 2007.

135. Al-Oula, June 20, 2007.

136. Oman, June 18, 2007.

137. *Al-Watan*, January 12, 2008.

138. Al-Sharja, July 12, 2007.

139. Al-Hiwar, May 12, 2007.

140. Nile News, May 4, 2007.

141. *Rose El-Yossef*, December 1, 2007.

142. *Al-Ayyam*, April 21, 2007.

143. *Ad-Dustour*, January 10, 2008.

144. *Al-Sabah*, March 26, 2005.

145. *Al-Osboa*, September 29, 2007.

146. Al-Manar, May 4, 2007.

147. *Akhbar Al-Khaleej*, June 5, 2007.

148. LBC, December 24, 2007.

149. *Al-Ayam*, June 2, 2007.

150. Bahaa Taher, *Love in Exile* (Cairo: Dar Al-Hilal, 1995). [In Arabic.]

151. *Akhbar Al-Khaleej*, June 5, 2007.

152. *Al-Thowrah*, November 28, 2006.

153. Oman, May 30, 2007.

154. *Akhbar Al-Khaleej*, June 5, 2007.

155. Al-Manar, July 13, 2007.

156. Syria, June 5, 2007.

157. Al-Jazeera Mubasher, June 11, 2007.

158. Al-Adala, June 3, 2007.

159. Future, July 12, 2007.

160. Al-Adala, June 21, 2007.

161. Oman, May 30, 2007.

162. Syria, June 5, 2007.

163. *Al-Hayat*, August 15, 2006.

164. *Akhbar Al-Khaleej*, June 5, 2007.

165. Al-Nasser, *America*.

166. *Arab Affairs*, Spring 2007.

167. Al-Baghdadia, June 21, 2007.

168. Jordan, June 11, 2007.

169. Goebbels said: "The lie can be maintained only for such time as the State can shield the people from the political, economic, and/or military consequences of the lie. It thus becomes vitally important for the State to use all of its powers to repress dissent, for the truth is the mortal enemy of the lie, and thus by extension, the truth is the greatest enemy of the State." For more on the propaganda techniques used by Goebbels, see Robert McChesney, "Springtime for Goebbels," *Z Magazine,* December 1997, http://www.zmag.org/Zmag/articles/dec97Mcchesne.htm (accessed 30 April 2004).

170. Al-Jazeera, April 17, 2007.

171. Al-Mehwer, May 9, 2007.

172. Al-Jazeera, May 29, 2007.

173. Al-Baghdadia, June 21, 2007.

174. Abu Dhabi, June 19, 2007.

175. Sout Al-Arab, September 8, 2007.

176. Al-Sharqiya, May 5, 2007.

177. Al-Jazeera, May 11, 2007.

178. *Al-Khaleej*, June 5, 2007.

179. Al-Jazeera, May 29, 2007.

180. Jordan, June 11, 2007.

181. *Akhbar Al-Khaleej*, June 5, 2007.

182. *Al-Massa*, April 19, 2007.

183. *October*, August 5, 2007.

184. *Al-Gomhuria*, September 19, 2007.

185. *Almussawar*, September 21, 2007.

186. Jordan, June 11, 2007.

187. Al-Jazeera Mubasher, June 11, 2007.

188. Al-Sumaria, June 18, 2007.

189. *Al-Shabiba*, January 13, 2008.

190. *Al-Osboa*, September 29, 2007.

191. *Al-Khaleej*, April 23, 2007.

192. Al-Sumaria, June 18, 2007.

193. *Al-Riad*, January 25, 2008.

194. *Akher Saa*, July 18, 2007.

195. Al-Jazeera, April 26, 2007.

196. *Al-Ahram*, November 6, 2007.

197. *As-Safir*, January 15, 2008.

198. *October*, August 5, 2007.

199. *Al-Khaleej*, April 23, 2007.

200. *Akhbar Al-Khaleej*, June 5, 2007.

201. *Al-Shabiba*, January 13, 2008.

202. *Al-Gomhuria*, September 29, 2007.

203. *Al-Thowrah*, January 12, 2007.

204. Hatr, *Iraqi Resistance*.

205. Mohamed Hasseinein Heikel, *The American Age: From New York to Kabul* (Cairo: Egyptian Company for Arab and International Publishing, 2002), 184. [In Arabic.]

206. *Al-Ahram*, December 27, 2007.

207. *Al-Gomhuria*, December 27, 2007.

208. *October*, September 30, 2007.

209. Al-Sharja, July 12, 2007.

210. *Al-Khaleej*, June 5, 2007.

211. *Al-Masry Al-Youm*, September 22, 2007.

212. Al-Mehwer, May 9, 2007.

213. Future, June 21, 2007.

214. Al-Sharqiya, May 5, 2007.

215. *Al-Arab Al-Yawm*, March 19, 2007.

216. *Al-Hilal*, July 2004.

217. *Al-Ahram*, August 1, 2006.

218. *October*, July 29, 2007.

219. *Al-Thawara*, January 7, 2007.

220. *Rose El-Yossef*, June 30, 2007.

221. *Al-Arab Al-Yawm*, March 13, 2007.

222. *Asharq Al-Awsat*, October 20, 2007.

223. *Almussawar*, September 21, 2007.

224. *October*, September 16, 2007.

225. *Al-Ittihad*, March 8, 2008.

226. *October*, July 29, 2007.

227. *Asharq Al-Awsat*, January 15, 2008.

228. *Al-Sabah*, January 13, 2008.

229. *Al-Arab Al-Yawm*, March 2, 2007.

230. *Al-Wafd*, December 29, 2007.

231. *Al-Ittihad*, January 14, 2008.

232. *Akhbar Al-Khaleej*, June 5, 2007.

233. *Akher Saa*, July 18, 2007.

234. Al-Adala, June 3, 2007.

235. *Al-Hayat*, December 27, 2007.

236. Al-Sharqiya, May 5, 2007.

237. *Almussawar*, October 5, 2007.

238. *Al-Khaleej*, April 2, 2007.

239. *Al-Masry Al-Youm*, April 11, 2007.

240. *Asharq Al-Awsat*, January 15, 2008.

241. Al-Jazeera, January 20, 2008.

242. *October*, July 29, 2007.

243. Al-Arabiya, January 24, 2008.

244. Future, August 13, 2007.

245. *Almussawar*, October 5, 2007.

246. Nile News, July 31, 2007.

247. *Al-Afkar*, January 14, 2008.

248. *Almussawar*, September 21, 2007.

249. *Rose El-Yossef*, December 1, 2007.

250. *October*, September 16, 2007.

251. Nile News, May 4, 2007.

252. Nile News, June 2, 2007.

253. *Al-Riyadh*, January 12, 2008.

254. *Arab Affairs*, Spring 2007.

255. Jordan, June 11, 2007.

256. Jordan, June 11, 2007.

257. *Al-Arabi*, July 29, 2007.

258. *Almussawar*, September 21, 2007.

5. Questioning American Democracy

1. Amin, *The Laughing America*.

2. Mahmoud, *Days in America*, 253.

3. *Al-Hilal*, August 1964.

4. Cited in Mona Shaheen, *Street of the Press* (Cairo: Akhbar El-Yom, 1978), 140. [In Arabic.]

5. Shaheen, *Street of the Press*, 116.

6. Al-Saddani, *America Wika*, 8.

7. Khafagi, *The American Personality*, 68.

8. Ibid., 71.

9. Amin, *The Laughing America*, 13.

10. Al-Ghamri, *Who Rules America*.

11. Amin, *The Laughing America*, 15.

12. Hatr, *Iraqi Resistance*, 317.

13. Inayet, *America to Where!*, 25.

14. Zakaria, *Arabs and the American Model*, 5.

15. Ibid., 6.

16. Ibid., 8.

17. Ibid., 85.

18. Thabit and Al-Anani, *Arabs and the American Imperial Inclination*, 101.

19. Salaheddine Hafez, *Forbidding Politics and Criminalizing Journalism* (Cairo: Dar El-Shorouk, 2008). [In Arabic.]

20. Al-Lawandi, *The Greater Middle East*, 10.

21. Gharbal, *Rise and Fall of Egyptian-American Relations*, 156.

22. Basheer, *Culture of Blood*.

23. Inayet, *America to Where!*, 103.

24. *Al-Ahram*, January 11, 2008.

25. *Al-Arab Al-Yawm*, May 28, 2007.

26. *Al-Ahram*, July 29, 2007.

27. *Al-Qabas*, November 10, 2006.

28. *Al-Hayat*, December 29, 2007.

29. *As-Safir*, January 15, 2008.

30. *Al-Arabi*, November 14, 2006.

31. *Al-Ittihad*, February 26, 2004.

32. *Al-Gomhuria*, November 24, 2007.

33. *Akhbar Al-Khaleej*, June 5, 2007.

34. *October*, July 29, 2007.

35. *Sabah El-Kheir*, August 4, 2007.

36. *Sabah El-Kheir*, May 15, 2007.

37. *Al-Watan*, January 12, 2008.

38. *Al-Ittihad*, April 8, 2007.

39. *As-Sabeel*, January 20, 2007.

40. Al-Nasser, *America.*

41. *Al-Arab Al-Yawm*, March 8, 2007.

42. *Al-Hayat*, July 17, 2006.

43. Islamonline.net, December 2, 2007.

44. *Rose El-Yossef,* February16, 2008.

45. *Nahdt Misr*, December 8, 2007.

46. *Tishreen*, January 15, 2008.

47. Al-Jazeera, June 7, 2007.

48. *Al-Hayat*, April 8, 2008.

49. *Al-Ittihad*, September 25, 2003.

50. *Al-Watan*, January 25, 2008.

51. *Akhbar Al-Khaleej*, April 18, 2007.

52. *Al-Masry Al-Youm*, April 11, 2007.

53. ANB, May 29, 2007.

54. *Al-Thowrah*, June 14, 2007.

55. *Al-Bayan*, January 15, 2008.

56. *Al-Rai*, September 12, 2008.

57. *Al-Osboa*, September 29, 2007.

58. *Al-Gomhuria*, September 29, 2007.

59. *Al-Arab Al-Yawm*, May 31, 2006.

60. Nile News, February 9, 2008.

61. *Al-Thowrah*, January 29, 2007.

62. *Al-Ahram*, August 1, 2007.

63. *Sabah El-Kheir*, August 4, 2007.

64. *Al-Ittihad*, April 8, 2007.

65. *Al-Qabas*, January 12, 2008.

66. *Al-Quds Al-Arabi*, January 5, 2008.

67. *Al-Ahram*, June 8, 2007.

68. *Akher Saa*, July 18, 2007.

69. *Asharq Al-Awsat*, December 3, 2007.

70. Al-Oula, June 17, 2007.

71. *Asharq Al-Awsat*, July 22, 2007.

72. *Al-Ayam*, January 12, 2008.

73. Al-Oula, June 17, 2007.

74. Al-Jamahiriya, June 16, 2007.

75. *Al-Ahram*, January 18, 2008.

76. *Al-Sahwa*, April 21, 2007.

77. Khafagi, *The American Personality*, 87.

78. Al-Maceer, *Earthquake of September 11*, 28.

79. Zakaria, *Arabs and the American Model*, 19.

80. Mohamed Basyouni and Yaser Hussein, *Holy Wars: America and Zionist Christianity* (Cairo: El-Boroug, 2006). [In Arabic.]

81. Al-Saddani, *America Wika*, 7.

82. Heikel, *The American Empire*, 19.

83. Al-Jazeera, June 6, 2007.

84. *Asharq Al-Awsat*, October 20, 2007.

85. Al-sahwa-yemen.net, April 25, 2007.

86. *Al-Ahram*, February 1, 2008.

87. *Al-Masry Al-Youm*, October 11, 2007.

88. Al-Oula, June 17, 2007.

89. *Al-Qabas*, November 10, 2006.

90. *Al-Arai*, April 21, 2007.

91. *Al-Ittihad*, April 5, 2007.

92. *Rose El-Yossef*, March 31, 2007.

93. Lebanon, May 5, 2007.

94. *Rose El-Yossef*, July 29, 2006.

95. Al-Jazeera, May 29, 2007.

96. Hatr, *Iraqi Resistance*, 93.

97. *Al-Gomhuria*, June 14, 2007.

98. *Rose El-Yossef*, July 29, 2006.

99. Al-Oula, June 17, 2007.

100. *Al-Bayan*, January 15, 2008.

101. *Rose El-Yossef*, March 31, 2007.

102. Al-Jazeera, June 7, 2007.

103. *El-Dostour*, June 6, 2007.

104. Al-Arabiya, January 21, 2008.

105. Al-Jazeera, July 12, 2007.

106. Al-Oula, June 17, 2007.

107. Alarabiya.net, March 20, 2008. It is worth noting that American officials later apologized and denied any prior knowledge of the atrocities committed at the Iraqi prison.

6. The Land of Dreams

1. Al-Ghamri, *Who Rules America*, 10.

2. Hammouda, *The American Dream*, 10.

3. Al-Saddani, *America Wika*, 8.

4. Heikel, *The American Age*, 25.

5. Heikel, *The American Age*, 37.

6. Ibid., 5.

7. Hammouda, *The American Dream*, 126.

8. Ibid.,125.

9. Ibid.,125.

10. Amin, *The Laughing America*, 5.

11. Ibid.,14.

12. Ibid.,15.

13. Ibid.,16.

14. Hammouda, *The American Dream*, 14.

15. Ibid., 17.

16. *Asharq Al-Awsat*, March 18, 2007.

17. *Al-Doha*, April 2008.

18. Ibid.

19. A Sa'edi is an inhabitant of the southern part of Egypt with a heavy Arabic accent.

20. For more on this, see *Al-Doha*, April 2008.

21. Al-Lawandi, *The Greater Middle East*.

22. Al-Saddani, *America Wika*, 8.

23. Basheer, *Culture of Blood*, 7.

24. *October*, October 29, 2007.

25. *Rose El-Yossef*, March 31, 2007.

26. *Al-Akhbar*, December 31, 2007.

27. Hilal, *The American Empire*.

28. Al-Ghamri, *Who Rules America*, 86.

29. Mageed, *America's Wars*, 7–8.

30. Ibrahim Nafie, *The September Explosion: Between Globalization and Americanization* (Cairo: The General Egyptian Book Organization, 2002), 17. [In Arabic.]

31. Heikel, *The American Empire*, 35.

32. Ahmed Al-Mossali, *American Foreign Policy and Islamic Politics* (Cairo: Dar El-Thakafa, 2006), 15. [In Arabic.]

33. Arab Thought Forum, *Arab Speech*, 117.

34. Said, *Arabs and September 11*, 36.

35. Mageed, *America's Wars*.

36. Al-Lawandi, *The Greater Middle East*, 7.

37. Said, *Arabs and September 11*, 14.

38. Al-Ghamri, *Who Rules America*, 273.

39. Al-Ghamri, *Who Rules America*, 101.

40. *Al-Masry Al-Youm*, September 11, 2007.

41. Sout Al-Arab, September 8, 2007.

42. *Ad-Dustour*, April 18, 2007.

43. *October*, September 16, 2007.

44. *Rose El-Yossef*, July 29, 2006.

45. *Al-Ahram*, August 1, 2007.

46. *Al-Hayat*, April 6, 2008.

47. *Al-Thowrah*, January 19, 2007.

48. *Asharq Al-Awsat*, December 10, 2007.

49. *Al-Bayan*, September 11, 2008.

50. *Al-Ahram*, September 25, 2008.

51. *Almussawar*, August 17, 2007.

52. *Al-Hayat*, February 21, 2008.

53. *Al-Gomhuria*, June 16, 2007.

54. *Rose El-Yossef*, July 7, 2007.

55. Nile News, September 11, 2007.

56. *Al-Arabi*, November 14, 2006.

57. Al-Arabiya, June 6, 2007.

58. Al-Jamahiriya, June 16, 2007.

59. *Rose El-Yossef*, August 11, 2007.

60. *Asharq Al-Awsat*, October 3, 2008.

61. *Almussawar*, August 10, 2007.

62. Sout Al-Arab, September 12, 2007.

63. Mahmoud, *Days in America*.

64. Khaled Abu Bakr, *War of Breaking Will: Between Resistance and the American-Zionist Project* (Beirut: Arab Scientific Publisher, 2007), 7. [In Arabic.]

65. See Samuel P. Huntington, *The Clash of Civilizations and the Remaking of World Order* (New York: Simon and Schuster, 1996).

66. Samuel P. Huntington, "The Clash of Civilizations?" *Foreign Affairs* 72, no. 3 (Summer 1993): 22–39.

67. Arab Thought Forum, *Arab Speech*, 27.

68. Al-Ghamri, *Who Rules America*.

69. Nafie, *The September Explosion*, 17.

70. Al-Maceer, *Earthquake of September 11*, 5.

71. Basyouni and Hussein, *Holy Wars*, 11.

72. Al-Mossali, *American Foreign Policy*, 104.

73. Arab Thought Forum, *Arab Speech*, 274.

74. Al-Maceer, *Earthquake of September 11*, 4.

75. Ibid., 5.

76. Hafez, *Forbidding Politics*.

77. Amin, *Age of Defaming Arabs and Muslims*, 19.

78. Ibid., 28.

79. Bernard Lewis, *The Crisis of Islam: Holy War and Unholy Terror* (London: Weidenfeld and Nicolson, 2003).

80. Amin, *Age of Defaming Arabs and Muslims*, 75–76.

81. Ibid., 134.

82. Arab Thought Forum, *Arab Speech*, 38.

83. Basheer, *Culture of Blood*, 25.

84. Ibid., 11.

85. *Al-Arab Al-Yawm*, May 28, 2007.

86. *Arab Affairs*, Spring 2007.

87. *Al-Ahali*, February 28, 2007.

88. *Al-Hilal*, November 1998.

89. *Al-Hilal*, November 2005.

90. *Al-Waei*, June 18, 2006.

91. See Aljazeera.net, April 11, 2006.

92. *Al-Masry Al-Youm*, October 26, 2007.

93. *Arab Affairs*, Fall 2007.

94. *Ad-Dustour*, June 4, 2007.

95. *As-Safir*, January 15, 2008.

96. *Al-Masry Al-Youm*, July 27, 2007.

97. *As-Safir*, January 15, 2008.

98. *Al-Ayam*, April 21, 2007.

99. *Al-Rai*, April 21, 2007.

100. *Al-Ahram*, December 24, 2007.

101. *Al-Arab Al-Yawm*, March 19, 2007.

102. *Rose El-Yossef*, July 29, 2006.

103. *Al-Hilal*, July 2004.

104. *Al-Khaleej*, April 24, 2007.

105. *Al-Masry Al-Youm*, September 11, 2007.

106. *Al-Ahali*, February 28, 2007. Al-Shayeb is referring to Francis Fukuyama, *End of History and the Last Man* (New York: Penguin, 1992).

107. *Ad-Dustour*, August 2, 2006.

108. *Ad-Dustour*, August 8, 2006.

109. *Al-Ittihad*, March 28, 2008.

110. *Rose El-Yossef*, September 15, 2007.

111. For more on this, see *Al-Ahali*, December 12, 2007.

112. *Al-Ittihad*, April 20, 2007.

113. *Al-Wafd*, December 22, 2007.

114. *October,* July 29, 2007.

115. Nile News, 9 August 2007.

116. Almotomar.net, January 12, 2008.

117. *Al-Hilal,* July 2004.

118. *Al-Hayat,* April 7, 2008.

119. Arab Thought Forum, *Arab Speech.*

120. Heikel, *The American Age,* 184.

121. Amin, *Age of Defaming Arabs and Muslims.*

122. Inayet, *America to Where!.*

123. *Asharq Al-Awsat,* January 13, 2008.

124. *Al-Bayan,* September 8, 2008.

125. *Al-Hayat,* January 28, 2008.

126. *Al-Arabi,* November 14, 2006.

127. *Sabah El-Kheir,* March 8, 2005.

128. *Al-Quds Al-Arabi,* January 5, 2008.

129. *Al-Khaleej,* April 13, 2007.

130. *As-Safir,* September 2, 2008.

131. *Al-Hayat,* April 8, 2008.

132. *Al-Bayan,* January 14, 2008.

133. *Al-Hilal,* July 2004.

134. *Akher Saa,* August 22, 2007.

7. What Do Arabs Want from Obama?

1. *Al-Qabas,* November 6, 2008.

2. *Al-Ahram,* November 7, 2008.

3. *Al-Ahram,* November 12, 2008.

4. *Ad-Dustour,* November 6, 2008.

5. *Al-Ittihad,* November 10, 2008.

6. There are two newspapers carrying the same *Al-Watan* name; one is Omani and the other is Qatari.

7. *Al-Watan,* November 6, 2008.

8. *Al-Iktisadia,* November 10, 2008.

9. *Al-Ahram*, November 7, 2008.

10. *Al-Watan*, January 22, 2009.

11. *Ad-Dustour*, November 8, 2008.

12. *Al-Thawara*, November 6, 2008.

13. *Al-Watan*, January 22, 2009.

14. *Ad-Dustour*, November 6, 2008.

15. Three newspapers from three different countries have similar titles. They are the Yemeni *Al-Ayam*, Bahraini *Al-Ayam*, and Palestinian *Al-Ayyam*. To avoid confusion I define each paper's ownership throughout the chapter.

16. *Al-Ayam*, January 6, 2009.

17. *Asharq Al-Awsat*, November 6, 2008.

18. *Alnilin*, November 6, 2008.

19. *Al-Masaa*, January 22, 2009.

20. *Al-Ahram*, November 6, 2008.

21. *Attajdid*, January 22, 2009.

22. *Al-Bayan*, February 1, 2009.

23. *Alnilin*, November 6, 2008.

24. *Al-Ittihad*, November 10, 2008.

25. *Al-Anwar*, January 22, 2009.

26. *Al-Ayyam*, January 24, 2009.

27. *Ad-Dustour*, January 26, 2009.

28. *Al-Watan*, January 22, 2009.

29. *Al-Ahram*, November 5, 2008.

30. *Al-Baath*, November 11, 2008.

31. *Al-Baath*, January 27, 2009.

32. *Ad-Dustour*, November 9, 2008.

33. *Ad-Dustour*, January 26, 2009.

34. *Al-Watan*, November 6, 2008.

35. *Asharq Al-Awsat*, November 7, 2008.

36. *Al-Watan*, November 6, 2008.

37. *Al-Baath*, January 28, 2008.

38. *Asharq Al-Awsat*, November 6, 2008.

39. *Asharq Al-Awsat*, November 7, 2008.

40. *Al-Hayat*, January 22, 2009.

41. *Al-Baath*, November 9, 2009.

42. *Al-Watan*, November 6, 2008.

43. *Ad-Dustour*, November 8, 2008.

44. *Asharq Al-Awsat*, November 7, 2008.

45. *Al-Watan*, January 22, 2009.

46. *Asharq Al-Awsat*, January 23, 2009.

47. *Al-Baath*, November 6, 2008.

48. *As-Safir*, January 26, 2009.

49. *Al-Ayam*, November 9, 2008.

50. *Al-Watan*, November 6, 2008.

51. *Alnilin*, November 6, 2008.

52. *Al-Hayat*, January 28, 2009.

53. *Alnilin*, January 21, 2009.

54. *Al-Jazira*, November 1, 2008.

55. *Ad-Dustour*, November 6, 2008.

56. *Al-Watan*, January 22, 2009.

57. *Ad-Dustour*, November 6, 2008.

58. *Al-Watan*, January 21, 2009.

59. *Al-Anbaa*, November 12, 2008.

60. *Al-Watan*, January 22, 2009.

61. *Al-Ayyam*, November 6, 2008.

62. *Ad-Dustour*, November 9, 2008.

63. *Al-Ayam*, November 8, 2008.

64. *Alnilin*, November 6, 2009.

65. *Al-Arab*, December 7, 2008.

66. *As-Safir*, January 23, 2009.

67. *Al-Ittihad*, November 10, 2008.

68. *Asharq Al-Awsat*, November6, 2008.

69. *Al-Thowrah*, January 21, 2009.

70. *Al-Watan*, January 23, 2009.

71. *Al-Ayyam*, January 24, 2009.

72. *Ad-Dustour*, November 8, 2008.

73. *As-Safir*, January 26, 2009.

74. *Alnilin*, November 6, 2008.

75. *Al-Thawara*, November 6, 2008.

76. *Alnilin*, January 21, 2009.

77. *Attajdid*, January 22, 2009.

78. *Al-Watan*, November 7, 2008.

79. *As-Safir*, January 23, 2009.

80. *Al-Sabah*, January 21, 2009.

81. *As-Safir*, January 20, 2009.

82. *Al-Ahram*, December 31, 2008.

83. *Al-Hayat*, January 31, 2009.

84. *Al-Ahram*, November 5, 2008.

85. *As-Safir*, January 30, 2009.

86. *Al-Baath*, November 9, 2008.

87. *As-Safir*, January 30, 2009.

88. *Al-Ahram*, November 12, 2008.

89. *Al-Akhbar*, December 31, 2008.

90. *Al-Hayat*, January 22, 2009.

91. *Al-Watan*, November 6, 2008.

92. *Al-Ayyam*, November 6, 2008.

93. *Al-Ittihad*, November 10, 2008.

94. *Al-Ahram*, December 31, 2008.

95. *Al-Baath*, January 27, 2009.

96. *Attajdid*, January 22, 2009.

97. *Asharq Al-Awsat*, January 24, 2009.

98. *Ad-Dustour*, November 9, 2008.

99. *Al-Ittihad*, November 10, 2008.

100. *Al-Thowrah*, January 21, 2009.

101. This argument was raised in the Qatari newspaper *Al-Arab* on December 7, 2008.

102. *As-Sabeel*, November 11, 2008.

103. *Al-Ahram*, December 31, 2008.

104. *Ad-Dustour*, November 8, 2008.

105. *Ad-Dustour*, January 26, 2009.

106. *Al-Anbaa*, November 14, 2008.

107. *Al-Akhbar*, December 31, 2008.

108. *As-Sabeel*, November 11, 2008.

109. *Ad-Dustour*, November 9, 2008.

110. *Al-Anbaa*, January 21, 2009.

111. Dream II, December 31, 2008.

112. *Al-Qabas*, January 17, 2009.

113. *Ad-Dustour*, November 6, 2008.

114. *Asharq Al-Awsat*, January 24, 2009.

8. Toward a Better Future

1. Hammouda, *The American Dream*, 10.

2. *Arab Affairs*, Fall 2007.

3. Al-Arabiya, January 9, 2008.

4. *Al-Anbaa*, April 10, 2007.

5. *Arab Affairs*, Spring 2007.

6. Eisenhower told Britain and France that there would no more support for their still shaky currencies.

7. Fisk, "Mohamed Hasseinein Heikel."

8. *Arab Affairs*, Fall 2007.

9. Al-Sharqiya, January 9, 2008.

10. Al-Arabiya, January 9, 2008.

11. *Ad-Dustour*, August 8, 2006.

12. Al-Oula, June 2, 2009.

13. See, for example, the Al-Jazeera television interview with Abdel Moneim Abu Al-Fatouh, an Egyptian physician and member of Egypt's banned Muslim Brotherhood group, aired on April 8, 2007.

14. *Akhbar Al-Khaleej*, January 12, 2008.

15. *Ad-Dustour*, June 14, 2007.

16. *Al-Khaleej*, April 13, 2007.

17. Waheed Abdel Mageed, *Terrorism, America, and Islam: Who Puts the Fire Out?* (Cairo: Dar Misr El-Mahrossa, 2004), 181. [In Arabic.]

18. Ibid., 183.

19. *Ad-Dustour*, September 14, 2006.

20. *Al-Thowrah*, January 29, 2007.

21. *Al-Ahram*, October 31, 2007.

22. *Al-Ahram*, September 19, 2006.

23. Nile News, August 9, 2007.

24. Heikel, *The American Empire*, 10.

25. Khafagi, *The American Personality*, 112.

26. *October*, August 5, 2007.

27. See United Nations Development Program, *Arab Human Development Report, 2002*, http://hdr.undp.org/en/reports/global/hdr2002 (accessed May 5, 2007).

28. Arab Thought Forum, *Arab Speech*, 49.

29. *Al-Hayat*, April 8, 2008.

30. World Economic Forum, *Islam and the West: Annual Report on the State of Dialogue, January 2008*, http://www.weforum.org/pdf/C100/Islam_West.pdf (accessed May 7, 2008).

31. *Asharq Al-Awsat*, March 1, 2007.

32. *Al-Ahram*, May 29, 2009.

33. Al-Oula, June 2, 2009.

34. *Al-Hayat*, June 5, 2009.

35. *Ad-Dustour*, June 8, 2009.

36. *Al-Anbaa*, June 7, 2009.

37. *Asharq Al-Awsat*, June 8, 2009.

38. *Al-Quds Al-Arabi*, June 7, 2009.

39. *Al-Khaleej*, June 9, 2009.

Postscript

1. Barack Obama (speech, Cairo University, Cairo, Egypt, June 4, 2009), http://www.whitehouse.gov/the-press-office/remarks-president-cairo-university-6-04-09.

2. Barack Obama (speech, University of Indonesia, Jakarta, Indonesia, November 10, 2010), http://www.whitehouse.gov/the-press-office/2010/11/10/remarks-president-university-indonesia-jakarta-indonesia.

3. *Al-Watan*, January 22, 2009.

4. Barack Obama (remarks, White House, Washington, DC, February 11, 2011), http://www.whitehouse.gov/the-press-office/2011/02/11/remarks-president-egypt.

5. *As-Safir,* May 21, 2011.

6. Barack Obama (remarks, State Department, Washington, DC, May 19, 2011), http://www.whitehouse.gov/the-press-office/2011/05/19/remarks-president-middle-east-and-north-africa.

7. Quoted in Hamza Hendawi, "Islamic Scholars Criticize Bin Laden's Sea Burial," Associated Press, May 2, 2011, http://www.cbsnews.com/stories/2011/05/02/501364/main20058892.shtml (accessed June 16, 2011).

BIBLIOGRAPHY

Al-Awadli, Salwa Mohamed Yehia. "Image of the United States among University Youth after September 11." *Egyptian Journal of Mass Communication Research* 14 (January–March 2002): 139–82.

Al-Fiqi, Mustapha. *Renewal of National Thought.* Cairo: The General Egyptian Book Organization, 1996. [In Arabic.]

Al-Ghamri, Attif. *Who Rules America: The Hawks Group and Their View of Arabs and Israelis.* Cairo: Al-Maktab Al-Masry Al-Hadith, 2002. [In Arabic.]

Ali, Fateen Ahmed Fareed. *American-Egyptian Relations: Second Part from 23 November 1963 to 28 September 1970.* Cairo: Police Printing, 2002. [In Arabic.]

Al-Lawandi, Said. *The Greater Middle East: An American Conspiracy against Arabs.* Cairo: Nahdt Misr, 2005. [In Arabic.]

Al-Maceer, Mohamed Said Ahmed. *Earthquake of September 11 and Its Intellectual Consequences.* Cairo: Nahdt Misr, 2003. [In Arabic.]

Al-Mossali, Ahmed. *American Foreign Policy and Islamic Politics.* Cairo: Dar El-Thakafa, 2006. [In Arabic.]

Al-Nasser, Abdullah Mohamed. *America: The Armed Mentality.* Beirut: Dar Riyadh Al-Reece, 2007. [In Arabic.]

Al-Rasheedi, Hassan. "Money Warfare to Control Satellite TVs and Newspapers." *Al-Akhbar,* August 2, 2007. [In Arabic.]

197

Al-Saddani, Mahmoud. *America Wika*. Cairo: Akhbar El-Yom, 1997. [In Arabic.]

Alterman, Jon B. *New Media, New Politics? From Satellite Television to the Internet in the Arab World*. Policy Paper no. 48. Washington, DC: Washington Institute for Near East Policy, 1998.

Amin, Galal. *Age of Defaming Arabs and Muslims: We and the World after 11 September 2001*. Cairo: Dar El-Shorouk, 2004. [In Arabic.]

Amin, Galal. *Egypt and Egyptians in the Mubarak Era (1980–2008)*. Cairo: Merit, 2009. [In Arabic.]

Amin, Hussein Y. "The Arab States Charter for Satellite Television: A Quest for Regulation." *Arab Media & Society* (March 2008). http://www.arabmediasociety.com (accessed January 12, 2009).

Amin, Mustapha. *The Laughing America*. Cairo: Akhbar El-Yom, 1996. [In Arabic.]

Anderson, Jon W. "Technology, Media, and the Next Generation in the Middle East." Paper delivered at the Middle East Institute, Columbia University, New York, September 28, 1999.

Arab Thought Forum. *Arab Speech: Content and Style*. Amman: Almuntada, 2003. [In Arabic.]

Bakr, Khaled Abu. *War of Breaking Will: Between Resistance and the American-Zionist Project*. Beirut: Arab Scientific Publisher, 2007. [In Arabic.]

Bakri, Mustapha. *Creative or Destructive Chaos: Egypt in America's Target*. Cairo: El-Shorouk International, 2005. [In Arabic.]

Basheer, Nazzar. *Culture of Blood: Chapters of the History of American Terrorism*. Cairo: Al-Zahra'a for Arab Media, 2003. [In Arabic.]

Basyouni, Mohamed, and Yaser Hussein. *Holy Wars: America and Zionist Christianity*. Cairo: El-Boroug, 2006. [In Arabic.]

Bishtami, Adel S. *Manifest Destiny of Imperial Decline: A History of American Injustice*. Beirut: Arab Institute for Studies and Publication, 2007. [In Arabic.]

Burdick, Eugene, and William Lederer. *The Ugly American*. New York: Norton, 1958.

Elshamy, Anwar. "Annual Doha Dialogue of Islamic Sects Urged." *Gulf Times*, January 22, 2007. www.gulf-times.com (accessed January 28, 2007).

Essam, Shawki. "I Hate Israel and I Am Not in Need of America." *Rose El-Yossef*, April 21, 2007. [In Arabic.]

Fisk, Robert. "Mohamed Hasseinein Heikel: The Wise Man of the Middle East." *The Independent*, April 9, 2007. http://news.independent.co.uk/world/fisk/article2434980.ece (accessed April 28, 2007).

Freedom House. *Freedom in the World 2008*. Washington, DC: Freedom House, 2008.

Fukuyama, Francis. *End of History and the Last Man*. New York: Penguin, 1992.

Gharbal, Ashraf. *Rise and Fall of Egyptian-American Relations: Secret Contacts with Abdel Nasser and Sadat*. Cairo: Al-Ahram, 2004. [In Arabic.]

Ghareeb, Edward. "New Media and the Information Revolution in the Arab World: An Assessment." *Middle East Journal* 54, no. 3 (2000): 396–412.

Habermas, Jurgen. *Structural Transformation of the Public Sphere: An Inquiry into a Category of Bourgeois Society*. Cambridge: Massachusetts Institute of Technology, 1994.

Hafez, Salaheddine. *Forbidding Politics and Criminalizing Journalism*. Cairo: Dar El-Shorouk, 2008. [In Arabic.]

Hammouda, Abdel Aziz. *The American Dream*. Cairo: The General Egyptian Book Organization, 2002. [In Arabic.]

Hatr, Nahed. *Iraqi Resistance and Crisis of American Imperial Project*. Cairo: Merit, 2004. [In Arabic.]

Heikel, Mohamed Hasseinein. *The American Age: From New York to Kabul*. Cairo: Egyptian Company for Arab and International Publishing, 2002. [In Arabic.]

Heikel, Mohamed Hasseinein. *The American Empire and Its War on Iraq*. 6th ed. Cairo: Egyptian Company for Arab and International Publishing, 2006. [In Arabic.]

Hilal, Rida, ed. *The American Empire: Pages from the Past and the Present*. Cairo: El-Shorouk International, 2002. [In Arabic.]

Hudson, Michael C. "'Creative Destruction': Information Technology and the Political Culture Revolution in the Arab World." Revised version of a paper presented at the Conference on Transnationalism, Amman, Jordan, June 19–21, 2001.

Huntington, Samuel P. "The Clash of Civilizations?" *Foreign Affairs* 72, no. 3 (Summer 1993): 22–39.

Huntington, Samuel P. *The Clash of Civilizations and the Remaking of World Order*. New York: Simon and Schuster, 1996.

Inayet, Raji. *America to Where!* Cairo: Nahdt Misr, 2006. [In Arabic.]

Ismail, Narmeen Zakaria. "The Picture of the United States of America among Egyptian Public." Master's thesis, Cairo University, 2001. [In Arabic.]

Khafagi, Bassem. *The American Personality*. Riyadh: Center for Humanities Studies, 2005. [In Arabic.]

Lasswell, Harold. "The Structure and Function of Communication in Society." In *The Communication of Ideas*, edited by Lyman Bryson. New York: Cooper Square Publishers, 1948.

Lewis, Bernard. *The Crisis of Islam: Holy War and Unholy Terror*. London: Weidenfeld Nicolson, 2003.

Mageed, Waheed Abdel. *America's Wars from Bin Laden to Saddam Hussein*. Cairo: Dar Misr El-Mahrossa, 2003. [In Arabic.]

Mageed, Waheed Abdel. *Terrorism, America, and Islam: Who Puts the Fire Out?* Cairo: Dar Misr El-Mahrossa, 2004. [In Arabic.]

Mahmoud, Mustapha. *The American Civilization*. Cairo: Al-Ghad Publishing, 1995. [In Arabic.]

Mahmoud, Zaki Naguib. *Days in America*. 2nd ed. 1955. Reprint, Cairo: Angelo, 1957. [In Arabic.]

McChesney, Robert. "Springtime for Goebbels." *Z Magazine,* December 1997. http://www.zmag.org/Zmag/articles/dec97Mcchesne.htm (accessed 30 April 2004).

Nafie, Ibrahim. *The September Explosion: Between Globalization and Americanization*. Cairo: The General Egyptian Book Organization, 2002. [In Arabic.]

Nua Surveys. "How Many Online." http://www.nua.ie/surveys (accessed June 8, 2002).

Pintak, Lawrence. "Taking Stock." *Arab Media & Society* (January 2008). http://www.arabmediasociety.com (accessed December 25, 2008).

Sadeq, Samia. *Kidnapping of a President*. Cairo: Arab Cultural Center, 2004. [In Arabic.]

Said, Abdel Moneim. *Arabs and September 11*. Cairo: The General Egyptian Book Organization, 2003. [In Arabic.]

Said, Edward. *Orientalism*. New York: Vintage, 1979.

Salama, Salama Ahmed. *Press Over a Hot Tinplate*. Cairo: Al-Ain, 2009. [In Arabic.]

Salem, Rania, and Nehal Balal. "From Dream to Mehwar, O.T.V., Life and C.T.V.: Satellite TV Channels are a New Hobby for Businessmen." *Almussawar*, December 7, 2007. [In Arabic.]

Shaheen, Mona. *Street of the Press*. Cairo: Akhbar El-Yom, 1978. [In Arabic.]

Taher, Bahaa. *Love in Exile*. Cairo: Dar Al-Hilal, 1995. [In Arabic.]

Taher, Bahaa. *Sunset Oasis*. 3rd ed. Cairo: Dar El-Shorouk, 2007. [In Arabic.]

Thabit, Ahmed, and Khalil Al-Anani. *Arabs and the American Imperial Inclination*. Cairo: The General Egyptian Book Organization, 2007. [In Arabic.]

Tuchman, Gaye. *Making News: A Study in the Construction of Reality*. New York: Free Press, 1978.

United Nations Development Program. *Arab Human Development Report*, 2002. http://hdr.undp.org/en/reports/global/hdr2002 (accessed May 5, 2007).

World Economic Forum. *Islam and the West: Annual Report on the State of Dialogue*, January 2008. http://www.weforum.org/pdf/C100/Islam_West.pdf (accessed May 7, 2008).

Zakaria, Fouad. *Arabs and the American Model*. Cairo: Egyptian Library, 1991. [In Arabic.]

INDEX

ABOUT THE AUTHOR

Mohamed El-Bendary is a native Egyptian and naturalized U.S. citizen who was educated in both the United States and Great Britain. He is the author of *The Egyptian Press and Coverage of Local and International Events* (Lexington Books, 2010). An independent journalist, he has published nearly a hundred articles in major American newspapers, including the *Philadelphia Inquirer*, *San Francisco Chronicle*, *St. Louis Post-Dispatch*, *Los Angeles Times*, *Dallas Morning News*, and *Editor & Publisher* magazine, among others. He has taught journalism and international relations in the United States and New Zealand. His research focuses on political communication, global journalism, and foreign affairs. He holds an MA in journalism and public affairs from American University in Washington, D.C.; a postgraduate certificate in Arabic-English translation studies from the University of Westminster in London; and a BA in media communications from Webster University in St. Louis, Missouri.